Exotic Journeys

BECOMING MODERN:
NEW NINETEENTH-CENTURY STUDIES

Series Editors:

Sarah Sherman
Department of English
University of New Hampshire

James Krasner
Department of English
University of New Hampshire

Rohan McWilliam
Anglia Polytechnic University
Cambridge, England

Janet Polasky
Department of History
University of New Hampshire

This book series maps the complexity of historical change and assesses the formation of ideas, movements, and institutions crucial to our own time by publishing books that examine the emergence of modernity in North America and Europe. Set primarily but not exclusively in the nineteenth century, the series shifts attention from modernity's twentieth-century forms to its earlier moments of uncertain and often disputed construction. Seeking books of interest to scholars on both sides of the Atlantic, it thereby encourages the expansion of nineteenth-century studies and the exploration of more global patterns of development.

Stephen Carl Arch, *After Franklin: The Emergence of Autobiography in Post-Revolutionary America, 1780–1830* (2001)

Justin D. Edwards, *Exotic Journeys: Exploring the Erotics of U.S. Travel Literature, 1840–1930* (2001)

Exotic Journeys

Exploring the Erotics

of U.S. Travel Literature,

1840–1930

Justin D. Edwards

University of New Hampshire

Published by University Press of New England • Hanover and London

University of New Hampshire

Published by University Press of New England, Hanover, NH 03755

© 2001 by University of New Hampshire

Printed in the United States of America

5 4 3 2 1

Library of Congress Cataloging-in-Publication Data

Edwards, Justin D., 1970–
Exotic journeys : exploring the erotics of U.S. travel literature,
1840–1930 / by Justin D. Edwards.
p.   cm. — (Becoming modern)
ISBN 1–58465–115–6 (alk. paper)— ISBN 1–58465–116–4 (pbk. : alk.
paper)
1. Travelers' writings, American—History and criticism.
2. American prose literature— 19th century—History and criticism.
3. American prose literature— 20th century—History and criticism.
4. Erotic literature, American—History and criticism.
5. Americans—Travel—Foreign Countries—History.
6. Exoticism in literature. 7. Sex in literature. I. Title. II. Series.
PS366.T73 E39   2001
810.9'355—dc21   00–012464

For my loving travel partner, Ellen

CONTENTS

Contents

ACKNOWLEDGMENTS

I am grateful to my family, friends, and colleagues for contributing in countless ways to the writing of this book. Discussing literature with George Piggford, Ellen Servinis, Joel Baker, Jennifer Westlake, Sarah Wight, Andrew Connochie, Mustapha Fahmi, Rainier Grutman, Katherine Roberts, and Douglas Ivison has stimulated and enhanced my work for the past eight years. The editorial suggestions of Ellen Servinis and Brian Lynch were insightful, intelligent, and enlightening; I owe much to their attentive reading of the manuscript. My parents, David and Cecilia, deserve much credit for their financial support and tireless patience. I must also thank my sister Madeleine for her emotional support.

This book began as a dissertation. I had the good fortune of working with a wonderful committee at the University of Montreal; each member enhanced my writing in many ways. Richard Cavell helped me to think about the theoretical framework of my project by giving me excellent advice concerning my original argument. Amaryll Chanady's comments provided a comparative perspective that strengthened my work. Lianne Moyes gave me important encouragement and advice throughout the project. Jay Bochner's close reading and informed criticisms were valuable; his support gave me the courage to pursue publication of this book. And, most important, Robert K. Martin was an exemplary adviser. His teaching and profound readings of American literature stimulated my interest in travel writing; without his comments and encouragement this book would never have been written.

This project was generously funded by the Social Sciences and Humanities Research Council of Canada. The University Press of New England has made the publication of this project a pleasure: Phyllis Deutsch, Sarah Way Sherman, and Richard Abel have done an excellent job in helping me to improve the final product. Thanks must also go to Brigitte Bailey for her outstanding suggestions for revision. Parts of chapter 1 appeared in *ARIEL: A Review of International English Literature* (April 1999, University of Calgary), and an earlier version of chapter 8 appeared in *American Modernism across the Arts* (Peter Lang Publishing, 1999).

J. D. E.

Exotic Journeys

Introduction

Erotic Spaces

Tennessee Williams's play *Suddenly Last Summer* (1958)* depicts two journeys to exotic locales. The first is described when Violet Venable tells Dr. Cukrowicz about the trip she took to the Galapagos Islands with her son Sebastian: "He [Sebastian] read me Melville's description of the Encantadas, the Galapagos Islands . . . and said that we had to go there" (15). The mother and son, upon arriving on the island's shores, discover that there is much more to "the enchanting Encantadas" than Melville had represented. Violet states: "But on the Encantadas we saw something that Melville *hadn't* written about. . . . [We witnessed] the hatching of the great sea-turtles and their race to the sea" to escape the flesh-eating birds (15). "The birds hovered and swooped to attack," Violet continues, "they were diving down on the hatched sea-turtles, turning them over to attack their soft undersides, tearing the undersides open and rending and

---

* Dates given in the text are original publication dates. Page numbers refer to the edition listed in Works Cited at the back of the book.

I

eating their flesh" (16). Violet is horrified by this primal scene and nearly faints as she conveys the story.

This journey to the "terrible Encantadas," as Violet calls them, fore-shadows Sebastian's death (15). Every summer Sebastian travels to an exotic location in order to engage in sexual affairs with young men. During "last summer's" trip to Cabeza de Lobo, however, Sebastian is overcome by a group of "primitive" young men who chase him through the city streets, begging him for money and bread. When the chase is over, Sebastian is found dead, "devoured" by the "flock of featherless little black sparrows" (92). In the words of his cousin Catherine, Sebastian's body was found naked and mutilated, for the young men had "devoured parts of him . . . [and] torn bits of him away and stuffed them into their gobbling fierce little empty black mouths" (92).

Williams's treatment of Americans in foreign countries incorporates numerous travel discourses that are central to nineteenth- and early-twentieth-century American travel literature. For instance, Williams invokes the tropes of liberation from American civilization: journeys that comprise searches for exotic spaces, primitive lands that are met with a mixture of awe and anxiety, identities that are engulfed (literally consumed) by the citizens of a foreign place. Most important, though, is Williams's use of eroticism and sexual emancipation in the context of travel. Sebastian's pursuit of sexual opportunities in southern countries frames travel as a source of erotic freedom; foreign spaces function as stages where he can enact his sexual fantasies. But the pursuit of sexual emancipation comes at a price: Sebastian's confrontation with the young men inspires him to experience a vibration of dread that arises out of his fear of the unknown, a fear of the Other, which is suggested by the cannibalistic images of his death.

These intersections of travel motifs with motifs of interracial same-sex desire and anxiety reverberate throughout American literature. As early as 1923, D. H. Lawrence, in his *Studies in Classic American Literature,* asserted that "the mythos of immaculate male love" in the American literary canon was intimately tied to representations of escape, liberation, and travel (151–52). And Leslie Fiedler suggests that the themes of displacement, interracial love, and the symbolic marriage of men are so common in American literature that they must be taken together and analyzed as such (152). The cross-cultural male couple traveling through the American wilderness (Huck and Jim) or on the high seas (Ishmael and Queequeg) is, for Fiedler, a recurring trope that works to disavow the restrictions of a repressed and conservative culture that has alienated itself from the so-called natural primitivism of man. Furthermore, Constance Penley notes that stories about American travel, whether in the form of texts, films, or television programs, frequently pose "questions of sexual difference and sexual relations, which [are] repeatedly addresse[d] alongside other kinds of differences" (103).

But I would argue that interracial sexuality—not just homosexuality—is a common feature of American narratives of travel. For instance, Richard Henry Dana's *Two Years before the Mast* (1840) probes "sex relationship[s] . . . with[in] the great circuit of men and women" (Lawrence 124). In fact, what D. H. Lawrence admires in Dana's text is his portrayal of the "Aikane," a "Kanaka practice" that combines heterosexual relationships with passionate bonds between men (124). My intention here is not to situate American travel narratives within a heterosexual frame; rather, I would say that literature of travel (and dislocation) includes a contact zone between cultures (whether in the wilderness, on the high seas, or in a foreign nation) that is presented in erotic terms—an eroticism that is at times homosexual and at other times heterosexual. The erotics of travel, that is, cannot be molded into a universal image; erotic modes of representation, like depictions of sexual desire, are often fluid, not fixed. But before pushing further into the wilderness that constitutes the erotics of travel literature, the terrain of generic convention must be surveyed and mapped out.

Generic Conventions

Textual representations of a journey, at least since the *Odyssey,* have been staple metaphors not only for life itself but also for any event in which time is applied to space (Butor 4). In fact, the journey is one of the basic elements in the production of narrative, and its position in time and space gestures toward what Bakhtin called "chronotope," his name for "the intrinsic connectedness of temporal and spatial relationships that are artistically expressed in literature" ("Forms of Time" 84). "The chronotope in literature," Bakhtin goes on to say, "has an intrinsic generic significance" because it "defines genre and generic distinctions" (85). In other words, spatial and temporal positioning—Bakhtin's "space and time"—come to define a narrative's genre. But there are many journey-chronotopes in literature: the quest, the exploration, the picaresque journey, the road narrative, and so on. Thus, the various forms of chronotopes in literature will profoundly influence a text's structure and meaning; as a result, Bakhtin's formulation provides an access route into the complicated subject of generic convention and travel literature.

Bakhtin's comments navigate a clear space through the obscurities of a genre that is usually characterized as undefinable. Terry Caesar, for instance, states that travel writing does not "suggest any generic expectation" because it is "subsumed in a textual practice that defies definition" (102). Likewise, Sarah Wright states that "travel writing" is at the very least "a hybrid genre" (Introduction 9). Paul Fussell, though, attempts to convey the formalistic qualities of travel writing by claiming that

> a travel book . . . is addressed to those who . . . require the exotic or comic anomalies, wonders, and scandals of the literary form romance. . . . Travel books are a sub-species of memoir in which the autobiographical narrative arises from a speaker's encounter with distant or unfamiliar data, and in which the narrative—unlike that in the novel or romance—claims literal validity by constant reference to actuality. (203)

American travel literature fits fairly well into the general coordinates that Fussell sets out here, but the question of genre remains a complicated one. If, as Fussell claims, a clear contrast exists between the romance and the travel sketch based on authentic experience, how would Fussell categorize a hybrid text like Hawthorne's *Marble Faun*? Because *The Marble Faun* is a "romance," which incorporates substantial passages from Hawthorne's Roman travel notebooks, it upsets the stability of Fussell's distinctions between romance and travel narrative. This instability speaks to the difficulty of imposing discrete generic conventions on texts about travel.

The limits to Fussell's vision of travel writing have led me to take my cue from more recent critics, who place the genre alongside discourses of imperialism. As Sara Mills points out in *Discourses of Difference* (1991), "travel writing is essentially an instrument within colonial expansion and served to reinforce colonial rule" (2). This view is supported by Mary Louise Pratt, who shows how "travel books by Europeans about non-European parts of the world went (and go) about creating the domestic subject of Euroimperialism" (4). And Douglas Ivison argues that in the nineteenth century the "practice of travel writing, and that of reading travel books, was intertwined with the creation and maintenance of European imperialism" (1). These critics, though, often omit discussions of the American strand of the genre, focusing primarily on European travel writing and European imperialism. My intention is to build on these studies by looking at the connections between imperialism, sexuality, and travel writing in the American history of imperial expansion. Travel books, I suggest, are not just a European tool of imperialism; they also contribute to the expansion of an American empire in the South Pacific, Europe, and even at home.

Analyzing the relationship of imperial expansion and American travel narratives is complicated by the fact that travel books published in the nineteenth-century United States joined what Eric Savoy calls "a literature of exhaustion" (290). This remark is explained by A. M. Metwalli's assertion that "almost every individual [in nineteenth-century America] who left home—even for a hike in the mountains—committed his impressions and experiences to paper and inflicted them upon the reading public" (15). Viewed under this light, American travel literature may be seen as a purely democratic mode of literary production that came to accommodate numerous textual frameworks: popular and personal experiences written in an epistolary style, intellectual and belletristic techniques to depict literary travels, travel narratives that were written in place of guidebooks, and so on. Such diverse literary practices appealed to nineteenth-century audiences, and the success of books such as Bayard Taylor's *Views A-foot* (1846), which went into twenty editions less than a decade after its first printing, encouraged other travelers to try their hand at recording journeys.

Furthermore, the popularity of nineteenth-century travel writing arose partially out of a Victorian compulsion to classify, taxonomize, and control the natural world. Thus, American travelers often performed the service of charting, mapping, and disclosing the secrets of exotic lands. The strange insects and plants of foreign lands were often dutifully described and classified for the armchair traveler back home; similarly, American travelers writing about France and Italy frequently classified and categorized the best sights and routes to be sought out during a European tour. Such writing appealed to the voyeuristic reader who desired a peep into unfamiliar cultures without leaving the confines of his or her home. But the processes of classification, mapping, and charting, as Peter Raby points out, also became an instrument of power used in the imperial project of conceptualizing and controlling foreign terrains. "If the world . . . were charted," Raby states, "the empire could control it" (5).

Within the specifically American context, though, the popular genre of travel writing was linked to the strong conscious need for a national identity. Given that nineteenth-century Americans possessed a short historical past, tradition and culture had to be developed in relation to other places (Withey 93). Thus, at the heart of American travel texts one usually finds a serious interest in the history and secrets of faraway lands. Discovering these secrets in American travel literature corresponded with American growth and imperialism that began in the 1840s. Unlike the early-nineteenth-century travel sketches by such American writers as Washington Irving,[1] the travel literature of the 1840s (and thereafter) paralleled the development of American expansionism. In fact, in the 1840s, Americans acquired Texas, and the 1846 war with Mexico cleared Spain out of California, thus providing Americans with western ports from which to expand into the South Pacific (Oliver 140). Such imperial gestures, as they were captured in American travel literature, performed the purpose of distinguishing America from foreign nations and past historical moments, while at the same time asserting the superiority of the American nation and justifying colonial expansion (Metwalli 18). This expansionism, though, was also partially responsible for the increased American tourist industry abroad—an industry that had begun in 1815 but became a fixture in American culture during the 1840s (Dulles 28).

The increase in the nineteenth-century tourist industry inspired many travelers and Americans citizens in general to reflect upon their national identity. For some Americans the cultural institutions of the United States were insignificant. Perhaps recognizing that, as Henry James believed, "the items of high civilization" lay outside the American nation, privileged Americans of the nineteenth century developed travel into a lucrative business that provided tours of European landmarks (43). After the European wars that grew out of the French Revolution and the Napoleonic Wars, up to 1815, Americans began to visit European cities with a vigor that lasted into the twentieth century. Although Mary Chapman correctly points out that the young American republic was anxious in the aftermath of the French Revolution and that early writers such as Charles Brockden Brown saw the French Revolution as a "reign of terror," many Americans toured France and England after 1815 (Chapman 20). Such journeys are all the more surprising when we consider Jenny Franchot's assertion that a large number of Americans considered European countries undemocratic because of their antiquated aristocratic political structures (28). Other American travelers, though, applauded the French Revolution and all subsequent efforts toward creating and re-creating republican government. Visitors in the early nineteenth century were still close enough to their own revolution to recall with gratitude the importance of French support in winning American independence. (Withey 81)

While the French Revolution inspired an ambivalent mixture of anxiety and admiration, Rome's republican revolution of November 1848 was celebrated by many Americans as an expression of the revolutionary ideals of 1776. Maria Sedgwick and Julia Ward Howe, for example, became acquainted with Italian revolutionaries exiled in the United States and visited their families and friends while in Europe. And Margaret Fuller declared that the Roman revolution was "one of terrible justice," manifesting "a spirit which cheers and animates mine. I hear earnest words of pure faith and love. I see deeds of brotherhood. This is what makes *my* America" (*Sad* 230). The number of Americans who were able to take the time for the long voyage and who could afford the high costs of travel inevitably remained very small by modern standards. Yet the number was large enough by 1818 to warrant a regularly scheduled transatlantic service between New York and Liverpool. Competition among transatlantic steamers soon arose with the increase in passengers, and the tourist industry expanded to the extent that by 1850 it was estimated that as many as thirty thousand Americans traveled to Europe each year (Dulles 1).

But the popularity of American travel writing was not limited to those works chronicling travelers' experiences on the European Grand Tour. Audiences were also fascinated by adventure narratives such as Melville's *Omoo* (1847), whose first printing of three thousand copies sold out in one month. Martin Green places such narratives in the subgenre of "adventure travel" by claiming that they are unique in their presentations of "a series of events, partly but not wholly accidental, in settings remote from the domestic and probably from the civilized" (23). For my purposes, this subgenre is apropos to describe American literature about the South Seas: Herman Melville, Charles Warren Stoddard, and Jack London all textually delve into the "uncivilized" areas of the South Pacific, where they are confronted with life-threatening adventures. Such dramatic narratives have been contrasted to other forms of travel writing, particularly those that capture itineraries of voyages developed as consumer products, best represented by writing about the European Grand Tour.

The tourist, then, did not seek out remote spaces (as the adventurer does), but "move[d] toward the security of pure cliché" (Fussell 39). The traveler, on the other hand, existed in the area between these two poles (the adventurer and the tourist) by seeking out excitement and that which is unpredictable, while always knowing where he or she is (39). James Buzard uses Wordsworth to show that the distinction between tourists and travelers was a nineteenth-century phenomenon. Tourists, he shows, were thought to pass "superficially through districts they little know, nor long remember . . . [while] irrevocably alter[ing] the landscape. In contrast, the traveler . . . [seeks] a distinctly meaningful and lasting contact with the visited place" but does not provoke any constitutive changes (28). The traveler sees things as they are and leaves them as they were; the tourist sees what he is told to see and leaves a trail of business in his or her wake designed to accommodate like-minded pleasure seekers (Frow 151).

Such categories, though, are fragile at best. For example, many American tourists, particularly those who participated in the European Grand Tour, considered the act of writing about their touristic forays as textual evidence of their identification with other travelers, not tourists. Within the traveler/tourist dichotomy, then, the nineteenth-century travel book worked to authenticate the experience of the tourist and had the (imagined) power to convert him or her into the traveler. Here, the ease with which travel writers transformed themselves from one identity to another exposes the arbitrary nature of the distinctions between the subgenres of travel writing. For Buzard, moreover, the distinction between the tourist and the traveler was based on an antitourist sentiment that constructed the myth of "a certain number of real travelers—a select few—[who] could distinguish themselves on the basis of purity of motive" (154). The distinction, he goes on to say, was a product of an imagination that sought to place the capacities of one individual over another. Once this was realized, the difference between tourist and traveler fell away as an artificial means of imposing hierarchies and class distinctions.

The similarity of the discourses in texts by tourists, travelers, and adventurers also reveals the interconnectedness (and artificiality) of the three literary modes. Eroticized rhetoric is common to all of these textual forms, and thus readings of eroticism are an appropriate frame of analysis for illustrating the connections between various kinds of travel literature. For instance, Catherine Maria Sedgwick's "An Incident in Rome" (1845), a tale about British tourists in Italy, presents what Brigitte Bailey calls "the myth of Italy's seduction" and charged sexuality ("Visual" 1).

The text's protagonist, Murray Bathurst, commences a tour of Italy. During this trip, Bathurst is seduced by Italy; he begins to think of the country as his "lover," and he becomes insane when a fever reduces him to groping the Roman ruins and wandering the Italian countryside as a beggar (C. M. Sedgwick 23). Although the tale concludes with the "rescue" of Bathurst by his faithful mother, Sedgwick's message is clear: the erotic appeal of Italy has the seductive power to "emasculate" the British tourist by reducing him to a defenseless beggar (Bailey, "Visual" 1).

A similarly erotic, though less threatening, image of foreign spaces (and unfamiliar women) is depicted in David Dorr's *Colored Man round the World* (1858). Dorr, unlike Sedgwick's characters, makes a point of defining himself as a traveler, not a tourist.[2] During his European travels, which he frames as "a promiscuous voyage," Dorr meets a "beautiful [English] girl of fifteen," Mary, who works at a Liverpool hotel (15). Dorr describes his sexual attraction to Mary as making him "a good deal like a dog" who has just met "his sexual mate" (15). While Mary "takes care" of him, Dorr warns his male readers that the erotic appeal of English girls may force the American traveler to become "uncommonly savage in his nature" (15–16). These erotic images are also present in the adventure narratives written by Mark Twain during his trip to Hawaii. Hawaiian women, Twain asserts, are "given to sexual licentiousness and sexual freedom" and participate in "orgies of total abandon" that are simultaneously attractive and shocking (132). Thus, on one fundamental level the similarities of erotic discourse in narratives by tourists, travelers, and adventurers unite the three textual forms.

In returning to Fussell's three categories it is also important to note that they leave no room for discussions of other forms of travel writing. For example, the urban explorer—the writer who uses travel discourse to describe the different neighborhoods of his or her city—is not present in Fussell's analyses. The urban travel text arose as a distinct textual form during the substantial growth of American cities in the 1840s.[3]

Texts by writers such as George Lippard and George G. Foster adopted the form of the travel narrative to explore the urban geography of the United States. Foster's *New York Naked* (1850), for instance, includes the voice of an urban explorer who claims the ability to "strip off the mask" of the city and guide the reader through the secret streets of New York (26). Here, Foster uses the language of exoticism and eroticism to describe his journey: the secrets of the city will be revealed, and the city will lie naked and exposed before the reader's gaze. Similar diction is used more than fifty years later in Henry James's *The American Scene* (1907), which takes the reader on an exotic trip to "a beer cellar" that is filled with "local colour"; while there, James mingles with "the baser patrons," including the "strong men and lovely women, prize-fighters and *ballerine*" who crowd together in the "deep bosom" of the billiard room (150, 153). The clearly demarcated gender distinctions (the prizefighter and the ballerina) are placed alongside the sexualized imagery of the "deep bosom" and the bodies that are "squeezed together," and such images clearly work to convey the exotic side of these "irrepressible animals" (151). The eroticism that James and Foster import to describe the American cityscape, then, is akin to the sexual images used by other American travelers in their accounts of foreign places.

Travel Discourse

Although totalizing views of American travel writing remain problematic, the similarities between the subgenres of travel literature constitute what one might call travel discourse, a label that brings together the rhetoric of travel in order to enlighten our readings of the discursive allegiances between power and sexuality. Throughout this study, the term *discourse* is employed to refer to the rhetoric of travel and the linguistic tropes of imperialism. *Discourse,* a word that has become common currency in literary theory but that frequently goes undefined, can be adopted from Foucault's tripartite definition: "The word discourse . . . [can be defined] sometimes as the general domain of all statements, sometimes as an individualizable group of statements, and sometimes as a regulated practice that accounts for a number of statements" (*Archaeology* 80). Foucault thus gives us a range of meanings. First, discourse constitutes all utterances and texts that work to structure our understanding of the world. This broad definition is coupled with his second explanation of discourse, which brings together a group of statements based on common linguistic structures; using this second definition, it is possible to identify a discourse of travel or a discourse of imperialism. Foucault's third definition of discourse lays the groundwork for analyzing the rules and structures that produce various utterances and texts. And here Foucault is less interested in the actual texts/utterances than in the rule-governed nature of a particular discourse.

Discourses, however, are not monolithic: they frequently include tensions and contradictions that must be taken together in order to fully understand the functions of particular discursive structures. Travel discourses, for instance, are often fraught with gaps, contradictions, and inconsistencies that destabilize the unified modes of representation persented by travelers. Many American travel writers of the nineteenth and early twentieth centuries produced discourses of travel that were both related to and in conflict with dominant discursive strategies. As Sara Mills correctly argues in her reading of nineteenth-century women's travel writing, "women writers in this period" produced texts that were "in conflict" with dominant travel discourses; but these same women, Mills goes on to say, often contradicted their rebellious statements by reinscribing conservative notions of gender and imperialism (*Discourse* 99). While it is true that the discursive conflicts for male travel writers were distinct in that the subject positions mapped out for colonial travelers were predominantly masculine, we find similar subversions of traditional discourses of gender, sexuality, and imperialism among those men who identified themselves in opposition to conventional sexual categories. For example, Charles Warren Stoddard's *Cruising the South Seas* does not simply repeat established views of gender, sexuality, or colonial expansion. Despite the fact that some of his accounts seem to uphold conventional discourses, Stoddard frequently challenges imperial projects that work to colonize same-sexuality and nonvirile masculinities. His travel narratives, then, present a range of discourses that mark them with disjunctions and fissures, making them less cohesive as colonizing documents. I would suggest therefore that, as in the work of some nineteenth-century women travel writers, travel writing by a number of American men at times drew on counterdiscourses.

Discourses of travel, however, are sometimes supportive of imperial projects. Mary Louise Pratt's *Imperial Eyes: Travel Writing and Transculturation* (1992) has been an essential guide to exploring travel writing's reinscriptions of the particular event sequences that structure colonial texts. She notes that travel texts shared with other colonial narratives the discourses and rhetorical structures that gesture toward potential imperial exploitation: the land is often naturalized, described as fertile, and lacking indigenous peoples (49). Building on Pratt's ideas, I would argue that travel discourses and imperial rhetoric are similar in that they both use the textual strategies of paranoia, structures of difference, expressions of intense desire, objects of sexual fetishism, primitivism, eroticism, and exoticism.

Nathaniel Hawthorne's *Marble Faun,* for example, foregrounds these discourses by describing the Italian character, Donatello, in erotic terms while simultaneously maintaining Donatello's ethnic difference from the American characters. More specifically, Hawthorne's erotic depictions serve as homoerotic posturing of a kind that finds its way into many male travel texts. But Pratt's work tends to overlook these issues of travel and same-sex desire. While she is sensitive to questions of gender and sexualized spaces, Pratt relegates same-sexuality to a footnote, suggesting that "the figure of the scientific explorer was bound up with heterosexual paradigms of masculinity," thus negating the possibility of same-sexual contact between travelers and natives (236). Here, Pratt seems to be following Edward Said's oversight when faced with the "East" as an eroticized space; Said's recognition that the Orient provided ground to explore heterosexual fantasies leaves no room for homoeroticism within the colonial context.[4]

Eroticism, then, is a trope that assumes various guises in nineteenth-century American travel literature. Frequently, the American traveler describes the native Other as an erotic spectacle that is viewed as anomalous in relation to the Western norm. Under these circumstances the native is denied subjectivity and becomes a source of erotic fantasy, an image that frames him or her as sexually accessible to the imperial traveler. The American gaze, which works to undermine foreign subjectivities in this way, casts the Other into an inferior mold by conceiving him/her as vulnerable to penetration and possession. In other instances, erotic images are used by the American traveler to critique imperial projects. This imagery is foregrounded in Melville's *Typee* by drawing attention to the "erotic paradise" and the "noble savage" as positive alternatives to American industrial capitalism. Melville thus uses eroticism to question Euro-American superiority and to critique imperial infiltrations into the cultures of the South Pacific. These anticonquest narratives, though, are often discursively corrupt; as Pratt points out, the "imperial eye" does not passively admire the erotic aspects of foreign cultures. Rather, these gazes construct typologies that categorize foreign lands and peoples within the cultural framework of "norm" and "Other" (30). The act of witnessing, then, often assumes objective knowledge of a foreign locale—enough knowledge to place that locale within a taxonomized system based on the general observations filtered through the traveler's imperial lens.

Travel Literature

In the chapters that follow this introduction it is not my intention to es-tablish a norm of travel literature or travel discourse—the rhetoric of travel is far too complex for there to be a single norm—but to provide a context in which alternative patterns of experience can be compared. This context is based on a tendency to think about travel literature, sexu-ality, and racial (or ethnic) differences as intimately connected. I have chosen to read these discursive patterns in diverse texts that might best be placed in the sweeping category of American travel literature, a category that comprises everything from Herman Melville's *Typee* (1846) to Claude McKay's *Home to Harlem* (1928). Such a broad grouping can be conceived as including three unique but not discrete subsections. The first of these is the conventional travel narrative (William Wells Brown, Edith Wharton, and Djuna Barnes) wherein the traveler transforms his or her experiences into a textual form that chronicles the events set out by an itinerary. In these narratives the fictions of linearity and chronology trans-form into the truth of the travel narrative (D. E. Johnson 6). The second of these subsections is the hybrid travel text (Herman Melville, Charles Warren Stoddard, and Nathaniel Hawthorne), which may be read as a pastiche of autobiographical travel accounts and fictional techniques. Hybrid travel narratives work to expose travel as intimately connected to the tradition of storytelling and suggest that "storytelling itself is the in-separable companion to any serious literary depiction of travel" (Whetter 443). Touristic fiction (Jack London, Carl Van Vechten, and Claude McKay) is the label that I have given to the third subsection of travel lit-erature. Within this grouping, a narrator/observer moves through a for-eign space while he or she captures and interprets the landscape of the story's setting. Thus, the touristic novel is guided by the narrator's didac-tic imperative to disclose the surrounding "foreign" scenes, a procedure that is integrated into the fictional necessities of the plot.

These subsections are not, of course, mutually exclusive. In fact, all of them share the stylistic devices of eroticism, exoticism, primitivism, and the employment of structures of difference. Furthermore, texts from at least two of these categories were used as guidebooks: Edith Wharton states that Hawthorne's *Marble Faun* was "the last word on Italy" and an essential guidebook for "the average well-to-do traveler" (*Backward*

Glance 44); likewise, as critics of the Harlem Renaissance have noted, Carl Van Vechten's *Nigger Heaven* "became a guidebook, and visitors carried it in their pockets as they went to Harlem" (Ikonné 29).

What brings all of these texts together, though, is their participation in the thematic and rhetorical interface between travel and eroticism. While American travel to foreign regions is usually presented as a commodious signifier, providing everything from civilization to primitivism, freedom to danger, and fulfilment to corruption, the images of eroticism remain a constant trope. The foreign land and its citizens, whether in Melville's descriptions of the Typees or Margaret Fuller's encounters with Italian men, are presented with erotic currency that typically goes hand in hand with the motif of sexual liberation. Nevertheless, recent studies of travel writing tend to gloss over issues of eroticism and sexuality. Although Mary Louise Pratt's *Imperial Eyes: Travel Writing and Transculturation* (1992), James Buzard's *The Beaten Track: European Tourism, Literature, and the Ways to Culture, 1800–1918* (1993), William W. Stowe's *Going Abroad: European Travel in Nineteenth-Century American Culture* (1994), and Mary Suzanne Schriber's *Writing Home: American Women Abroad, 1830–1920* (1997) touch upon the erotics of travel as tangential subjects, my study provides a sustained analytical reading of these issues. By consistently focusing on the operations of eroticism and its rhetorical effects, I identify previously unnoticed or ignored (but nonetheless important) dimensions of the writing practices of American travelers from 1840 to 1930.

PART 1
Cruising the
South Seas

The South Pacific

In *Tales of the South Pacific*, the 1949 collection of stories by James A. Michener set in the "exotic" South Seas during the Second World War, the handsome Lieutenant Joseph Cable, from Philadelphia, journeys to the "forbidden" romantic island of Bali-ha'i and immediately falls in love with Liat, a beautiful young Polynesian woman. Because the American military classifies Bali-ha'i as off-limits, Cable must go back to the base, but he keeps returning to visit Liat and courts her with the promise of marriage. Their joyous future together is ruptured, though, when Liat's mother, Mary, suggests that the happy couple unite in wedlock.

Cable's response is to state: "Oh God! Mary, I love her, but I can't" (182). Cable then decides to flee; he runs to his boat and returns to his life on the military base. Joseph Cable simply desires (to use Herman Melville's words) an exciting "peep at Polynesian life"; he wants a fleeting romantic liaison, not a lifetime commitment.

An untroubled Orientalist fantasy, *Tales of the South Pacific* illustrates an American tradition of imperial control and sexual adventure on South Pacific islands—a tradition with generic conventions that were already in place in 1846, when Herman Melville published his first novel, *Typee*. Michener's text deploys many of the same discourses and tropes as Melville's: the Polynesians are presented in terms of idealized beauty; they are erotic and sexually accessible to the Western traveler; the American traveler is simultaneously attracted and repulsed by the Othered beauty of the natives; and the main character flees when he fears being initiated into Polynesian culture. Echoing *Typee* is Joshua Logan's 1958 film, *South Pacific* (based on Michener's tales), which presents the Polynesian islands as sites where the American characters can engage freely in homosocial bonds and experiment with alternative gender performances. During a Thanksgiving party, for instance, the hypermasculine character, Bullis, performs a drag show while the men in the audience attempt to slap his buttocks and fondle his false breasts. Logan's film, then, may be read as a 1950s version of the fertile landscapes, the preindustrial peacefulness, and the polymorphous sexuality that have been projected onto Polynesian culture throughout the Euro-American era of empire that began during the eighteenth century (Young xi).

One could argue that American imperialism began as early as 1803 with the expansionist policies that resulted in the Louisiana Purchase and

continued with the acquisition of Alaska in 1867. Yet there can be no denying that the occupation of Texas and the 1846 war with Mexico
marked a significant moment in American expansionism; while the journalist John L. O'Sullivan would call it Manifest Destiny, his political rhetoric simply put a new face to the old visage of European imperialism (E.
Wright 129). Because the Mexican War cleared Spain out of California,
the port of San Francisco became available to Americans as a base from
which to expand trade and establish republicanism in the South Pacific.
Increased trade, combined with the enlarged borders, meant that it was
no longer possible for Americans to conceive of themselves as isolation-
ists. In fact, expansion into the Pacific became a necessary outlet for the
growing industrialization of the United States. By 1870, American ex-
ports had become a fundamental aspect of the economy, and there continued to be a steady rise in the manufactured goods for foreign trade
(Oliver 101). As this industrial system took shape, the need for foreign
markets added impetus to the demand for American political control of
the South Sea Islands.

The United States was thus becoming a significant power in the Pacific.
In 1868, for instance, Secretary Seward arranged for the United States to
annex the Midway Islands off the coast of Hawaii, and in 1878 the
Americans established a protectorate over the Samoan Islands (E. Wright
132). Acquisition of the Hawaiian Islands in 1898 was the result of
forces similar to those that brought the United States colonial respon-
sibilities in Samoa. As early as 1820, American missionaries had established themselves on a number of Hawaii's islands, and their descendants
grew into a sizable American population in the area. Political instability
and fluctuations in the sugar trade caused President McKinley to push for
Hawaiian annexation in 1897.[1] Acquisition of the Hawaiian Islands, he
claimed, would stop Hawaii from falling under foreign control and
would provide opportunities for commercial and naval expansion (Oliver 143). These arguments were reinforced in the minds of many citizens
by the belief that it was the Manifest Destiny of the United States to control the Pacific and that the nation had a duty to bring Christianity and
democracy to the native population of this area. There were also those
Americans who sanctioned the acquisition of Hawaii because they believed it to be an unspoiled "Golden Island," an earthly paradise (Rennie
180). Mythic renderings of Hawaii (and other South Sea islands) generated what Neil Rennie refers to as "far-fetched facts," whereby Western

culture imposes its values on these islands while persuading itself that it wants to throw off the trappings of civilization (182).

A complex relationship between imperial ideology and an idealized "natural" space can be found in numerous sexualized narratives that present a Western subject embracing and penetrating the symbolic Otherness of Polynesian culture. These narratives assume different forms. As Gregory Woods points out, one such typical narrative depicts a Western man who journeys to a "golden island" inhabited by sexually accessible women, an island where the man can experience a "natural heterosexuality" that is accompanied by uncomplicated divisions of traditional gender roles (126). In other South Sea narratives, Western men travel to foreign islands in order to form close bonds with the landscape and the elements, while relating homosocially and homoerotically with the Polynesian men; inherent to these narratives is a renegotiation of the character's masculinity before he returns to a homeland that is defined by its whiteness and heterosexuality. Whatever form these narratives may take, the theme of sexual liberation among cultures that are defined as natural and primitive become defining qualities that unite such texts.

American colonial expansion in the South Seas during the mid-nineteenth century provided opportunities for American men to participate in these "exotic" experiences and create mythic narratives of their adventures. The texts by Herman Melville, Charles Warren Stoddard, and Jack London that I have chosen to discuss in this section provide three distinct contributions to erotic narratives of travel in the South Pacific. Melville's *Typee*, for example, combines an eroticization of the racially Othered women and men of the Polynesian island of Typee, producing what we might now call a bisexual fantasy. Charles Warren Stoddard, on the other hand, finds among the Hawaiian islands a male-centered space where he can explore homoerotic bonds with feminine young men. Jack London, writing during the early twentieth century, when homosexuality "began to speak in its own behalf," searches among the hypermasculine Polynesian men for homosocial bonds that are unruptured by homophobic ideology (Foucault, *History* 101). In analyzing these texts, I will focus on the threads of eroticization, exoticization, racial ideology, and imperial discourse that bind these texts together in a tradition of travel writing about the South Seas.

CHAPTER 1
Melville's Peep Show; or,
Sexual and Textual Cruises in *Typee*

> So pure and upright were they in all relations of life, that entering
> their valley, as I did, under the most erroneous impressions of their
> character, I was soon led to exclaim in amazement: "Are these the
> ferocious savages, the blood- thirsty cannibals of whom I have
> heard such frightful tales!"
>
> (*Typee* 132)

Counterallegiances?

At a crucial moment in *Benito Cereno* (1855) the narrator asks: "Who
ever heard of a white so far a renegade as to apostatize from his very species almost, by leaguing in against it with negroes?" (Melville 254).
Christopher Lane has read this passage as an example of Melville's horror when faced with the possibility of an imperial subject fostering a
counterallegiance with a colonized group (2–3). Such readings, though,
disregard the ironic voice that is so often present in Melville's narrator—
a voice that destabilizes Lane's argument. A closer reading of *Benito Cereno* might highlight Melville's ironic narrator as maintaining a much
more ambiguous position, for he is exposing the limits of Captain
Delano's views on racial difference. It is Delano, not Melville or the narrator, who is inspired by terror at the thought of the two races joining

together. The narrative thus speaks with a forked tongue: on the one hand, the rhetoric associated with speciesism is uttered by Delano; on the other hand, the narrator views Delano's utterance through an ironic lens. Such ambiguity allows for a potential critique of racist discourse while avoiding an absolute allegiance with another race.[1]

The narrator of *Typee* (1846) holds a similar position: Melville's first novel combines anticolonial statements and an anxiety about being consumed by Typee society. In this chapter, I want to inquire into this structural tension that underlies *Typee,* an inquiry that examines the combination of Melville's unique anti-imperial assertions—based on his exotic and erotic attractions to the island—with his appropriation of colonizing discourses from contemporaneous travel narratives set in the South Pacific.

Melville's Lie

According to Charles Anderson's *Melville in the South Seas* (1939), Melville lied when he claimed that he spent three months among the natives of a Polynesian island. The biographical information that we have regarding Melville's travels suggests that this fabrication resulted in other half-truths, particularly regarding the sources that he read while composing the novel. The details that scholars, such as T. Walter Herbert, have collected concerning Melville's Polynesian trip include the following facts: after completing a voyage to Liverpool as a deckhand in 1839, Melville acquired a job on board a whaling vessel; leaving from Fairhaven, Massachusetts, in January 1841, the ship arrived at what would become the fanciful island of Typee eighteen months later.[2] Melville and his shipmate, Toby Greene, deserted their vessel soon after it arrived. But they were eventually separated, and Melville returned to the coast approximately one month after his desertion. This three- to four-week residence on the island became loosely translated into *Typee,* a text that he published in John Murray's Home and Colonial Library as a narrative of "authentic" experience (Anderson 20–30).

The research compiled on Melville's South Sea adventures leads the contemporary reader to speculate about his motives for lying about the amount of time he spent on Typee; one might also ask why Melville adamantly asserted the authenticity of his text. There are undoubtedly numerous possible motives for Melville's fabrications; perhaps one such motive was that publishers found it "far-fetched" and almost "impossible to believe" (Woodcock 7). In fact, when Melville submitted an early copy of his manuscript to the Harper publishing house in New York, the narrative was rejected on the grounds that it was "too fanciful" (7–8). In light of this experience, Melville sent his manuscript to the English publisher John Murray, accompanied by a letter that vehemently upheld the authenticity of his narrative: "I have stated such matters just as they occurred and leave every one to form his own opinion of them" (qtd. in Woodcock 8). As well as making *Typee* more attractive to potential publishers, Melville's deception enabled him to identify himself as an expert concerning Typee culture. That is, if he had not lied about the length of time he spent on this island, readers might have questioned his expertise and the legitimacy of his narrative. But still some readers were skeptical concerning the authenticity of *Typee:* contemporary British critics indicated that Melville was a gentleman, "so he could never be a beachcomber." And many American missionaries identified Melville as a "lewd deceiver, whether he was a gentleman or not" (Herbert, *Marquesan* 181).

Furthermore, by attempting to convince his readers that *Typee* was a "real" travel narrative, Melville was trying to establish a framework from which he could broach political issues that were points of debate within mid-nineteenth-century American culture. In the guise of an authentic travel narrative, that is, Melville was able to denounce American and European expansionist policies that threatened to colonize the islands of the South Pacific. Authenticity, moreover, meant that Melville could critique the powerful ideological forces that privileged American "civilization" over the "uncivilized" islands of the South Pacific.

The popularity of travel writing in mid-nineteenth-century America also helps us to understand Melville's assertions of authenticity. Texts about authentic travel experiences were fashionable because they provided American readers with voyeuristic "peeps" into foreign lands unrestricted by American social and sexual codes; under the guise of scientific observation, in other words, travel writing explored exotic and erotic sites that titillated American readers with half-naked natives and fertility festivals.[3]

Melville's declarations of accuracy, however, led to further deceptions, for, by way of capturing verisimilitude, Melville consulted a number of contemporary travel narratives—narratives that he in turn attempted to hide from his audience. David Porter's *Journal of a Cruise Made to the Pacific Ocean, in the U.S. Frigate Essex, in the Years 1812, 1813, 1814* (1815), Charles Stewart's *Visit to the South Seas, in the U.S. Ship Vincennes, during the Years 1829 and 1830* (1831), and William Ellis's *Poly-*

nesian Researches (1833) were among the sources that Melville consulted before writing *Typee*.[4] Melville even writes of consulting David Porter's narrative; but perhaps in an attempt to undermine Porter's influence on *Typee,* Melville supplied an incorrect title for Porter's text (38). I would suggest that these sources are significant for reading *Typee,* in that they provided Melville with an imperial frame of reference, which inevitably resulted in *Typee*'s reinscription of the same colonizing attitudes that Melville claimed to be critiquing.

Erotic Journeys

The epistemological and fantastic modes of *Typee* work to two distinct ends: the former enables Melville to critique colonial Euro-American discourses; the latter permits him to utilize contemporary rhetorical strategies that constructed Polynesian culture as an earthly paradise. The extent to which Melville borrowed images from travel narratives by such voyagers as Nicholas Dorr, David Porter, Charles Stewart, and William Ellis is uncertain. What is certain, though, is that Melville's representations of sexuality and eroticism were influenced by such travelers. For example, one of the images that Melville takes from Dorr, Porter, and Stewart is the depiction of Typee women swimming out to greet the ship. Nicholas Dorr, in 1791, was the first to record this practice of Polynesian women: "The girls were permitted on board without hesitation. They were in general small and young, quite naked and without exception the most beautiful people I ever saw" (qtd. in Heath). Porter also records similar images in his 1815 travel narrative:

> The old chief directed the young girls to swim off to us. . . . The young men
> led them to the water, where they were soon divested of every covering and
> conducted to the boat. . . . [O]n their entering the boat, the seamen threw
> their handkerchiefs to the beautiful naked young women for covering. (13)

Melville, borrowing from Dorr and Porter, draws on these voyeuristic accounts to present the naked "nymphs" of Typee swimming out to meet the sailors of the *Dolly:*

> We were still some distance from the beach, and under slow headway,
> when we sailed right into the midst of these nymphs, and they boarded us

at every quarter. . . . All of them succeeded in getting up the ship's side, where they clung dripping with brine and glowing from the bath, their jet-black tresses streaming over their shoulders, and half enveloping their naked forms. . . . What a sight for us bachelor sailors! How avoid so dire a temptation? (48–49)

By referring to these women as naked temptations, Melville titillates his readers, an erotic strategy that is continued when he describes the women's arrival as "wholly given up to every species of riot and debauchery," for the women were irresistible due to their "graceful figures" and "softly moulded limbs" that "seemed as strange as beautiful" (49–50).

Melville's debt to Dorr and Porter is increased by his lingering descriptions of Polynesian beauty:

> The Marquesan girls are beautiful in the extreme . . . [with their] luxuriant locks . . . anointed with fragrant oil. . . . Their appearance perfectly amazed me; their extreme youth, the light clear brown of their complexions, their delicate features . . . and free unstudied action. (49)

Such descriptions function as typical Orientalist fantasies wherein dark otherness and "unlimited sensuality" transform these Marquesan girls into "creatures of male power-fantasy" (Said, *Orientalism* 207). And Charles Stewart furthers these exotic myths by commenting on the sexual accessibility of these women; he is, in fact, so dismayed by the sexual prowess of the Polynesian women that he is shocked into silence. "The scenes of licentiousness exhibited in our presence," Stewart exclaims, "were too shocking ever to be narrated by either pen or tongue" (132).

Melville, who consistently invokes the conventions of earlier travel narratives, also paints erotic pictures of his male Polynesian characters. He draws, for instance, on Charles Stewart's 1815 report of a beautiful Marquesan prince: "Piaroro is a prince by nature as well as blood—one of the finest looking men I ever saw—tall and large, not very muscular, but of admirable proportions, with a general contour of figure . . . that would do grace to Apollo" (259). Echoing Stewart, Melville describes Marnoo in similar terms of classical and effeminate beauty: "Marnoo was built like a Polynesian Apollo [with] curling ringlets, which danced up and down [on the] feminine softness of his cheek" (147).

If, as Edward Said and others have argued, the assigning of feminine attributes to peoples perceived as Other by a dominant and patriachally configured society is a way of usefully pressing them into an inferior mold, we must assume that Melville was participating in a pervasive discourse that assumed the effeminacy and inferiority of Polynesian culture. Such a discursive strategy was common in nineteenth-century travel writing. In 1853, for instance, Captain John Erskine published his *Journal of a Cruise among the Islands of the Western Pacific* (1853), a text that provides detailed accounts of Polynesian culture by focusing on the feminine features of Polynesian men. The most striking example of this occurs in a lithograph, published among the first few pages of the book, entitled *Girls and Man of Uea—Loyalty Islands* (reproduced below). This illustration, by J. A. Vinter, shows three Polynesians drinking from a large round cask; the two women are erotically presented through a lack of clothing; their breasts are completely revealed to the viewer, and only a thin band of material covers their waists. More interesting, though, is the image of the Polynesian man: his slim features, his long blond hair, his facial characteristics, and his feminine body all combine to blur his gender identity. Indeed, upon first seeing this figure a viewer could easily mistake him for one of the Polynesian women. By positioning the man's back to the viewer, moreover, the artist enhanced his effeminate appearance by hiding his genitalia from view. Thus, the only indication of his biological sex exists in the caption that accompanies the lithograph.

Furthermore, because the gaze of the nineteenth-century audience of adventure and exploration narratives was often assumed to be masculine, Vinter's presentation of this Polynesian man disseminates colonial ideology while presenting a sexually charged image for the potential homoerotic spectator. While critics often point out that feminizing projections function as forms of cultural imperialism, they often overlook the homoerotic nature of such representational strategies. Although Edward Said astutely argues that the "East" has existed as a psychological space where heterosexual men can erect illicit sexual fantasies and explore "sexual experience[s] unobtainable in Europe" or America, he ignores same-sexuality as part of this "different type of sexuality" imposed upon Eastern cultures (*Orientalism* 190). Joseph Boone, remarking on these oversights, claims that "the possibility of sexual contact with and between men [during voyages to the East] underwrites and at times even explains the historical appeal of orientalism as an occidental mode of male perception, appropriation and control" ("Vacation" 90). With this in mind, we may approach Vinter's lithograph from the perspective of the homoerotic. Through the feminizing depiction of a Polynesian man, the

J. A. Vinter's lithograph depicting the "Girls and Man of UEA-
Loyalty Islands." From John Erskine's *Journal of a Cruise Among
the Islands of the Western Pacific* (1853). Special Collections,
McLennan Library, McGill University, Montreal, Quebec, Canada.

artist conveys a sexually obtainable object, an object that symbolized a form of sexuality that was proscribed to an American spectator.

Melville's depiction of Marnoo, like Vinter's lithograph, combines feminine features with the conjecture of same-sexual opportunity. Marnoo, for example, is described as displaying an androgynous figure that stimulates Tom's sexual desire. We are also told that Marnoo's appearance consists of a Polynesian charm combined with classical forms of beauty, all of which culminate in a "matchless symmetry of form" (193). Melville also refers to Marnoo as "an antique bust" that displays a striking "feminine softness" (193). Upon seeing Marnoo for the first time, Tom's desire is immediately stimulated, but he soon becomes distraught when this "elegant" and "beautifully formed" man chooses to keep his distance:

> Struck by his [Marnoo's] demeanour . . . [I] proffered him a seat on the mats beside me. But . . . the stranger passed on utterly regardless of me. . . . Had the belle of the season, in the pride of her beauty and power, been cut in a place of public resort by some supercilious exquisite, she could not have felt greater indignation than I did at this unexpected slight. . . . His conduct, however, only roused my desire. (193–95)

Here Melville's narrator, the adventurous explorer, is transformed into the "belle of the season" when his desire is aroused by the "exquisite" beauty of Marnoo. Such representations of fluid gender identities and same-sexual desire in *Typee* can be traced to earlier South Pacific travel narratives. As Robert K. Martin points out, Melville's reference to "Buggery Island" in a brief descriptive passage about the South Sea isles signals his knowledge of the Polynesian institutionalization of male kinship as it came to him through Henry Dana's 1840 travel book, *Two Years before the Mast* (Martin, *Hero* 63). In Dana's text, the narrator describes the Polynesian system of male kinship known as *aikane,* a system wherein every man has "one particular friend . . . [whom he is] bound to everything for . . . in a sort of contract—an alliance" (Dana 153).

A similar form of male kinship is reported by William Ellis, who asserts that foreign visitors to Polynesian islands are immediately presented with male companions:

> On the arrival of strangers, every man endeavoured to obtain one as a friend and carry him off to his own habitation, where he is treated with the

greatest kindness by the inhabitants of the district; they place him on a high
seat and feed him with abundance of the finest food. (132)

Tom, upon arriving on Typee, is presented with Kory-Kory, a young man
who provides Tom with food and shelter. This Polynesian friend, moreover, expresses a sexual attraction to Tom and becomes "jealous" when
Tom's body is anointed and massaged by Fayaway and "the young
nymphs" (163). Directly following this passage, Kory-Kory begins light-
ing a fire; the sexual images that Melville uses in this scene suggest auto-
erotic behavior on Kory-Kory's part, which stands in for a deferral of his
sexual desire for Tom:

> [Kory-Kory] rubs . . . slowly up and down . . . quite leisurely, but gradually
> quickens his pace, and waxing warm in the employment . . . approaches the
> climax of his effort, he pants and gasps for breath, and his eyes almost start
> from their sockets with the violence of his exertions. (165)

Further textual allusions to Polynesian same-sexuality can be found in
Charles Stewart's account of his visit to Nukuheva. This narrative includes the description of a particular scene that disgusted him more than
his earlier experiences with the sexual practices of the South Pacific natives. During a visit to a so-called unknown tribe, Stewart observed a sexual festival of "pure heathenism" that plays out "the absolute of human
depravity":

> There was less of licentiousness in the dance than I had expected; but in a
> hundred things else there were such open outrages upon all decency, that I
> hurried away in horror and disgust, with a heart too much humbled for the
> race to which I belong, and too much depressed at the depravity and guilt
> of man, to think or feel upon any other subject. (262)

Here Stewart, as in his other descriptions of Polynesian sexuality, refuses
to give a detailed account of the festival. This experience is, however, distinct in that this ceremony causes him to suffer the greatest "horror and
disgust." Stewart goes on to inform us that the festival was "limited to
male Polynesians, including only those women who participated in the
erotic dances" (263). Because he establishes this ceremony as male-
centered, it seems probable that Stewart's horror and disgust arose out of
his panic regarding same-sexual desire. Eve Kosofsky Sedgwick notes

that "homosexual panic" may account for "the Unspeakable," the secret of that which remains hidden and ungraspable (*Epistemology* 204). This form of "panic" would explain Stewart's silence about and profound outrage at the events of this particular festival, an outrage so intense that he was forced to "question his Christian faith, for the acts of the ceremony mar[red] the highest glory of man" (263).

Melville's Imperialism

Throughout *Typee,* Melville is consistent in his harsh critiques of imperialist and missionary projects in the South Seas—projects led by missionaries like Charles Stewart. Thus, Melville uses anticonquest rhetoric to condemn colonial expansion. The conclusion to chapter 2, for instance, denounces the "European invasion" of the South Sea islands:

> Alas for the poor savages when exposed to the influence of these polluting examples! Unsophisticated and confiding, they are easily led into every vice, and humanity weeps over the ruin thus remorselessly inflicted upon them by their European civilizers. Thrice happy are they who . . . have never been brought into contaminating contact with the white man. (50)

Melville's progressive, anticolonial discourses are undermined, however, by the narrator's choice of diction; the very use of the term *savage,* for example, functions as a projection of Western constructions of Otherness by forcing a taxonomous system of that which is civilized and that which is uncivilized upon Typee society. Such binaristic language designates a boundary with which the concepts of what is extrinsic or intrinsic to a culture come into forceful play. It follows, then, that *Typee* is involved in what Homi Bhabha calls "a strategy of disavowal," whereby the trace of what is disavowed is "not repressed but repeated as something different" (114). That is, the "splittings" implied in Tom's articulations of displacement and dislocation are structured around the ambivalence of denial and repetition. *Typee's* narrator expresses such inconsistencies by placing overt disavowals of imperialism within the very structures of difference that are central to the rhetoric of colonial projects.

Furthermore, the tattoos of the various characters become distinct markers for constructing boundaries of cultural and racial difference.

While Tom claims to refuse tattooing for aesthetic reasons, his repulsion indicates an aversion beyond the aesthetic; for if he were tattooed, one of the central distinctions separating him from the Polynesian native would blur. As Elizabeth Grosz points out, tattooing often "offends Western sensibility . . . [because it does not] map a particular psyche or subjectivity but designate[s] a position, a place, binding the subject's body to that of the collective" (138, 140). Following Grosz, Tom's fear of being tattooed signals a much greater fear: the fear of becoming permanently marked as a member of the Typee community, thus losing his privileged position as traveler. Tom's tattoo panic, moreover, may be brought back into the realm of desire by linking it to the sexual panic expressed in Charles Stewart's narrative. If, as theorists have suggested, tattooing transforms an individual's "sexual zones by extend[ing] and proliferate[ing] them, creating the whole abdomen, arm, back, neck, leg, or face—whichever surface is tattooed or marked—as an erotic site," we may account for Tom's panic as partially based on a fear of increasing the erotic sites on his body (Grosz 140). A multiplication of erotogenic space, in other words, would disrupt his culturally specific notions of erotic zones, subsequently disrupting the fundamental constructions of Euro-American sexuality that mark his difference.

Refusal of tattooing, like the discursive power exerted by Melville's use of taxonomy, helps to stabilize cultural barriers that are reinforced by Tom's fear of cannibalism. His anxiety about losing his identity and being consumed—culturally and physically—by the Typees constitutes yet another discursive model that originates within the nineteenth-century system of connotations and assumptions of the traditional travel narrative. Melville's depictions of cannibalism, then, also were inspired by his sources. Gananath Obeyesekere, for example, argues that, while certain South Sea cultures may have ritualized ceremonies of anthropophagy, many early British and American ethnographers exaggerated the accounts of Polynesian cannibalism due to "the Euro-American tradition of cannibalist discourses." Nineteenth-century American audiences of the traditional travel text, in other words, associated ocean voyages (including shipwrecks) with human consumption, and "cannibalism during an exploration among native peoples or after a shipwreck was so much taken for granted in England and America that often ordinary innocuous survivors had trouble denying that it had taken place" (Obeyesekere 638–39). Melville, in compliance with audience expectations, echoes the conventions of the shipwreck narrative by implying that after leaving the

Dolly, Tom and Toby contemplate consuming one another. When they arrive on Typee, Tom and the crew suffer from starvation, for they have exhausted their fresh provisions and been reduced to eating only sea biscuit (35). The hungry crew is described as symbolically consuming itself, and once Tom reaches the island, body parts take on edible qualities: Tom's hurt leg is referred to as being "in the same condition as a rump-steak" (127); Tom's misshapen pieces of biscuit become like "midshipman's nuts" (75); Toby is said to be "ripe for the enterprise"; and when meeting the Typees, Tom and Toby are imagined to be "a couple of white cannibals" (113). Here, as with the threat of tattooing, the civilized-savage dichotomy threatens to collapse, but the narrative structure stabilizes such anxieties by reasserting the binary through Tom's anxiety regarding a ritualized ceremony for which he believes he will become the main course.

Gananath Obeyesekere links cannibalism with male sexuality by suggesting that nineteenth-century discourses surrounding anthropophagy, particularly as they were articulated after a shipwreck, were often infused with sexual currency. "In popular [Euro-American] thought," he states, "the black man, the Spaniard and the Portuguese were highly sexed libidinous creatures. They represented sexuality and life power; by consumption of their flesh one could introject these powers" (640). It is not surprising that Melville affiliates cannibalism with sexuality, for, by the mid-nineteenth century, a long discursive tradition had linked anthropophagy with sodomy. Epiphanius, for instance, condemned the Borborites for practicing both cannibalism and sodomy, and Thomas Aquinas connected sodomy with cannibalism in his descriptions of the sins that "exceed the mode of human nature" (Bergman 142). In *Totem and Taboo* (1913), moreover, Freud connects cannibalism with homosexuality in his explanation of the transition of patriarchal power from father to son. He asserts that in "primitive societies" the father's control over the harem forces his sons to engage in homosexuality; however, when the father's strength falters with age, the sons combine to overcome the father: "one day the expelled brothers joined forces, [and] slew and ate the father" (83). David Bergman's claim that Melville's reference to the consumption of the "midshipman's nuts" provides a frame in which cannibalism is given sexual currency is compelling. Such a framing partakes in the system of connotations and assumptions that conflate cannibalism and same-sexuality as potential violations of an American body. As a result, the feared physical taboos of sexuality and cannibalism inspire Tom's panic, for these possible transgressions threaten to disrupt his imagined identity as a "civilized" American. Yet, as Caleb Crain notes, it is likely that Melville's depiction of cannibalism on Typee was yet another mid-nineteenth-century legend that he borrowed from popular discourses (27).

Melville's representations of cannibalism, along with Melville's eroticization of the Typees and his critiques of Western civilization, not only function as tropes of difference but also assume an empirical understanding of Typee culture. As a traveler, though, Melville's presumed knowledge places him in the position of the "seeing-man," a man who symbolizes the "Euro-American male subject . . . whose imperial eyes passively look out and possess" a particular culture (Pratt 7). Tom may thus be read as a seeing-man who "peep[s] at Polynesian life" without disenfranchising the imperial rhetoric inherent to the nineteenth-century travel narrative. Tom, read as *Typee*'s seeing-man, might be considered a precursor to the twentieth-century sexual tourist, for the island serves as a space where he can explore different forms of eroticism while resisting a loss of self or cultural identity. Likewise, as a Western traveler exploiting the sexual freedom of Typee, Tom's critiques of imperialist expansion are implicitly corrupt. This, however, is not surprising when one considers the sources that Melville consulted while writing *Typee*, sources that inspired and reinscribed the very imperialist rhetoric concerning the South Seas that he claimed to denounce.

CHAPTER 2

Primitivism and Homosexuality: The Search for the "Natural" in Charles Warren Stoddard's *Travel Sketches*

And it is only through travel literature's permissiveness that
Charles Warren Stoddard can take us on a far more exotic journey
to the world of homosexual expression and freedom.
(Gifford 9)

Primitivism and Homosexuality

In his 1873 travel sketch, "In a Transport," a sketch that blends autobiography with fiction, Charles Warren Stoddard's narrator remarks that the mysteries of the South Pacific islands were unraveled by the author of *Typee:* "Herman Melville has plucked out the heart of its [the South Seas] mystery, and beautiful and barbarous Typee lies naked and forsaken" (*Cruising* 151). The language that Stoddard bestows on his narrator here is typical of the conventional nineteenth-century American travel text in that it assumes that exotic mysteries can be solved through

33

Western rationality. Furthermore, by referring to the nakedness of the island, Stoddard's reference to Typee rhetorically conceptualizes the South Seas as a sexual space, a space that the narrative voice ultimately renounces through the textual coupling of "naked" with "forsaken." More important, though, is the primitivist rhetoric of the narrator's allusion to the "beautiful and barbarous" island, which reflects an idealization of nonindustrial culture and thus echoes Melville's primitivist discourses.

In this chapter, I want to draw on what Marianna Torgovnick refers to as "primitivist discourse"—discourse that disseminates primitive tropes that are meant to distinguish between the Western sense of self and Other. I also wish to examine how particular tropes of the primitive function in Charles Warren Stoddard's representations of the South Pacific. Central to my analysis will be the issue of Stoddard's sexual attraction to men, an attraction that his narratives paradoxically define as both "Natural" and "*un*-natural." Contrary to John Crowley's claim that Stoddard did not define his same-sex desires as unnatural prior to the early-twentieth-century medical paradigm of homosexuality, I would like to suggest that (particularly in his later travel narratives) Stoddard's need to articulate his sexual desires led him to use terms such as "natural" and "unnatural" (Crowley, Editor's Introduction xl). This chapter, then, attempts to illustrate how Stoddard's search for a textual expression of same-sex desire inspired him to turn to the rhetoric of "primitivism," "prodigality," "childishness," "normalcy," and "abnormality" to fill the textual vacuum of nineteenth-century homosexual discourse.[1]

By tracing Stoddard's discussions of same-sexuality, I will argue that his autobiographical stories constitute a search for the natural, a term that I will use to refer to two central concepts in Stoddard's work. My first demarcation of the natural comes out of nineteenth-century conceptions of primitivism, which defined the primitive as man's *natural* state prior to the growth of industrialism and capitalism.[2] My second demarcation of the natural is that in Stoddard's later sketches the term usually implies sexual preference: heterosexual unions are defined as natural; homosexual experiences are labeled unnatural. Throughout Stoddard's writing, therefore, his search for "the Natural" constitutes both a desire to return to a world unblemished by modern industry and a desire to become natural by overcoming his own (and his autobiographical characters') same-sex desires. Thus, while Stoddard's sketches are, at times, of a piece with the discourses of imperialism, Stoddard's linking of homosexuality with primitivism also depicts homosexualities as colonized by an oppressive culture that classifies same-sexual attraction as abnormal. As Thomas Yingling puts it, Stoddard depicts the discursive colonization of the homosexual in ways similar to those of "the discourse of Orientalism [whereby] the Other [the homosexual] is positioned (but in this case by the discourse of heterosexualism) as the site of the uncivilised or primitive practices that are rejected as inferior and yet are essential to the definition and ideological construction of the civilised and the culturally superior" (92).

In light of Yingling's comments, I would suggest that inherent to Stoddard's representations of a "natural same-sexuality" and to the colonizing forces of heterosexual ideology is the emergence of a homosexual identity in late-nineteenth-century America. Indeed, Stoddard's South Sea sketches, published from 1873 to 1904, serve as important documents in tracking the development of an American homosexual identity, for the sketches were influenced by and in turn influenced turn-of-the-century sexual theories; Xavier Mayne, for example, quoted from *South-Sea Idyls* (1873) in his 1908 defense of homosexuality.

Following on the European sexological studies of homosexuality by Havelock Ellis, Magnus Hirschfeld, and Richard Krafft-Ebing, American doctors of the late nineteenth and early twentieth centuries began treating homosexuals and developing theories regarding "unnatural" sexual desires. The American psychiatrist Charles H. Hughes, for instance, wrote a 1904 article titled "The Gentleman Degenerate: A Homosexualist's Self-Description and Self-Applied Title," which defined homosexuality as "an unnatural hereditary perversion" (68). As treatment for this so-called unnatural biological disorder, Hughes believed that he could "cure" inverts by severing their pudic nerves or by castrating his patients in order to generate "sexual relief" (Gifford 60). Even the homosexual defender, Edward Prime Stevenson ("Xavier Mayne"), wrote in *The Intersexes* (1908) about the unnatural "Uranian . . . as [a] degenerate and criminal." More interesting, however, is Stevenson's use of Stoddard's *South-Sea Idyls* as evidence that not all "Uranians" were degenerate, for, according to Stevenson, certain of them were artistic and thus worthy of praise (383). Stevenson's quoting of *South-Sea Idyls* in defense of same-sexuality suggests that Stoddard's tales expressed an alternative to the unnatural or degenerate models of same-sex desire that were popular among American sexologists. What Stevenson recognized in *South-Sea Idyls* was that Stoddard, by linking homosexuality with primitivism, was able to depict the South Sea islands as a space outside civilization—a "Natural" space that was not always subject to the colonizing influences of heterosexuality or modern industry.

Stoddard's belief that the South Seas provided a liberating space from heterocolonization is expressed in a letter he wrote to Walt Whitman in 1890. Here, Stoddard states that he was unable to find peace in the United States and is turning to Tahiti in search of satisfaction:

> In the name of CALAMUS listen to me! . . . [I am] sailing towards Tahiti in about five weeks. I know there is but one hope for me. I must get in amongst people who are not afraid of instincts and who scorn hypocrisy. I am numbed with the frigid manners of the Christians; barbarism has given me the fullest joy of my life and I long to return to it and be satisfied. (Stoddard to Whitman, qtd in Katz 506–7)

While Stoddard reveals his internalization of imperial rhetoric in the structures of difference expressed through his delineation of "barbarian" and "civilised" cultures, this passage illustrates a connection between Tahitians and nineteenth-century homosexuals ("In the name of CALAMUS").[3] Stoddard's letter, moreover, asserts a primitivist stance by idealizing "barbarism" and privileging it over American culture; like many of his travel sketches, Stoddard's letter aligns primitivism with same-sexuality through the implication that, in order to find emotional fulfilment, the homosexual must flee the "frigid manners" of America and embrace the "instincts" of Tahiti.

Similarly, Paul Clitheroe, the homosexual hero of Stoddard's 1903 autobiographical novel, *For the Pleasure of His Company,* is unable to find gratification in his native America and so escapes to the homoerotic bliss of the ideal South Seas, accompanied by "three naked islanders" (188). The novel ends with this "escape from America," and the reader is led to assume that Paul's "Gilded Exit" is a permanent one, through which he has finally found satisfaction on "an island of sexual enchantment" (Gifford 29). Clitheroe's same-sexual desires place him outside the norms of American culture; consequently, he must seek out an alternative to the repressive patterns of nineteenth-century American thought and action, an alternative for which Stoddard was constantly searching in his travel writings.

Nineteenth-Century Primitivism?

According to Marianna Torgovnick, primitivism is difficult, if not impossible, to define because "the primitive . . . [is] an inexact expressive whole—often with little correspondence to any specific or documented societies" (*Gone Primitive* 20). Primitivist ideologies, in other words, are merely products of Euro-American thought and therefore shed more light on Western cultures than on those of so-called primitive locales such as the islands of the South Pacific. Yet the elusiveness of definitions of the primitive does not preclude the possibility of reading primitivist tropes—tropes that originate in Euro-American images and ideas about preindustrialist societies. Marianna Torgovnick articulates primitive tropes as follows:

> Primitives are like children, the tropes say. Primitives are our untamed selves, our id forces—libidinous, irrational, violent, dangerous. Primitives are mystics, in tune with nature, part of its harmonies. Primitives are free. Primitives exist at the "lowest" cultural levels; we occupy the "highest," in the metaphors of stratification and hierarchy. (*Gone Primitive* 8)

Torgovnick's description of primitivist discourses provides a helpful access route into Stoddard's South Sea sketches, but Torgovnick reminds us that we must historicize the primitive; nineteenth-century primitivism differs from that of other periods in American history.

In fact, primitivism was much more pervasive in nineteenth-century American social thought than during other historical moments. Although it was always linked to questions of race and ethnicity, the concept of primitivism was often taken from "savage" cultures and applied to other European and American societies as an instrument for gauging the advancement of a nation or a social class (Bentley 920). Inherent to nineteenth-century American theories about the rise of civilization from primitive societies were middle-class ideals about the industrialized principles of human progress (Stocking 53). George Stocking illustrates how these principles focused on the ideals of self-discipline, sexual restraint, and rational control over instincts and emotions. J. S. Mill's 1873 essay, "Nature," for example, claims that the "savage" has failed to find progress and that "civilized" man must repress physical pleasures and sexual gratification in order to commit himself to social and industrial progress (18). Euro-Americans who lacked self-restraint were therefore thought of as bereft of "moral nature" and given to "childish mirthfulness" (Bentley 921). Edward B. Tylor's *Primitive Cultures* (1871) summed up this discourse best by saying that "the savage" had "the mind of a child with the passions of a man" (27).

Because homosexuality was often defined in terms of uncontrolled instinct, same-sex desire found its way into primitivist tropes. Charles Hughes, for instance, rhetorically conflated primitivism with homosexuality by characterizing Uranians as "pigmies [*sic*] in the pathway of the giants" who needed to overcome their primitive passions if American culture was going to "progress" (Neurological 378). The discursive link between primitivism and so-called sexual deviance, then, was established by nineteenth-century doctors like Hughes, a link that may have been the origin of Stoddard's association of primitivism with same-sexuality. More interesting, however, is that the nineteenth-century rhetoric that defined the primitive as "childish" was also reserved for homosexuals; Hughes, for instance, warns his homosexual patients that they must overcome their "child-like behaviors" by controlling their "reverse sexual instinct[s]" (68). As John W. Crowley has shown, Stoddard's peers often used metaphors of childhood and immaturity when referring to Stoddard's same-sexual relationships and his homoerotic writing. Samuel Clemens's assessment of the "poor, sweet, pure-hearted, good-intentioned, impotent Stoddard," for example, characterizes the homosexual writer as an unworldly and childlike individual (qtd. in Crowley, "Howells" 69). Likewise, Walt Whitman describes Stoddard as having "a simple direct naive nature" (qtd. in Katz 507). William Dean Howells echoes Whitman's description by referring to Stoddard as "that veteran babe and suckling." And finally, the nature of the correspondence between Stoddard and Howells caused Crowley to remark that "Stoddard the child would [often] submit to Howells's parental authority" ("Howells" 77, 79).

Howells and Clemens accounted for Stoddard's childlike state by conflating his "sexual impotence" with his attraction to the South Seas (69). Although they were perhaps using the excuse of sexual inertia as a non-threatening explanation for Stoddard's bachelorhood and pursuit of male companionship, these inadequacies came to define his "childish" behavior in the eyes of his fellow writers. And the virile Clemens and the masculine Howells soon grew to scorn Stoddard's "impotence" and "childish frailties" (69). Stoddard's "sexual impotence," however, was not the only aspect of his personality that defined him as immature, for his affiliation with the South Pacific natives also caused his peers to consider him childlike and effeminate. T. J. Jackson Lears sheds light in the gendered implications of Stoddard's "childishness" in relation to his friendships with "the savages":

> In the *fin-de-siècle* imagination, many of the "childlike" qualities associated with the premodern character, and with the unconscious, were also linked with femininity. . . . [And] the premodern unconscious generated androgynous alternatives to bourgeois masculinity. Those options especially appealed to the men and women who were most restive under bourgeois definitions of gender identity. (223)

Effeminacy, then, became a primitivist trope within the nineteenth-century rhetoric of gender, and this trope came to define feminine men like Stoddard as both childish and unrestrained. Yet this discursive strategy resulted in one inconsistency: the "savage" was considered natural, while Stoddard's same-sex desire was defined (in American sexological terms) as unnatural. Although this rhetorical incongruity was partially responsible for Stoddard's search for a "Natural" life in the South Seas, the conflation of homosexuality with primitivism also illustrates how nineteenth-century imperial discourse was used to colonize both same-sexualities and nonindustrial societies.

Stoddard's South Sea Sketches

As Roger Austen puts it, "perhaps the greatest degree of homoeroticism can be found in [Stoddard's] 'Chumming with a Savage,' based on [his] 1869 visit to Molokai" (Introduction 13). Indeed, this autobiographical sketch describes Stoddard's relationship with Káná-aná, a Hawaiian adolescent with whom Stoddard fell in love. An example of Stoddard's portrayal of same-sexuality in the South Seas arises when he first meets Káná-aná:

> [W]e went . . . through the river to his hut, where I was taken in, fed, and petted in every possible way, and finally put to bed, where Káná-aná monopolized me, growling in true savage fashion. . . . I didn't sleep much, after all. I think I must have been excited. (*Cruising* 36)

While this passage is far from sexually explicit, the meaning is quite clear to the discerning reader: Stoddard and Káná-aná not only sleep together, but they also have a physical relationship which includes "petting" and sexual excitement. Disguised homoerotic scenes like this one are scattered throughout Stoddard's sketches, and they often constitute depictions of same-sex desire that is "natural" rather than a symptom of sexual perversion. Stoddard's writing, then, as E. I. Stevenson points out, provided an alternative to homophobic sexological models of same-sex desire.

Although many of these homoerotic scenes are depicted as being "natural," Stoddard's autobiographical voice occasionally condemns his own sexual attractions to the "savages." Stoddard, in a sketch titled "The Island of Tranquil Delights," for example, criticizes his attraction to the South Pacific islands as "childish." Here, Stoddard echoes Howells's and Clemens's critiques of his childlike naivete, for, when preparing to travel to Tahiti, Stoddard's autobiograpical narrator states:

> Again I turned towards my islands, and kept doing this sort of thing until it grew monotonous, and then I said to myself, Young fellow this must be stopped; cast yourself penniless upon some undiscovered island and work your passage home. The experience will, in all human probability, effect a permanent cure; you can then settle down and be as stupid as the great majority. I did it. (*Cruising* 159)

By referring to himself as a "Young fellow," Stoddard complies with those peers who labeled him as childish and sexually immature. Moreover, this passage implies that a "penniless" trip will "cure" his childlike behavior and make him a "normal" man. In fact, Stoddard's reference to being cured resonates with the sexological theories of Charles Hughes, who believed that homosexuals could rid themselves of their childish behaviors by undergoing medical and psychological treatment. Such a need to rid himself of his childish desires among "the children of nature" reflects Stoddard's longing to achieve that which nineteenth-century American ideology determined sexually normal: to "settle down" into a domestic lifestyle that precluded same-sex desire (*Cruising* 158).

The rhetoric conflating same-sexuality with the children of nature is prevalent in a number of Stoddard's other sketches, particularly "Chumming with the Savage" (1873), which amalgamates the sexual desires of the autobiographical protagonist with the biblical myth of the prodigal son. "So life flowed out in an unruffled current," the narrator states, "and so the prodigal lived riotously and wasted his substance" (*Cruising* 41). This sentiment is repeated in the conclusion of the sketch, when the narrator states:

> So I grew tired over my husks. I arose and went unto my father. I wanted to finish up the Prodigal business. I ran and fell upon his neck and kissed him, and said unto him, "Father, *if* I have sinned against heaven and in thy sight, I'm afraid I don't care much. . . . I'd give more this minute to see that dear little velvet-skinned, coffee-colored Káná-aná than anything else in the world. . . . He's about half sunshine himself; and, above all others, and more than any one else ever can, he loved your Prodigal." (44–45)

Although Stoddard's autobiographical character resists repentance in this passage, the repeated identification of himself with the prodigal son places him in a position of inferiority to the powerful figure of the father. Stoddard's character thus assumes the identity of the childish son, whose "riotous" and unrestrained actions with Káná-aná retain their adolescent features. Stoddard's rhetoric of same-sexuality, then, forces him into the same textual category as the childlike primitive: they are both characterized as children who must be controlled and educated by the colonial patriarch.

Furthermore, "Chumming with the Savage" presents "the Doctor," who functions as a policing force in the text, a force that imposes American morality on the autobiographical narrator and Káná-aná.[4] In order "to stop and be natural" among the natives, Stoddard must avoid the Doctor's gaze, and his evasive maneuvers serve as comic moments in the sketch. However, even when he escapes the Doctor's surveillance, Stoddard cannot shed the Doctor's moral influence. In an expression of internalized patriarchal morality, for example, the narrator states: "For the first time that summer I began to moralize a little. Was it best to have kicked against the Doctor's judgment? Perhaps not!" (32). When the Doctor finally becomes aware of Stoddard's sexual liaisons with Káná-aná, he is "filled with disgust" and he attempts to take Stoddard "over to the paths of virtue and propriety" (35). Thus, the Doctor, who is bestowed with the "voice of civilization," engenders Stoddard's "hating [of] civilization" and forces him to reject "the formalities of society" (35). Stoddard's dismissal of a culture that condemns homosexuality illustrates, once again, the rhetorical allegiance that Stoddard maintains between homosexuality and primitivism, an allegiance that is conceived out of colonial oppression and imperial surveillance.

Unfortunately, by referring to his sexual desires in terms of prodigal behavior, Stoddard performs a discursive slippage wherein same-sex desire is established as morally questionable. Homosexuality, within these rhetorical confines, is relegated to an unrestrained and decadent practice that is reprehensible to the ideological framework of nineteenth-century America. In accordance with the Victorian imaginary, then, the language that Stoddard uses to define his "prodigal love" is derived from the sphere of the "unnatural," thus implying that it must be conquered by restraint. As a result, while Stoddard's South Sea sketches depict an early identificatory system for same-sex relationships, this system is fraught with contradictory language and paradoxical assumptions. Stoddard's writing thus presents the reader with an alternative to the "unnatural" model of same-sexuality theorized in nineteenth- and twentieth-century sexology while simultaneously implying that same-sex attractions are childish and prodigal. These seemingly paradoxical positions suggest that although Stoddard was searching for a "natural" identity of same-sex desire, his internalization of the colonial practices of nineteenth-century America cannot be shed.

Stoddard's sketch entitled "Kane-Aloha" (1904) is typical of the discursive tension between the natural and the unnatural that runs throughout his work. This sketch, in which Stoddard depicts his love for a Hawaiian youth, opens with the statement "God made me!" and continues by describing the "natural love" that develops between the narrator and Kane-Aloha (68). This reference to God in the opening line echoes contemporary homosexual sympathizers who claimed that inverts should be considered natural because they had been created by God; a perfect God, in other words, could never create an unnatural being.[5] Stoddard continues by rhetorically uniting his natural love for Kane-Aloha with the nineteenth-century primitivist tropes that presuppose the "natural state" of the Hawaiians:

> There was a natural throne set upon a rock above the river . . . [where Kane-Aloha and I] rejoiced together; and there, laying aside such artifices as civilization and the new dispensation had forced upon them, returned again to that state of Nature which is nothing if not innocence exemplified. With what rapture my beauty-loving eyes fed upon this animated scene. Those children of the wilds were as modest in deportment as if their souls were guiltless of the knowledge of sin. (70–71)

Here, a tension develops between the "natural" and the "unnatural" in the textual slippage from their "natural love" to their guilty souls. While this paragraph begins by rejecting civilization in favor of the "state of Nature" of "children of the wilds," Stoddard's acceptance of primitive space is undermined by the condemnation of the final phrase: "their souls" are guilty of sin. Sin and guilt, that is, contradict Stoddard's earlier statement that the natives are free from the "artifices of civilization," for if these natives are guilty of sin, they must have been touched by Christian civilization—a civilization that stands outside that which is tropologically articulated as natural.

Furthermore, at the end of "Kane-Aloha," Stoddard contradicts his "natural love" for the Hawaiian natives. Regarding his love for Kána-aná, for instance, Stoddard tells his reader: "I have not written in vain if I, for a few moments only, have afforded interest or pleasure to the careful student of the Unnatural History of Civilization" (81). Here, the narrative undermines his declarations of natural love by turning to the contemporary discourses of sexology. By referring to the homosexual as the "student of . . . Unnatural History," that is, Stoddard chooses to reject his prior "natural" model of same-sexuality in favor of the sexological theories that defined same-sex attraction as transgressive.

Cruise Control

Stoddard, in fact, was far from innocent when it came to participating in imperial discourses. His internalization of the ideologies that colonized homosexualities cannot be divorced from an internalization of the American rhetoric used to justify the colonization of Hawaii and other South Sea islands. If, as Marianna Torgovnick states, "primitivist discourse . . . [is] a discourse fundamental to the Western sense of self and Other," Stoddard cannot be exempt from a nineteenth-century colonial practice that idealized the primitive (*Gone Primitive* 8). Such idealization of and fascination with "savages" certainly contributed to the work of imperialism, but it also provided an outlet and a locus for alternative impulses and desires. Stoddard can thus be conceptualized as inhabiting a space in which imperial practices were in conflict with an alternative impulse to merge with the colonized culture. Conversely, those making policy in nineteenth-century America knew what they wanted to do with Hawaiians and other Polynesian natives: control and colonize them, exploit them, convert them to Christianity, and use them as workers for industrial expansion (Torgovnick, *Primitive Passions* 15). While he expressed his anger at these imperial ideologies, Stoddard also identified (at least partly) with those Americans who were articulating colonial policies, which Stoddard at times condemned and at other times disseminated.

Stoddard's primitivism, then, is partially allied with the discourses of imperialism. In fact, throughout his sketches the Polynesian men are as much servants as they are lovers. In the sketch entitled "Joe of Lahaina" (1873), for instance, Stoddard first meets Joe, with whom he falls in love, and the two men live together in terms that can only be described as a master-servant relationship. Although Joe is Stoddard's lover, the narrator tells us: "Joe was my private and confidential servant"; and, as a servant, Joe must do all the "housekeeping," which the narrator itemizes for the reader:

> Joe would wake up in the middle of the night, declaring to me that it was morning, and thereupon insist upon sweeping out at once, and in the most vigorous manner. Having filled the air with dust, he would rush off to the baker's for our hot rolls and a pat of breakfast butter, leaving me, meantime, to recover as I might. Having settled myself for a comfortable hour's reading, bolstered up in a luxurious fashion, Joe would enter with breakfast. (48)

Joe's servitude in this passage is consistent with Stoddard's treatment of his other Polynesian lovers, for, in "Chumming with the Savage," Stoddard refers to Káná-aná as his "devoted servant" who will do anything for his master (42). Regarding these asymmetrical power relations, Crowley remarks: "The combination of racial darkness with devoted service and knowing silence was the ideal for Stoddard in his Island lovers" (Editor's Introduction xxx).

Stoddard justifies such master-servant relationships by using the imperial rhetoric of white supremacy. Upon arriving in Hawaii, for instance, Stoddard states:

> I was quite alone with two Hundred dusky fellows, only two of whom could speak a syllable of English, and I the sole representative of the superior white within twenty miles. Alone with cannibals—perhaps they were cannibals. They had magnificent teeth, at any rate, and could bite through an inch and a half of sugar cane, and not break a jaw. (32)

By adopting the rhetoric of superiority, Stoddard negates his claims to reject civilization; as John Crowley puts it, "Stoddard never forgot that he was civilized at heart" (Editor's Introduction xxix). Furthermore, as in Melville's *Typee*, Stoddard's labeling of the Hawaiians as cannibals buys into contemporary white mythologies of Polynesian culture and forces a structure of difference between the civilized American and the savage Hawaiian. Racial differences are reinforced in the final sentence of the paragraph, with its image of the animal-like and "magnificent teeth," an image that is later juxtaposed with the delicate features of the civilized American narrator.

Participation in nineteenth-century imperial discourse also emerges in Stoddard's feminization of the Polynesian men. In a move similar to Melville's representation of Marnoo, Stoddard describes Káná-aná's "ripe and expressive" lips and his "girlish face" (33). In "Joe of Lahaina," moreover, the gendering of Joe is developed in Stoddard's use of the feminine pronoun in reference to his breath: "*her* [Joe's] breath [was] sweeter than the sweet winds . . . of Lahaina" [emphasis mine] (47). Finally, in a sketch entitled "The Island of Tranquil Delights" (1904), the men of the Spice Islands are said to express a "genteel . . . [and] feminine fondness" for each other (161). By attributing feminine characteristics to Hawaiian men, Stoddard borrows from nineteenth-century American ideology in which "the primitive was coded as metaphorically feminine . . . and civilization was coded as masculine" (Torgovnick, *Primitive Passions* 14). David Spurr explains this gendered rhetoric as establishing a system of metaphors based on imperial penetration of the colonial subject, metaphors that established a discursive system for labeling colonies as feminine and thus, according to American patriarchal values, as inferior (125). Therefore, while many of Stoddard's travel sketches claim to despise and reject imperial ideologies, his gendering of Polynesian men contributes to the dissemination of metaphors that sanction imperial practices.

Consequently, Stoddard's repeated rejection of American civilization is never complete, for his autobiographical characters always return home to the United States.[6] In "Chumming with the Savage," for instance, Stoddard pays homage to the conclusion of Melville's *Typee* by having his American character flee a Polynesian island while being pursued by a native lover:

> There was Káná-aná rushing madly toward us; he had discovered all, and
> . . . ran after us like one gone daft, and plunged into the cold sea, calling my

name over and over as he fought the breakers. . . . I knew if he overtook us
I should never be able to escape again. . . . We lost sight of the little sea-god,
Káná-aná . . . [and] I didn't care for anything else after that, or anyone else,
either. I went straight home, and got civilized again. (44)

Like many of Stoddard's sketches, this passage depicts his fear of losing
affiliations with civilization and being consumed by Polynesian culture;
indeed, the narrator is said to "escape" the island so that he can return to
America and get "civilized." Such an escape, in addition to denoting a
lack of commitment to premodern cultures, signals a participation in the
erotics of imperial expansion. That is, Stoddard's actual and textual in-
dulgences in the sexual possibilities that he finds in the South Seas are
congruent with the exploitation of labor and natural resources by those
Americans who formed imperial policy: Stoddard could travel to Hawaii
or Tahiti, satisfy his sexual desires, and leave regardless of the consequences. As a result, Stoddard's textual rejections of civilization remain
linguistic gestures, never to become manifest in material practice. Crowley succinctly articulates this when he states: "Stoddard's notion of
'barbarism' was not only sentimental; it was also thoroughly in keeping
with the prevailing racialism and imperialism of the American Gilded
Age" (Editor's Introduction xxix).

Stoddard's travel sketches thus negotiate a paradoxical course
between the condemnation of American civilization (for its colonization
of same-sexuality) and the reinscription of imperial rhetoric. Homi K.
Bhabha sheds some light on this seemingly contradictory position by stating that these two levels—the idealization and colonization through
primitivism—are not always discrete but are often fused within colonial
discourse. In the words of Bhabha, "the colonial presence is always ambivalent, split between its appearance as original and authoritative and
its articulation as repetition and difference" (110). Imperial rhetoric,
Bhabha goes on to say, operates not only as an instrumental construction
of knowledge but also according to the ambivalent protocols of fantasy
and desire. Consequently, ambivalence depends upon a fluctuation
between wanting one thing and its opposite: a simultaneous attraction
toward and repulsion from an object, person, or action. Bhabha's theory
of ambivalence speaks to a representational space that is consistent with
Stoddard's seemingly paradoxical stance; he theorizes a gap that provides
room for fluctuations between oppressor and oppressed, colonizer and
colonized (Young 161).

Such ambivalence, moreover, explains Stoddard's characterization of homosexuality as both natural and unnatural, for his seemingly equivocal stance illustrates a dual position that concurrently attempts to forgo homophobic discourses while repeatedly returning to the American sexological models of same-sex desire. Although it is undoubtedly easy to condemn Stoddard's failed divorce from contemporary homophobic and colonial discourses, we should commend his valiant effort: not only does his search for a "natural" life function to critique imperial expansion, but it also contributes to the development of sexual theories by influencing sexologists like E. I. Stevenson to think about same-sexuality as a natural form of desire. Therefore, Stoddard's travel sketches were instrumental in developing a homosexual identity, an identity that could only have been explored through what James Gifford has called "travel literature's permissiveness" (Gifford 9).

CHAPTER 3

"Closer than blood-brothership": Male Homosocial Attachment in Jack London's *Tales of the South Pacific*

All my life I had sought an ideal chum—such things as ideals are
never obtainable, anyway. I never found the man in whom the
elements were so mixed that he could satisfy,
or come anywhere near satisfying my ideal.
(Jack London to Cloudesley Johns, qtd. in Sarotte 253–54)

Like a Brother

"Hawaii is a queer place," says the narrator of Jack London's 1912 short story, "Good-By Jack." Qualifying this statement, the male narrator describes the lack of social organization that characterizes Hawaii, and he goes on to define the archipelago as a "song," thus establishing it as an irrational space: "Everything socially is what I may call topsy-turvy. . . . Life in Hawaii is a song. That's the way Stoddard put it in his 'Hawaii Noi'" (111). While Hawaiian "queerness" may stem from a lack of social organization as London conceived of it, his narrator also condemns the American missionaries and "humble New Englanders" who attempt to "civilize the kanaka" by disseminating Christianity and American economic policies (111). London's reference to Charles Warren Stoddard's "Hawaii Noi," moreover, illustrates a direct link between the two authors: they both idealized Hawaii and condemned the colonial project that sought to corrupt the Polynesian islands with "civilization."[1] Such comments place London's South Sea stories in the tradition of the anti-conquest narrative in which the Western traveler/narrator critiques imperial projects and obstensibly renounces civilization while he simultaneously imposes Western values upon the foreign locale.

In addition to sharing Stoddard's denunciation of American imperialism, London's South Sea stories represent an exploration of alternative forms of male companionship; that is, London's Pacific tales, like his earlier fiction, express a love of masculinity that raises the issue of homoeroticism in his work. But unlike his earlier hypermasculine texts, which generate "identifiable strategies of homophobic displacement and suppression," London's South Sea stories explore a redefinition of conventional stereotypes and expectations concerning sex-role behavior (Derrick 118).[2] Part of this refiguration of male kinship, I would suggest, includes London's desire for close male friendships and homosocial attachments—attachments that he was able to explore through the "queerness" of Hawaii.

This chapter, then, examines the homosocial attachments that are developed in two of London's 1909 South Pacific stories: "The Sheriff of Kona" and "The Heathen." Past readings of these neglected texts have failed to position London's representations of colonization alongside or in relation to his depictions of same-sexuality.[3] Recent theories of sexuality and postcolonialism, moreover, provide a theoretical frame that facilitates inquiry into the rhetorical structures and ambivalent negotiations of London's texts: "national and sexual identification," as Christopher Lane points out, are often brought together in colonial narratives so that "the diverse subjective and symbolic meanings of masculine identity and desire" become embedded in imperial rhetoric. What follows is a reading of London's two texts in the context of Sedgwickian theories of sexuality and Bhabhaian notions of colonial practice. Along the way, I question the rigidity of Eve Sedgwick's theory of the homosocial continuum and combine Bhabha's and Sedgwick's conjectures to interpret London's representations of colonial ambivalence and conflicted same-sexuality. London's depictions of homosociality show the ways in which sexual ambivalence is intertwined with ambivalence about racial difference and American imperialism in the South Pacific.

Although other texts by London depict male-male attachments similar to those in "The Sheriff of Kona" and "The Heathen," the two short stories express clearly the possibility of ideal masculine relationships that are unhindered by traditional constructions of American masculinity. I have also chosen to focus on these stories because, like Melville's *Typee* and Stoddard's travel sketches, they were inspired by London's own travels in the South Pacific.

Because of their autobiographical nature, any reading of these stories benefits from the wealth of letters and autobiographical materials he wrote at this time. One such letter, written to his wife, Charmian, articulates the same intense male companionship that is explored in the South Pacific stories:

> I have held a woman in my arms who loved me and whom I loved, and in that love-moment have told her, as one will tell a dead dream, of this great thing I had looked for, looked for vainly, and the quest of which I had at last abandoned. And the woman grew passionately angry. . . . For I had dreamed of a great Man Comrade. (*Letters*, 1:370)

London goes on to rapturously confess to Charmian that he has searched for a "closeness . . . whereby . . . [a] man and I might merge and become one for love and life" (371). Dreaming of a "great Man Comrade" signals London's dissatisfaction with monogamous heterosexual relations, as well as with those gender tropes that preclude intimate male attachments. It is this homosocial "quest" that London plays out in his tales of the South Pacific, a quest that he found more gratifying in his fiction than in his letters.[4]

London's South Sea stories examine the possibility of an alternative form of male kinship between men of different races.[5] London's presentations of interracial attachments differ from those by Stoddard in that they do not depict genital sexuality; thus, these relationships can best be defined by such terms as "romantic friendship" and/or "homosociality." Some clarity is gained, therefore, by following the example of recent literary critics who distinguish between "homosocial," referring to the entire range of same-sex bonds, and "homosexual," referring to that part of the homosocial continuum marked by genital sexuality. Although the homosocial/homosexual distinction is problematical at best, it has useful, if limited, descriptive value.[6] Eve Kosofsky Sedgwick helpfully describes homosociality as social bonds between persons of the same sex . . . [that are] obviously formed by analogy with "homosexual," and just as obviously meant to be distinguished from "homosexual.". . . To draw the "homosocial" back into the orbit of "desire," of the potentially erotic, then, is to hypothesize the potential unbrokenness of a continuum between homosocial and homosexual—a continuum whose visibility, for men, in our society, is radically disrupted. (*Between Men* 1–2)

Sedgwick's articulation of a "broken" homosocial continuum is significant for reading London's South Sea sketches in that the emerging identity of homosexuality of the late nineteenth century engendered a homosocial rupture that would undoubtedly have influenced London's representations of masculinity. In fact, it may have been this disruption that resulted in London's search for a "great Man Comrade" in Hawaii; American homophobic ideology would have negated any possibility of his finding an "ideal chum" at home.

It is clear that London was exposed to homophobic American discourses. Joseph Noel's *Footloose in Arcadia* (1940), for instance, reports a conversation between Jack London and Michael Monahan:

"They were soldiers that perverted Rimbaud?" Jack asked.

"Yes."

"Sailors are that way too. Prisoners in cells are also that way. Wherever you herd men together and deny them women their latent sex perversions come to the surface. It's a perfectly natural result of a natural cause."

Then he [London] told us of what he called the fo'castle lovers he had encountered on his early trip to the Far East. (132)

Here we see London's familiarity with the heterocentric language that characterized homosexuality as a perversion. This passage illustrates, moreover, the early rhetoric that related homosexuality with the absence of women: intimate male contact was seen as a mere substitute for heterosexuality, and men were thought to experience same-sex desire only in the absence of heterosexual possibilities. These discourses, as Sedgwick points out, disseminated a "fear and hatred of homosexuality" and enforced a disrupted rather than a continuous structure of male kinship in Euro-American culture (*Between Men* 1).

Homosociality and Hybridity

London's voyages to the South Pacific (similar to those made by Herman Melville and Charles Warren Stoddard) were inspired by his dissatisfaction with American materialist culture. Earle Labor and Jeanne Campbell Reesman attribute this dissatisfaction to London's primitivist aesthetic, an aesthetic that he developed out of the writings of contemporary scholars (*Jack London* 32). One such scholar was George Santayana, who labeled the "authentic primitivist" as "an extreme individualist" who

> disowns all authority save that mysteriously exercised over him by his deep faith in himself . . . [he will be] heir to all civilization, and, nevertheless . . . take life arrogantly and egotistically, as if it were an absolute personal experiment. (96)

Santayana's words fit London's persona, for, as well as being an individualist, London considered himself to be the "heir to all civilization." London also recognized that capitalism and material consumption had corrupted the spirit of the United States; he therefore traveled to foreign lands with the hope of "finding some form of spiritual fulfilment" (Labor and Reesman 30)

In December 1907 this search for "spiritual fulfilment" took London to the Marquesas Islands and, most significantly, to Typee (the valley of Hapaa), an island that he had been longing to visit since first reading Melville's novel as a youth (Sinclair 8).[7] On this voyage, London expressed a desire to experience relationships similar to those that Melville had formed on Typee: "I was bent on finding another Fayaway and another Kory-Kory" (*Snark* 157). He was, however, soon disappointed. Instead of finding a natural paradise of beautiful natives, London was confronted with a population that had been decimated by diseases brought on by contact with missionaries and traders; the few remaining natives were crippled and deformed by leprosy and tuberculosis. Expressing his disillusionment, London states:

> [S]trength and beauty has departed, and the Valley of Typee is the abode of some dozen wretched creatures, afflicted by leprosy, elephantiasis, and tuberculosis. . . . Life has rotted away in this wonderful garden spot, where the climate is as delightful and healthful as any to be found in the

world. . . . When one considers the situation, one is almost driven to the conclusion that the white race flourishes on impurity and corruption. (*Snark* 164, 169)

Imperial expansion, London goes on to say, had corrupted Typee. But he justifies the corruption of Typee by turning to "Darwinian terms of natural selection" and arguing that "the superior white race" had overpowered the Marquesan natives (Stasz 130). Nonetheless, London recognized that Euro-American imperial policies had destroyed the "beautiful golden people described by Melville," thus decimating his chances of finding another Fayaway or Kory-Kory (Labor, "Pacific World" 212).

London's South Pacific fiction attempts to capture these imagined "Golden Isles" and unruptured homosocial attachments even in the destructive wake of imperial expansion. "The Sheriff of Kona," for instance, depicts the relationship between Cudworth (an American) and Lyte, the Sheriff of Kona. Set after Lyte's exile from Kona, Cudworth tells of his great love for his friend: "He was a great man, my best friend, my more than brother" (123). Such a bond attempts to refigure male-male relationships by including verbal expressions of love. And this gender refiguration is also present in Cudworth's affectionate description of Lyte's hypermasculine physique:

He stood six feet three. His stripped weight was two hundred and twenty pounds, not an ounce of which was not clean muscle or bone. He was the strongest man I have ever seen. He was an athlete and a giant. He was a God. He was my friend. And his heart and his soul were as big and as fine as his body. (123–24)

Cudworth's attraction to Lyte's vitality and power expresses itself in this frank admiration of Lyte's body, which Cudworth goes on to label "magnificent" and "perfect" (125). Lyte's exemplary figure exudes virility and potency, arousing Cudworth's desire, but this attraction is permitted no sexual outlet, for the two men are never physically intimate and remain "loving friends" rather than passionate lovers.[8]

By describing Lyte's flawless masculinity and his fine "heart and . . . soul," Cudworth echoes London's quest for an "ideal chum" who combines hypermasculine features with a mild and loving temperament. "The Sheriff of Kona" seems to play out London's quest in that the Lyte-Cudworth relationship is undisrupted by homophobic sentiments. London, in fact, presents their love as conventional, but their intimacy is disrupted when Lyte is exiled to the leper colony. Even this rupture, however, cannot estrange Cudworth from his friend, for he passionately risks his life to liberate Lyte from the colony. Hence, the homosocial bond remains unharmed by the Euro-American "fear and hatred of homosexuality," and Lyte and Cudworth are free to form a romantic friendship that is not subject to homophobic attacks (Sedgwick, *Between Men* 1).

It is important to note that the Cudworth-Lyte homosocial attachment is complicated by Lyte's racial ambiguity: his racial heritage mixes American and Polynesian characteristics. Lyte, who "was born . . . on the Kona coast," thus stands outside both racial identities; although he is an American, he is "built like the chieftains of old Hawaii" (123). Such ambiguity appears in Cudworth's other descriptions of Lyte. We are told, for instance, that Lyte supported colonization in the South Pacific but that he was nonetheless loved by the Kona natives, who made him Kona's sheriff. And although he is said to be Anglo-Saxon, Lyte's racial identity is allied with the primitive tropes that come to define the "child-like natives" (127):

> He [Lyte] was a simple man, a boy that never grew up. His was no intricate brain pattern. He had no twists nor quirks in his mental processes. He went straight to the point, and his points were always simple. (125)

Cudworth's descriptions of Lyte, then, echo those passages in Stoddard's travel sketches that construct Polynesians as childish and primitive. Unlike Stoddard's American characters, though, Lyte is born on Kona and represents what Anne McClintock refers to as "a cultural hybrid" (69).[9] McClintock, taking up Homi Bhabha's idea of colonial ambivalence, asserts that colonial texts can, at times, "blur the distinction between colonizer and colonized" by depicting characters who, like Lyte, disturb racial and national identities (69).[10] Lyte, in fact, embodies a "colonial crisis of origins" in that his ambivalent racial heritage places him in the "inbetween" of colonial discourse: he cannot be clearly identified as either American or Polynesian (63). Lyte, by inhabiting this space between colonizer and colonized, illustrates what Bhabha calls an "epistemological splitting" that discloses the double vision of colonial discourse and thereby dislocates its authority (Bhabha 86). London's characterization of Lyte thus denotes the "rupture," the "disruption," and the "ambivalence" that subverts colonialism and infuses it with flawed discourses that reveal its own "strategic failure" (Bhabha 86).

McClintock, in her reading of Rudyard Kipling's *Kim* (1901), complicates Bhabha's delineation of hybridity and mimicry as strategies of anticolonial resistance. She stresses that Kim's ambiguous racial identity as "both cultural hybrid and mimic man" enables him "to suggest a reformed colonial control" (70). This means that the privileged position of whiteness results in an alliance with colonization; the white man who passes for the colonized Other, therefore, does so in order to better police and govern the colonized region. While McClintock's argument is convincing in relation to Kipling's text, it is not as persuasive when brought to bear on London's stories. Perhaps this is because Lyte's affiliation with imperial policy is less stable in "The Sheriff of Kona." For example, although Lyte polices the natives, he resists the imperial policy regarding the leper colony, a decision that leads him to reject the laws that govern the island and to sever his loyalty to colonial rule. Thus, London presents Lyte as both racially ambiguous and politically indeterminate: Lyte concurrently enforces and rejects imperial policies.

The positioning of Lyte in between colonizer and colonized engenders a textual exploration of male bonds within the boundaries of colonial policy. Likewise, the imperial dislocations that arise out of Lyte's racial ambiguity lessens his stake in colonization and sanctions a potential anticolonial subversion of early-twentieth-century American bonds between men. Such connections between homosocial attachment and imperial defiance are formed during the climax of the narrative, when, in an act of anticolonial resistance, Cudworth helps Lyte to escape the leper colony and flee to Shanghai, where Lyte spends his remaining years. Here, the intensity of the Cudworth-Lyte homosocial bond is illustrated in Cudworth's life-risking act of rescuing his friend, a rescue that functions as a symbolic rejection of colonial law and policy. The potential self-sacrifice of one man for the other denotes how Cudworth and Lyte are not necessarily subject to the ideologies that govern American male kinship.

Between Men, Between Race

"The Heathen" (1909) is another of London's South Sea stories that explore homosocial attachments and racial ambiguities: it focuses on the relationship that develops between the American narrator, Charley, and a native of Bora Bora, Otoo.[11] Charley and Otoo are thrown together during a shipwreck, and when the ship's captain, Captain Oudouse, refuses to save Otoo's life, Charley shows his compassion by rescuing "the black heathen" (168). Otoo, in return, saves Charley's life by providing him with food and shelter when they finally land on a deserted island. Subsequently, the two men become intimate friends and engage in a marriage-like ritual that binds them together for life:

> [W]e . . . performed the ceremony of exchanging names. In the South Seas such a ceremony binds two men closer than blood-brothership. The initiative had been mine; and Otoo was rapturously delighted when I suggested it. (171)

Such an exchange significantly shifts the structure of Western male kinship: the exchange is a symbolic bond that joins them together in love for eternity. Charley, in fact, reminds Otoo of the significance of this ceremony by stating: "To you I am Otoo. To me you are Charley. . . . And when we die . . . still shall you be Charley to me, and I Otoo to you" (172). The subsequent merging of their identities through an exchange of names echoes traditional Western marriages, but this particular ceremony does not preclude heterosexual unions. Instead, their homosocial devotion serves as an accompaniment to their unions with women, and heterosexual relations become congruent with, rather than disruptive of, homosocial bonds.

The Charley-Otoo relationship, like that between Lyte and Cudworth, resonates with London's desire for an unruptured homosocial bond. Otoo, in fact, is given the masculine qualities that London often idealized: we are told that Otoo had a hypervirile body that "stood nearly six feet . . . and was muscled like a gladiator . . . [and] a manhandler" (168). Reminiscent of the descriptions of Wolf Larsen in *The Sea-Wolf*, London goes on to idealize Otoo's great physical strength by championing his ability to "break a man's ribs and forearm within four minutes" (169). The narrator is quick to assert, however, that Otoo "was no fighter," for "he was all sweetness and gentleness, [and] a loving creature" (168). But he could defend himself easily against attacks from other men.

Such comments regarding Otoo's physical appearance and loving nature gesture toward homoeroticism, but London exempts references to sexual intimacy. Instead, a commitment to heterosexuality is signaled when Charley informs us that they both have wives and children whom they love dearly. Yet when Otoo discovers that his wife is dead, the homosocial bond between him and Charley is strengthened. Charley states:

I never had a brother; but from what I have seen of other men's brothers, I doubt if any man ever had a brother that was to him what Otoo was to me. He was brother and father and mother as well. And this I know: I lived a straighter and better man because of Otoo. I cared little for other men, but I had to live straight in Otoo's eyes. Because of him I dared not tarnish myself. He made me his ideal, compounding me, I fear, chiefly out of his own love and worship. (174)

Charley's assertion that Otoo combines the features of brother, father, and mother posits domesticity, rather than sexual desire, as the principal attribute of their attachment. While this statement may obstruct homoerotic conjectures about their relationship, domesticity does not rupture their continuous homosocial bond; domestic paradigms actually strengthen this attachment, for Charley tells us that "for seventeen years we were together; for seventeen years he was at my shoulder, watching while I slept, nursing me through fever and wounds" (174–75). Thus, Otoo and Charley are undisturbed by—or simply unexposed to—the homophobic and racist discourses that might have severed their companionship; instead, their interracial bond flourishes, resulting in Charley's emotional growth. Charley tells us, for example, that his bond with Otoo forces him to reform his behavior:

I am very much afraid that I kept later hours than were becoming or proper. No matter what the hour was when I left the club, there was Otoo waiting to see me safely home. At first I smiled; next I chided him. Then I told him flatly that I stood no need of wet-nursing. After that . . . I discovered that he still saw me home, lurking across the street among the shadows. . . . Insensibly I began to keep better hours. . . . Truly, he made a better man of me. (176)

The domestic nature of their relationship is complicated by similar racial distinctions that are present in "The Sheriff of Kona." That is, London chooses to deconstruct traditional Western tropes of savage and civilized in his depiction of homosocial attachment. According to primitivist discourses, the "savage Polynesian" needed to be "tamed" and brought under the conceptual control of Christianity and domesticity.[12] London discredits this trope by characterizing Otoo in terms of restraint, materialism and the traditional paradigms of American domesticity. Charley, on the other hand, turns his back on American ideals and chooses the life of a drunken wanderer who disdains domestic impulses. In effect, London's

presentation of the Otoo-Charley homosocial bond resists representational modes wherein American characters "go native"; rather, an ideological slippage occurs in which their relationship causes Charley to become "a better man" by American standards.

London's negative portrayals of the so-called civilized characters in
"The Heathen" further contribute to the deconstruction of the civil-
ized/savage dichotomy. White characters exist outside tropological constructions of Western "civilization" due to their cruel and savage actions;
the French captain, Oudouse, for instance, cruelly "hits and kicks" Otoo
when "the black heathen" attempts to save himself by joining the captain
on his life raft (167). Oudouse's violent reaction forces Charley to yell:
"For two centimes I'd come over there and drown you, you white beast!"
(169). Charley's reference to Oudouse as a white beast gestures toward
London's belief that the colonial project transforms imperial subjects into
cruel and violent "savages," a theme that is more common in London's
other South Pacific tales.[13] Such anticolonial sentiments in "The
Heathen" become amplified when Charley rejects the tropes of white
superiority by dismissing Otoo's claim that Charley is his "master"
(172). Charley, regardless of Otoo's racial background, prefers to view
him as his partner, not as a racial inferior. And when Otoo sacrifices his
life to save Charley from a potentially fatal shark attack, their devoted
partnership culminates in "the act of a loving friend, not as the toadying
gesture" of an inferior servant (Tietze and Riedl 60).

Masculine Imperialism

It is important to recognize that London, like Melville and Stoddard, was
not exempt from believing in American imperial projects. While "The
Heathen" complicates the civilization/savagery binary, the very title of
the text illustrates London's implication in the rhetoric of an empire in-
vested in promoting structures of difference between American Christians and Polynesian "heathens." Reading this title as an "ironic use of
racism," as Thomas Tietze and Gary Riedl do, is problematic because of
Charley's sincere references to Otoo as "a black heathen" throughout the
text (168). And Charley uses other forms of divisive language to mark the
racial distinctions between himself and the South Pacific natives, referring
to them at times as "woolly-headed cannibals," "niggers," "savages,"
"black boys," and "head-hunters" (180–81). Charley, as well as using

racist language, clearly subscribes to the notion that "whiteness" is a shorthand term for fairness, loyalty, and trustworthiness. For instance, he praises Ah Choon as "the whitest Chinese I have ever known" (152). Charley, though, does not describe Otoo's skin color, but he does inform us that Otoo is "a native of Bora Bora, the most westerly of the Polynesian Group" (168). Otoo's status as a "westerly" character is furthered by the narrator's comment that Bora Bora had long been colonized by Christians and that most of the Bora Borans had adopted Western beliefs (188). The narrator thus sanctions the Otoo-Charley bond by marking Otoo as "westerly," not "uncivilized."

The racial ambivalence reflected in the characterizations of Otoo and Charley is consistent with London's more general ambivalence regarding the South Pacific. In a 1913 letter to his relatives, London states: "Here's hoping you two will never go journeying to the rotten-beautiful and beautiful-rotten places of the South Seas" (qtd. in Labor, "Pacific World" 212). London found much beauty on these islands, but he was also troubled by the deterioration of the South Pacific caused by Western economic policies and diseases. However, London justified the "Western corruption" of the South Seas by claiming that racial conflicts were necessary for determining "the fittest race" (Moreland 6). For London, the white man, especially the Anglo-Saxon, was the most "worthwhile" race and thus far superior to the South Sea native: "I do not believe in the universal brotherhood of man . . . I believe my race is the salt of the earth, I am a scientific socialist, not a utopian" (qtd. in Joan London 212). In an 1899 letter to Cloudesley Johns, moreover, London states his commitment to social Darwinism by claiming to be "an Evolutionist believing in Natural Selection . . . [who] cannot but hail as unavoidable the Black and Brown going down before the White" (*Letters* 1:27).[14]

Social Darwinism thus formed London's rationale for imperial expansion. Darwinist ideologies, as they were popularized at the time, appealed to the Anglo-Saxon elite because they reinforced ethnocentric and evolutionist attitudes toward "primitive" peoples. While London's variety of social Darwinism was more complex than the popular view, London could not, as Clarice Stasz notes, "help absorbing the ideology's crude racist slant" (130). London's social Darwinist convictions led him to accept Benjamin Kidd's theory that "the natural inhabitants of the tropics . . . [are] peoples who represent the same stage in the history of the development of the race that the child does in the history of the development of the individual" (52). Echoing Stoddard's representations of "the child-like Hawaiians," London accepted the imperialist thesis, which claimed that, since the "immature" native population was unable to develop its own natural resources, it was the duty of the white man to "farm the tropics" and profit from these islands (Moreland 8). Exploitation of natives, London believed, was simply an unavoidable consequence of evolutionary necessity, a necessity that would eventually engender a beneficial result (Stasz 132).

By subscribing to these colonizing ideologies, London contradicts the anti-imperial statements of his South Sea tales. Taken together, these conflicting stances embody Bhabha's notion of colonial ambivalence, whereby what is discursively disavowed always reemerges in another rhetorical form. Strategies of disavowal, then, are inherently corrupt in that they are marked by contradictions and ambiguities. Furthermore, London's paradoxical assertions regarding imperial conquests affect his presentations of homosocial attachments in that his acceptance of white supremacy represents a repudiation of "the universal brotherhood of man." By accepting asymmetrical power structures between races, London forces a slippage wherein his earlier models of interracial homosocial desire are disavowed, thus sliding homosociality into the same paradoxical position as his colonial rhetoric. That is, London's assertions of Anglo-Saxon superiority complicate the male homosocial bonds that are explored in "The Sheriff of Kona" and "The Heathen," two texts that depict interracial attachments that are supposedly "closer than blood-brothership." Colonial ambivalence, then, governs London's intricately intertwined racial and homosocial representations. According to Joseph Boone, "London seems as vitally concerned with issues of sexual identity as Melville; yet his attempt to chart a more positive ideal through male bonding is fraught with ambiguities" (*Tradition* 266). As Boone points out, it is important to note that, while London's South Pacific tales present "male bonding" in a much less ambiguous manner than *The Sea-Wolf* does, the homosocial attachments of these texts illustrate London's hypermasculine sensibilities—sensibilities that exclude effeminacy. Homosociality, as it is experienced by Lyte-Cudworth and Otoo-Charley, allows for an expression of masculine love and a fetishizing of athletic bodies without transgressing traditional gender codes or heterosexuality. That is, neither man becomes effeminized by the physical eroticism or homosocial contact that London phobically rejected as "lower class filth" (Sarotte 256). His South Pacific tales attempt to distinguish between a homosocial love of men and an eroticism that is rejected as effeminate.

Such fears of effeminacy are prominent in *The Sea-Wolf*, where they disrupt homosocial bonds; however, in his South Sea tales, London attempts to contain these fears so that homosociality might remain continuous. He thus tries to split his views of homosocial love from his misogynistic tendencies by presenting his male characters passionately declaring their love and performing a marriage-like ceremony. Genital contact, though, is absent from London's depictions of male-male bonds: although Otoo and Charley sleep together following the shipwreck, they do not physically express their love. In addition, the conclusions to "The Sheriff of Kona" and "The Heathen" suggest that intense homosocial attachments cannot be sustained: they are presented as fleeting rather than enduring. Lyte, for instance, becomes dislocated because of his leprosy, thus erasing his bond to Cudworth. Otoo and Charley's attachment is similarly nullified during the story's ultimate scene, in which Otoo is killed by a shark. The fates of these two (in London's eyes) "racially inferior" characters function as symbolic dismissals of homophobia and taboos of miscegenation. London's textual decisions result in a strategic failure within the Sedgwickian model of homosocial desire. Because there is no fluid movement between male friendship and genital contact, a rupture occurs to prevent a smooth transition from homosociality to homosexuality. Lacking a fluid continuum, London is unable to present undisrupted male bonds, and his desire to achieve a continuous structure of male kinship is exhausted. Ambivalence, therefore, characterizes London's depictions of male homosocial attachments, for his articulations of a desire for unruptured male companionship are eventually undermined by an avoidance of portrayals of genital contact, resulting in an ambivalent homosociality that echoes London's conflicting positions on race and imperialism.

While for the most part these stories confirm Sedgwick's theory, the powerful bonds between their male characters inspire a question about Sedgwick's conception of the ruptured homosocial continuum: if Euro-American homosocial bonds are always subject to disruptions, at what point on the homosocial continuum do such ruptures occur? Because the imagined structures of male kinship in the South Seas allow for same-sex marriages and verbal expressions of love, they must be distinguished from American homosocial bonds that rupture prior to these ceremonial and verbal commitments. It seems problematic, then, to group *all* homosocial ruptures together without distinguishing between the distinct forms of male companionship that may develop on a broad continuum of homosocial desire. In short, although London privileges male bonds in his South Sea stories, the homosocial attachments remain ambivalent through the exclusion of physical passion. However, like Melville's representation of the cross-racial love of Ishmael and Queequeg in *Moby-Dick,* London's exploration of romantic male friendship provides an alternative paradigm of kinship between men—a paradigm that leads us to question the conformity of early-twentieth-century interracial bonds.

PART 2
Europe and
Beyond

Inglese Italianato, è un diavolo incarnato, that is to say, you remain men
in shape and fashion, but become devils in life and condition.
Roger Ascham
(of Englishmen traveling in Italy, 1570)

The Grand Tour

The eighteenth century witnessed a substantial increase in the number of British men and women traveling to France and Italy for pleasure. France and Italy were the touristic destinations of choice, not only because of their geographical locations (which made them easily accessible from England) but also because they provided cultural monuments (artistic, historic, architectural, etc.) and moral freedom. As Jeremy Black illustrates, British men of the eighteenth century traveled to Paris and Rome under the pretense of wishing to experience the painting, sculpture, and ruins that these European cities had to offer—a pretense that, more often than not, provided cover for activities involving gambling, drinking, and sex (189). The discourses surrounding the Grand Tour, therefore, constructed France and Italy as offering opportunities to experience "immoral pursuits." The most prominent discourse was that of sexual conquest, a notion that pervaded the travel writing, journalism, letters, and diaries by those men who took the Grand Tour.

British rhetoric about the Grand Tour constructed eighteenth-century Paris and Rome as cities of "loose morals," for both urban centers were notorious for prostitution. Fathers, according to Jeremy Black, would often warn their traveling sons of the "danger from Italian amours" that could presumably lead to same-sex encounters or venereal diseases. While the anxiety regarding homosexuality is not well documented, the fear of contracting a sexual disease in Rome was a common feature of eighteenth-century British travel writing. According to Black, a large number of English noblemen were infected with sexually transmitted diseases while visiting Rome; most notoriously, Charles Howard, Viscount Morpeth, died in 1741 of a venereal disease contracted in Italy (191). The cause of Howard's death was well publicized and compounded travelers' anxiety about the possible physical and moral corruption of those who participated in the Grand Tour. Such infections provided physical evidence of European sexual activities and contributed to the dissemination of France and Italy as morally corrupt spaces, a dissemination that continued into the nineteenth century.

The large numbers of British noblemen who participated in the Grand Tour during the late eighteenth century were not matched among American men of wealth, for, after the American Revolution, extreme American nationalism discouraged Americans from traveling to Europe (Withey

80–81). In declaring their independence, Americans had rejected Europe and chose to dissociate themselves from European institutions; thus, they thought that "refinement" and "culture" could be found at home rather than in "distant countries" (Dulles 2). Furthermore, late-eighteenth-century American nationalists considered European culture to be morally corrupt; Americans crossing the Atlantic were thought to be risking moral infection by exposing themselves to the vices of the Old World. It would seem, then, that the widely publicized sexual exploits of eighteenth-century Englishmen in Europe painted tourism in France and Italy as immoral within the American imagination.

But there was another side to the discourses disseminated by the nineteenth-century American traveler in Europe: they often represented European cities as providing opportunities that could not be encountered at home. According to Rhea Foster Dulles, Americans of the nineteenth century began to conceive of Europe as "a tumultuous playground," where one could enjoy a carefree vacation and escape the restraints of a country dominated by Victorian conventions (4). Travel in Europe, therefore, meant experiencing a "greater liberty": diversity instead of conformity, play instead of work, pleasure instead of duty. It would seem that many of the British discourses about European freedom, liberty, and opportunity—discourses that were established during the Grand Tours taken by British noblemen of the eighteenth century—were inherited by Americans of the nineteenth century. In fact, the European tour designed for Americans was modeled on the Grand Tour of the eighteenth century: Americans would sail to Liverpool, from which they would then travel to London, Paris, Switzerland, Germany, and Italy.

Early-nineteenth-century American travel texts on Europe tended to represent Paris as a beautiful, colorful, and lively city; it was the "longed-for Paris, gay Paris," George Hillard wrote with typical exuberance, "*la belle ville,* enchanting city" (qtd. in Dulles 74). Other American travelers commented upon "the vivid, almost weird, life of the Parisian streets" with their "well-dressed dandies with curling whiskers and round hats" (Dulles 74). While the boulevards and the museums (particularly the Louvre) were admired by American travel writers of the period, many American tourists were appalled by what they considered to be the lavish decadence of the architecture and sculpture. One American tourist, for instance, referred to the "spurting monsters" of the fountains at Versailles as "a disgusting and outrageous perversion"; another saw the whole scene as "a striking monument to the selfish lifestyle of kingcraft" (qtd. in Vance 26).

Yet some American travelers in Europe shared Emerson's view that Paris was "a place of the largest liberty . . . in the civilised world" (qtd. in Baker 66). One such liberty was the vibrant nightlife that could be found on the Champs Elysées and that many Americans wrote about in their journals and travel books. Thus, similar to the Grand Tours of the eighteenth century, the nineteenth-century European tours gained a reputation for vice and "immoral" activity. Travel accounts of this period often condemned the European enthusiasm for gambling and described gambling establishments such as the Palais Royal as "the most corrupt spot[s] on the face of the earth" (Baker 42). The Reverend John A. Clark's travel notebooks, for example, refer to the casinos as "those dreadful gambling houses—those fearful haunts—those hells" (qtd. in Baker 42).

As well as providing freedom to wager money, European cities also provided unique social opportunities that, at times, transgressed American conventions of gender and sexuality. Numerous travel accounts described the popular masked balls, where the identities of the participants were concealed throughout the evening. Quite often, such balls were occasions for individuals to conceal their gender by cross-dressing. These carnivalesque parties fascinated and outraged many American travelers; according to Rhea Foster Dulles, "Americans generally were scandalised by the popular mask balls (they hinted only vaguely of what they feared might take place)" (77). Paradoxically, several of the American travel texts that condemned these balls also described them in great detail, indicating that the travelers/writers had attended many of the "questionable" parties. In fact, Nathaniel Willis, after describing a number of masked balls, was inspired to pronounce: "I am not very particular, I think, but I would as soon expose a child to the plague as give either son or daughter free rein for a year in Paris" (53).

In my reading of the American participation in the Grand Tour, I have chosen to focus on three texts: Nathaniel Hawthorne's *Marble Faun* (1860), William Wells Brown's *Sketches of Places and People Abroad* (1854) and Edith Wharton's *In Morocco* (1919). While these works may seem more diverse than similar, all of them present Europe as a site of potential liberation for the American traveler. For Hawthorne, Rome's ethnic differences and avenues of liberation from nineteenth-century moral codes governing gender and sexuality ultimately inspire intense anxieties, which cause representational gaps and crises. On the other hand, for a fugitive slave such as William Wells Brown, Europe represents a space that provides both physical and psychological freedom, a space where he can explore a liberated identity in a so-called foreign homeland (132).

In reading Edith Wharton's *In Morocco,* I would suggest that she extends the European Grand Tour to include North Africa. Writing at a time of increased American tourism in Europe, Wharton journeys to Morocco in order to free herself from the mass of her fellow tourists. And as Lynne Withey points out, the European Grand Tour of the early twentieth century "moved east" to include Morocco and Egypt (223). Moreover, the French presence in Morocco provides a Eurocentric frame of reference through which she can explore the ancient Roman history that she sees lying in the background of Moroccan culture.

CHAPTER 4

Roman Holiday:
Discourses of Travel and Eroticism in
Nathaniel Hawthorne's *Marble Faun*

As Malcolm Bradbury notes, Nathaniel Hawthorne's 1860 novel, *The Marble Faun*, "became a kind of guide book" for the many nineteenth-century American tourists who "visited the sites, the paintings, the church interiors of . . . Rome" (Bradbury xlv). In fact, Thomas Ryan adds that Hawthorne's novel "is seriously fragmented by [the] inclusion of descriptive impressions of Italy which belong more properly to the tradition of the travel book than to the romance" (3). Paintings, sculptures, architecture, ruins—these are a few of the Roman sights that interrupt the narrative and provide the reader with touristic commentary, much of which was compiled during Hawthorne's own Roman vacation of 1858 and 1859.[1] The narrative voice of Hawthorne's novel, then, at times takes on the persona of the narrator-as-traveler who guides the reader through Rome, and it utilizes many of the literary techniques associated with the travel narrative. My intention in this chapter is not simply to itemize the guidebook elements of Hawthorne's novel but to examine how Hawthorne utilizes traditional discourses of travel to construct Rome as an exotic and erotic place for the American reader. I will argue that the formal structure of *The Marble Faun* enables Hawthorne to depict his erotic attraction to Rome and to inscribe his text with autobiographical experiences that correspond to the discourses of the traditional travel text. By asserting that *The Marble Faun* cannot be divorced from the representational devices of travel writing, then, this chapter will explore Hawthorne's appropriation of the colonizing rhetorical strategies that were deployed in traditional nineteenth-century travel literature. Finally, I will argue that Hawthorne participated in the rhetoric of eroticism, primitivism, idealization, and anxiety that characterized the discourses surrounding European tours, discourses that began during the Grand Tours of the eighteenth century.

Discourses of Travel

The entry dated February 7, 1858, in Nathaniel Hawthorne's Italian notebook expresses the representational difficulties he experienced when confronted with Rome: "I cannot get fairly into the current of my Journal, since we arrived in Rome; and already I perceive that the nice peculiarities of Roman life are passing from my notice before I have recorded them. It is a very great pity" (*French* 55). Passages similar to this one, proclaiming the representational limits of travel writing, appear throughout Hawthorne's notebooks and indicate his awareness of his own inability to capture in text his impressions of Rome. Hawthorne, therefore, recognized the impossibility of bridging the gap between experience and signifier, for language and the performance of writing became inadequate for disclosing his emotional reactions to the Roman scene.

The problem inherent to the genre of travel writing—translating personal experience into language—is further complicated in Hawthorne's Italian notebook by his complex and conflicting sentiments regarding Rome. Roman culture inspired both admiration and disgust in Hawthorne, conflicting emotions that he expresses throughout his travel writing. Upon arriving in Rome, for instance, Hawthorne is excited by the "brilliant frescoes" and the "beautiful pictures painted by great masters"; he also finds that the churches and palaces convey "an idea of splendour . . . never gained from anything else" (*French* 48–49). This passage, however, is juxtaposed with a paragraph that expresses Hawthorne's revulsion to the nineteenth-century city:

> I shall never be able to express how I dislike the place [Rome], and how
> wretched I have been in it. . . . Rome does seem to lie here like a dead and

mostly decayed corpse, retaining here and there a trace of the noble shape it was, but with a sort of fungous growth upon it, and no life but of the worms that creep in and out. (*French* 54)

Hawthorne's conflicting emotional reactions to Rome, combined with the representational problems of travel writing, contribute to his inability to record his Roman impressions through language and thus impede a disclosure of Rome's secrets.

Although Hawthorne lists the "cold, nastiness, evil smells, narrow lanes between tall, ugly, mean-looking, white-washed houses, sour bread, pavement, most uncomfortable to the feet, enormous prices for poor living, beggars, pickpockets, ancient temples and broken monuments with filth" as reasons for his aversion to Rome, he also dislikes the city for the eroticism of its art (*French* 54). Upon gazing at the "voluptuous" imagery of Paul Veronese's *Rape of Europa*, for instance, Hawthorne feels "cold and miserable, morally and physically" and experiences "a kind of half-torpid desperation" (*French* 114–15). According to William L. Vance, Hawthorne saw the "guiltless animal sexuality" in Italian art as "indistinguishable from late classical 'corruption' with tales of nymphs and satyrs—and their attendant fauns" (1:118). Apparently from a kind of fear, then, Hawthorne expressed discomfort in the face of the Faun of Praxiteles and other Roman or Greek sculptures. Paradoxically, though, the erotic elements of Italian art also inspire his admiration:

Close beside Beatrice Cenci hangs the Fornarina, a brunette, with a deep, bright glow in her face, naked below the navel, and well pleased to be so for the sake of your admiration—ready for any extent of nudity, for love or money,—the brazen trollope that she is. Raphael must have been capable of great sensuality, to have painted this picture of his own accord and lovingly. (*French* 93)

Hawthorne's Italian journal, then, expresses both admiration and moral protest when confronted with the eroticism of Italian art—conflicting emotions that correspond to his simultaneous adoration of and disgust with the Italian city. That is, Hawthorne's attraction to the erotics of Italian art is combined with a moral anxiety about the sexualized subject matter of these paintings and sculptures, an anxiety that threatens the "Victorian purity . . . [that was] a feature of the sexuality inscribed upon women's bodies" in nineteenth-century America (Herbert, "Erotics" 12).

The discourses that Hawthorne uses to construct Europe as exotic and erotic—describing Italian art as sexually explicit, for example—had already been established by earlier travel texts. For instance, the British travel writing from the European Grand Tours of the eighteenth century used erotic language to describe France and Italy. It seems possible, then, that Hawthorne used these eighteenth-century texts as literary models to overcome the representational difficulties he experienced when attempting to record his impressions of Rome.

European Tours

"Young man, *go to Europe!*" Grant Allen tells his reader on the opening page of his 1908 edition of *The European Tour*. Allen goes on to qualify this statement by asserting that "the most valuable education a man can obtain is a European trip, undertaken during the years most often devoted to a college course" (1). While he cites European art, architecture, and historical monuments as precious sources of education, Allen also refers to the importance of Europe's leisure activities, such as drinking beer, smoking cigarettes, gambling, and female companionship—all of which Allen lists as being quite acceptable for a young American in Europe. Allen's comments, then, suggest that the European tour provided not only an education in the humanities but also the "leisurely pleasures" that were unacceptable in America (265). Furthermore, Allen informs his reader that Rome ought to be the last stop on the European tour: "Don't go first to Rome. If you do, you will never understand Italy so well . . . to see Rome before Florence is *a fatal blunder.* . . . The moral is, *go last to Rome.* See it after you have learned what Italy aims at" (193–95). Although he explains this comment by stating that it is the best way "to study the evolution of the arts," his tenacity about visiting Rome last is rooted in the European "way of life" (195). In Allen's view, the American must become accustomed to the "impurity" of European morality before visiting the most morally "decadent" of all European cities (202).

The American discourses that constructed travels in Europe as educational in both "high culture" and "impure morality" had their origins in the Grand Tours of the eighteenth century, when there was "a substantial increase in the number of British men and women traveling abroad for pleasure" (Black 7). Jeremy Black illustrates how many of these British tourists indulged in excessive drinking and gambling during their brief stays on the Continent. The greatest attractions for British men, though, were the erotic possibilities that were said to exist in France and Italy. Travel writing of the period often disseminated stories of mythic erotic adventures in Paris and Rome, constructing French women, for example, as morally flexible and sexually available:

> It is observable, that the French allow their women all imaginable free-doms, and are seldom troubled with jealousy; nay, a Frenchman will al-most suffer you to court his wife before his face, and is even angry if you do not admire her person: And, indeed, by the liberties I have often seen a married lady use, I have been at a loss to distinguish her husband from the rest of the company. *(General)*

Newspaper articles of this kind were common in eighteenth-century England; likewise, British sexual conquests were recorded in many of the journals and letters belonging to the young men who went on the Grand Tour. The *London Evening Post,* for example, commented on these sexual exploits in 1737:

> Our gentry will make themselves . . . famous in making conquests among the French women. . . . We hear from Paris, that one of the dancers of the Opera, called La Salle, so remarkable for her chastity, as to have obtained the name of vestal, has at last surrendered to a young English nobleman, who was introduced to her at an assembly in woman's apparel, and so far insinuated himself into her favor, as to be permitted to take part of her bed.

This passage is particularly interesting, not only because it is an example of how articles described the Grand Tour in terms of sexual conquest but also because it establishes Paris as a place where gender divisions are not discrete. That is, Paris is portrayed as a city that accepts men who dress "in woman's apparel" in order to fulfill their sexual desires.

Those discourses of the Grand Tour that constructed French women as available for sexual encounters were also used in reference to Italian women. Rome, in particular, was known as a place where sexual adventures could be bought. According to Philip Francis, "in England the commerce between the sexes is either passion or pleasure; in France it is gallantry, sentiment or intrigue; in Italy it is a dull insipid *business*" (qtd. in Black, 196). Francis, of course, was referring to the Italian prostitution industry of the eighteenth century, an industry that became very popular among tourists; indeed, it was not long before Rome was considered by many Englishmen to be the "cockpit of sexual adventure in Italy" (196). Moreover, young travelers of the eighteenth century, according to Black, were often warned about the potential "dangers of Italian amours," including the homosexual encounters that were sold on the streets of Rome. Such sexual opportunities soon took on a mythic status, and the sexual currency associated with Paris and Rome was a common theme in most eighteenth-century travel narratives.

Like Hawthorne's Italian journal, the eighteenth-century discourses that constructed Italy as an erotic space were infused with anxieties about corruption. Much of this anxiety was expressed as a fear of the physical and moral corruption wrought by venereal diseases—a fear that was heightened in 1741 when Charles Howard, Viscount Morpeth, died of a sexually transmitted disease that he contracted in Rome.[2] This anxiety was intensified when the English noblemen Charles Hotham, Henry Pelham Clinton (earl of Lincoln), and John (second earl of Buckinghamshire) all contracted venereal diseases in Rome between 1734 and 1754 (Black 190). Although stereotypes created by British writers had constructed the Continent as an morally corrupt place, the Grand Tour reinscribed and disseminated these discourses, which later provided textual models for nineteenth-century Americans who chose to write about their own European tours.

During the nineteenth century, the Grand Tour continued with writers such as Byron, whose long poem *Childe Harold's Pilgrimage* (1818) was partly based on his travels in Italy. Byron's travel writing inspired a recreation of the eighteenth-century Grand Tour, in which many travelers followed the well-worn routes to Paris and Rome. However, these travelers were no longer the wealthy young men of Boswell's generation; for the first time, "women began traveling in large numbers, and . . . there were more family groups and more people of merely upper-middle-class means" (Withey 60). Indeed, Americans women like Margaret Fuller were free to travel throughout Europe unchaperoned, and James Fenimore Cooper traveled through England, France, and Italy with his wife and children. While these new conditions changed the experience of European travel, the discourses that had been disseminated during the eighteenth-century Grand Tour persisted. For instance, the rhetoric of European travel as a means to acquiring cultural capital remained prominent, and many American and British travelers were said to be inspired by the Continent's historical and cultural heritage (Dulles 27). Another persisting discourse was that of European freedom and liberation. Harriet Beecher Stowe observed that "French life was different from any other. Elsewhere you do as the world pleases; here you do as you please yourself" (2:146). And Bayard Taylor called Paris "an earthly Elysium," a place of entertainment and sensuous pleasures that was part of the Parisians' "exuberant gaiety of spirit" (436).

Many travelers who re-created the Grand Tour for the nineteenth century continued to comment on the exhilarating and unsettling sensuality of European capitals. Paris's Palais Royal, for example, became known as the center of European decadent entertainment because of its open policies on gambling and prostitution (Russell 187). Italy, too, continued to be an important destination on the nineteenth-century Grand Tour. And as Lynne Withey points out, "although history and art remained an important part of Italy's appeal, the sensual qualities of Mediterranean life that had so appealed to Boswell and Goethe became even more captivating to nineteenth-century visitors" (84).

These allegiances between the eighteenth-century travel discourses of the Grand Tour and the American travel writing of the nineteenth century have been further described by Eric Savoy. Savoy argues that "the discursive practices of the Grand Tour, with which American travel writings align themselves . . . crucially shaped the American travel essay of the later nineteenth century" (288–89). In fact, the eighteenth-century discursive strategies that defined Rome as an erotic space where a tourist "risked moral infection" became important features of American travel texts (Dulles 2). Paul Baker shows how the typical male American traveler considered Rome "the goal of his travels in Italy," for it was here that he could experience the "sensual pleasures" of life (always at the risk of moral infection) (62). Even Thomas Jefferson, who deeply appreciated European art and culture, believed that an American's virtue could be threatened by taking a European tour: "It appears to me . . . that an American, coming to Europe for his education, loses in his knowledge, in his health, in his habits, and in his happiness" (54). In nineteenth-century America, then, Rome was thought to provide "an escape from the restraints of a country dominated by Victorian conventions" but at the expense of moral corruption (Dulles 4).

Erotic images, along with anxious reactions to Roman culture, were inscribed into Hawthorne's Italian notebooks partly in response to Rome's erotic art. Returning to Paul Veronese's *Rape of Europa,* for example,

Hawthorne comments on its "magnificent frame" and asserts that it is a "joyous, exuberant, warm, [and] voluptuous piece of work" (*French* 114). Hawthorne goes on to say that some of the painter's work is "too voluptuous . . . for the public eye," and he claims that Veronese's depiction of Calypso and her nymphs (representing "a knot of naked women by Titan") is an "objectionable" painting (*French* 170). The erotic paintings and sculptures that Hawthorne viewed in Rome often offended his Victorian sensibilities, which, according to Walter Herbert, idealized sexual purity: "The Hawthornes had been startled," Herbert says, "by the nudity of the pictures and statues they viewed in Italy, and their minds insistently formed a judgment concerning the sexual interaction between artist and model" (*Dearest* 231). Similar to Hawthorne's anxious reactions to the eroticism of Roman art were his troubled responses to Rome's lack of domesticity, a value that he, like so many nineteenth-century Americans, cherished.[3] Meditating on Roman architecture, for example, Hawthorne asserts: "There was never any idea of domestic comfort—or of what we include in the name of home—at all implicated in such structures; they being generally built by wifeless and childless churchmen" (*French Notebooks* 58). For Hawthorne, then, Rome symbolized an erotic space that rejected Victorian sexual ideology as it was expressed in domesticity and moral purity, a space that incited a mixture of attraction and anxiety in the prudish Hawthorne.

Erotic Discourses

Lying in sharp contrast to Hawthorne's anxiety concerning Roman eroticism is Margaret Fuller's travel writing on Rome. In fact, William Stowe writes that, for Fuller, Rome was a city of "aesthetic pleasure," "political commitment," and "sexual fulfillment" (124). Indeed, passion and desire were central to her Roman travels: she writes of Rome as a place of "high desire" and a place where she is free to explore her sexuality by taking an Italian lover (*At Home* 106). And in her memoirs she meditates on the passionate feeling that "the men of Rome excite" in her (19). This excitement, of course, led to Fuller's relationship with Giovanni Angelo Ossoli. Ossoli certainly had the physical qualities to inspire excitement: Madeleine Stern writes that Fuller was intensely attracted by Ossoli's becoming "dark hair and olive skin, [as well as] his handsome and youthful form" (420). Moreover, Hawthorne's Italian notebooks describe Ossoli's "fine

figure" and "extraordinary good looks" (*French Notebooks* 155). Hawthorne and others, then, saw Fuller's relationship to Ossoli as a profoundly physical affair; Hawthorne even goes as far as to comment on
Ossoli's "lack of intelligence," saying that he does "not understand what
feeling there could have been [between Fuller and Ossoli], except the
purely sensual" (156).

Fuller's physical attraction to Ossoli was played out on a stage that did
not demand the same roles as did nineteenth-century America. That is,
her affair occurred out of wedlock, until she eventually had a child by
Ossoli and they subsequently married. But the openness of this unconventional affair shocked Hawthorne's American sensibilities, and he
called the relationship "unrefined" and "rude" (156). Rome, then, provided a space where Fuller could explore her sexuality and unconventional relationships that would not have been sanctioned in the United
States. Her relationship to Ossoli thus questioned two important ideologies of nineteenth-century American culture: the sanctity of women's purity and the strict gender roles imposed on women.[4] Such questioning
echoes her *Women in the Nineteenth Century*, which celebrates "inde-
pendent" women who are not afraid to express their "affections," and
this book even heralds gender transgressions by paying homage to the
cross-dressing of George Sand (163, 75). For the other American expatri-
ates in Rome, though, Fuller's writing about free love and gender bending
was one thing; to actually have an affair with a young Italian count was
another. Her questioning of nineteenth-century sexual and gendered categories through her relationship with Ossoli alienated her from the
American expatriate community in Rome. For instance, Hawthorne, a
longtime friend of Fuller, condemned her behavior; he writes of her as
having "fallen victim to lust" and of being corrupted by "animal impulses" (Herbert, *Dearest* 226). As a result, he cut off all social contact
with Fuller and openly repudiated her, a repudiation that clearly illustrates his anxieties concerning Roman eroticism. That is, Hawthorne sees
Rome as a place of liberation, but he also sees the city as a place of potential corruption. Rome, from his perspective, provided a liberatory space
for Fuller to explore her sexuality; however, for Hawthorne this space
also awakened Fuller's animal nature and the "rude potency" that led to
her moral and social downfall (*French Notebooks* 157).

This eroticism that "corrupts" Fuller found its way into *The Marble
Faun*. In the first chapter of Hawthorne's novel, for instance, the narrator
eroticizes the Faun of Praxiteles:

> The Faun is the marble image of a young man. . . . His only garment—a lion's skin . . . falls half-way down his back, leaving the limbs and entire front of the figure nude. The form . . . is marvelously graceful, but has a fuller and more rounded outline, more flesh and less heroic muscle, than the old sculptors were wont to assign to their types of masculine beauty. . . . The mouth, with its full, yet delicate lips . . . calls forth a responsive smile. The whole statue . . . conveys the idea of an amiable and sensual creature, easy, mirthful, [and] apt for jollity. (10)

The diction of this passage—the "graceful" and "full" outline of the body, combined with terms such as "sensual," "delicate," and "heroic"—signals the sexual currency of the sculpture. Furthermore, Hawthorne's attribution of both classically heroic and effeminate characteristics to this sculpture presents the nude image of the "young man" for the reader's erotic pleasure; the narrator asserts that Praxiteles' Faun provides the viewer with sexual possibilities because of its "lack [of] moral severity . . . [which is] endowed with no principle of virtue" (10).[5] By describing the faun's beauty as effeminate, the narrator legitimizes his erotic attraction to the sculpture. Likewise, the masculine erotics projected by Hawthorne's text onto Praxiteles' sculpture echo the erotic image that Hawthorne describes in his Italian notebooks. In an entry dated April 30, 1858, Hawthorne writes:

> The faun['s] . . . garment falls half way down his back, but leaves the whole front, and all the rest of his person, exposed, displaying a very beautiful form, but clad in more flesh, with more full rounded outlines, and less development of muscle, than the old sculptors were wont to assign to masculine beauty. . . . [The face has] beautiful and most agreeable features, but rounded, especially about the throat and chin; a nose almost straight, yet very slightly curving inward, a voluptuous mouth . . . in short, the whole person conveys the idea of an amiable and sensual nature. (191–92)

In both *The Marble Faun* and the Italian notebooks, then, Hawthorne attributes feminine features to the "sensual nature" of the sculpture. The lack of muscle and the artist's resistance to "masculine beauty" opt for a feminine beauty, which Hawthorne transposes onto the body of Donatello, *The Marble Faun*'s only significant Italian character. The narrator's erotic feminization of Praxiteles' faun, moreover, is superimposed on

Donatello when Kenyon, the text's American tourist, states that Donatello does not only resemble the faun but that "Donatello be actually he!"
(13). The text goes on to establish Donatello as symbolic of Rome's historic ancestry, for he is a combination of the paganism of ancient Rome
and the nineteenth-century Rome of corruption and decadence. Descriptions of Donatello, for instance, fluctuate between images of a "Dancing
Faun" and nineteenth-century American stereotypes of him as an "un-
washed ruffian" (14).

The Marble Faun, like the discourses surrounding the Grand Tour,
constructs Roman culture as feminine and accessibly erotic. Hawthorne's
depiction of Donatello echoes discourses of travel and imperialism in
which "a rhetorically constructed body . . . represents the colonized
world as feminine and which assigns to subject nations those qualities
conventionally assigned to the female body" (Spurr 170). Hawthorne's
rhetoric of gender difference can be seen elsewhere in nineteenth-century
American travel writing; George Hillard, for example, wrote that "the
image of Italy dwells in our hearts like that of a woman we have loved"
(qtd. in Dulles 68). By imposing feminine characteristics on the Italian
Other, Hawthorne, like Hillard, reinscribes the travel rhetoric of the
eighteenth century, rhetoric that considered Rome to be an Anglo-
American "playground," where sexual exploits were readily available
(Dulles 4). In this rhetorical strategy, differences in power are reformu-
lated as differences in gender, and colonization is naturalized as the relation between the sexes. I would suggest, then, that the discourses of travel
and eroticism in *The Marble Faun* force Rome into an inferior mold
through the novel's depiction of effeminate Roman men.

Hawthorne's gendering of Roman culture also furthers a structure of
ethnic difference that pervades *The Marble Faun.* Hawthorne delineates
textual boundaries that distinguish American characters from the European ones: Kenyon and Hilda are described in terms of innocence and
moral purity, whereas Donatello and Miriam are constructed as erotic
and morally corrupt.[6] The narrator explicitly marks this structure of difference at the end of the novel, when Hilda and Kenyon decide to return
home:

> [T]hey [Hilda and Kenyon] resolved to go back to their own land; because
> the years, after all, have a kind of emptiness, when we spend too many of
> them on a foreign shore. We defer the reality of life, in such cases, until a
> future moment, when we shall again breathe our native air. (365)

This passage reinforces the binary structure that separates "their own land" from the "foreign shore" of Italy, a binary that reminds us of the differences between the Americans and the Europeans. As such, Hawthorne's Italian novel corresponds with the aspect of travel discourse that imposes discrete features on different racial or ethnic groups. In other words, the Italian characters in Hawthorne's novel are clearly differentiated from the American characters, resulting in a structure of difference that is imposed on the Italian characters by the American narrator-as-traveler. As a result, Italy is reinterpreted and determined by the American observer so that the presentation of Italian life reflects the framework and values of the gazing American tourist.

The positions of power held by the American characters and the narrative voice, in addition, establishes the eroticism of Donatello in terms of nineteenth-century primitivism. While Donatello is often described as a feminine man, the narrator at times refers to him as a savage, "beautiful creature, standing betwixt man and animal": throughout *The Marble Faun,* Donatello is described as being "on the verge of Nature," like the "woodland elf" who occupies the space between modern man and animal (14, 16). The most striking depiction of Donatello's "strange animal qualities" appears in chapter 9, "The Faun and Nymph" (Bradbury xxxvii). Here, Donatello is said to use

> the language of the natural man; though laid aside and forgotten by other men, now that words have been feebly substituted in the place of signs and symbols. He gave Miriam the idea of being not precisely man, nor yet a child, but, in a high and beautiful sense, an animal; a creature in a state of development less than what mankind has attained, yet more perfect within itself for the very deficiency. (61)

The idealization of "natural man"—man who is untouched by the industrialization of Victorian culture—is prominent in this passage, for the narrator asserts that the animal-like Donatello is "more perfect" because of his connection to the mythic Europe of the faun and his lack of connection to modern Europe and America.

The narrator's use of primitivist rhetoric in reference to Donatello is congruent with Hawthorne's travel notes on Praxiteles' faun. Upon visiting the Roman sculpture gallery, Hawthorne claimed to take "particular note of the Faun" because he wanted to write "a little romance about it" (191). And in his itemized description of the statue, Hawthorne focuses on the Faun's primitive attributes:

The Faun has no principle, nor could he comprehend it, yet is true and honest by virtue of his simplicity; very capable, too, of affection. He might be refined through his feelings, so that the coarser, animal part of his nature would be thrown into the back ground, though liable to assert itself at any time. . . . All the genial and happy characteristics of the brute creature, seemed to be mixed in him with humanity—trees, grass, flowers, cattle, deer, and unsophisticated man. (192)

Like the rhetorical strategy of feminization, this primitivist depiction of Praxiteles' faun idealizes and eroticizes the Italian culture that Hawthorne experienced during his Roman holiday. Like discourses of the eighteenth-century Grand Tour, Hawthorne depicts Donatello and Praxiteles' faun as free from the moral laws of the nineteenth century and thus as open to erotic possibilities. By placing the Italian characters outside morality and rationality, Hawthorne suggests that they represent an alternative to nineteenth-century American values. The primitive faun and the animal-like Donatello, that is, represent a romantic nostalgia for a historical moment that existed prior to the advancement of industrial capitalism.

According to David Spurr, the ideology that characterizes primitive peoples as "children of nature" became a common feature of nineteenth-century travel writing (156). Hawthorne's text, like Melville's representation of the Typees, presents the Italian characters in terms of natural qualities and natural phenomena; after all, "trees, grass, flowers, woodland streamlets, cattle, deer, and unsophisticated man" characterize Donatello (11). This process of naturalization functions as a rhetorical device that imposes an identificatory system on the native cultures encountered by the travel writer. That is, although the concept of nature is idealized in Hawthorne's text, the process of naturalization forces the Other into an inferior position by defining him or her as nonrational, nonprogressive, and less developed. By describing Donatello as "natural," Hawthorne defines him as more immediate and spontaneous than his American counterparts, for Donatello is more given to expressing his passions and desires; he thus lacks the nineteenth-century American virtues of self-control and rationalism.

While Hawthorne may have been attracted to Donatello's freedom of expression, he was clearly anxious about the potentially destructive consequences of unleashed passion. For example, Donatello is referred to as a "wild" animal who displays "brute force" through "a trait of savageness"; it is this unrepressed desire, the narrator implies, that leads to the murder of Miriam's model. Hawthorne's anxiety arises .out of the nineteenth-century Victorian concept of "natural man" as an unproductive and debased being. J. S. Mill's 1873 essay, "Nature," for example, attempted to distinguish between natural man and modern man by defining the ideal nineteenth-century subject as committed to social and industrial progress. Mill's essay therefore disparages the idealization of mankind in its natural state and asserts that nature and natural instinct are precisely what humanity must learn to discipline: "The ways of Nature are to be conquered, not obeyed" (20). Thus, Hawthorne's idealization of Donatello as a natural man is undermined by his anxious feelings about not conquering nature, an anxiety that arises out of the Victorian position articulated by Mill (and represented by the murder of Miriam's model). By undermining his idealization of the primitive, Hawthorne, like J. S. Mill, reduces "the ways of nature" to a strategy of power and control whereby different cultures are classified and distinguished from one another: the Italians become taxonomized as natural, and the American characters retain their identities as modern.

Hawthorne's assigning of primitive attributes to his Italian characters is entirely unique, because this rhetorical strategy was typically reserved for non-Western cultures: as we have seen, Herman Melville and Charles Warren Stoddard used primitivist discourses in their descriptions of the aboriginal cultures of the South Seas. Nineteenth-century primitivism, moreover, was usually used in reference to cultural others defined through an established travel rhetoric of national-racial character. As Nancy Bentley points out, Hawthorne participates in the racialized discourses of travel writing by representing Donatello, Miriam, and the other Europeans in terms of their racial difference (912). The narrator, for example, defines Donatello's racial heritage as "[n]either man nor animal, and yet no monster, but a being in whom both *races* meet, on friendly ground!" (*Marble* 11 [emphasis mine]). Donatello is again depicted in terms of racial difference when the narrator alludes to him as "a beautiful creature, standing betwixt man and animal, sympathizing with each, comprehending the speech of either *race*" (13 [emphasis mine]). The narrative passages that construct Donatello's racial characteristics comply with the sections of Hawthorne's Italian notebook that refer to Praxiteles' faun. In the following passage, Hawthorne describes his inspiration and intention for regarding his depiction of Donatello's race:

The *race* of fauns was the most delightful of all that antiquity imagined. It seems to me that a story, with all sorts of fun and pathos in it, might be contrived on the idea of their species having become intermingled with the human race. (*French* 178 [emphasis mine])

Hawthorne employs the rhetoric of racial difference in both his travel notebooks and *The Marble Faun* to reinscribe the dichotomous relationship between native and foreign, natural man and modern man. In other words, Hawthorne constructs discrete racial identities for the racial characteristics of Americans (Hilda and Kenyon) and the Europeans (Donatello and Miriam). By making these racial identities discrete, he sets up a binary system whereby the text's American tourists are never in danger of "going native" or adopting the "savage" characteristics of "natural man." These dichotomous racial structures were common features of nineteenth-century American travel writing, for they created a shared "reality" between the writer-as-traveler and the American audience; in this discursive strategy, the authority of "we" (we Americans) was placed in a position of power and control over the racially othered group that was being observed.

But the merger of eroticism and racial difference is best illustrated in Hawthorne's depiction of Miriam. Like Donatello, Miriam's racial identity is constructed as the dark "foreign" figure, a figure that Nancy Bentley correctly links to a collection of racial types that flourished in travel books of the eighteenth and nineteenth centuries (Bentley 915). Miriam's specific racial identity, though, is never stated, and it remains a mystery throughout the text. Kenyon, for example, claims that Miriam "has Anglo-Saxon blood in her veins . . . but [she also features] much that is not English breeding, nor American" (19). The narrator, however, complicates Miriam's Anglo-Saxon traits by referring to a rumor that calls her "the offspring of a Southern American planter . . . [with] one burning drop of African blood in her veins" (20). This rumor concerning Miriam's mysterious racial identity enables Hawthorne to paint an erotic image of her by merging her Aryan features with a darkly exotic identity that is left unnamed. The eroticism that Miriam conveys through her "dark eyes . . . [and] black, abundant hair" is further developed by the "rich oriental character in her face," a feature that prompts rumors that she is "the heiress of a great Jewish banker" (20).

If, as Edward Said suggests, the "dark, oriental" woman frequently symbolized "unlimited sensuality" and sexual availability in nineteenth-century American and European texts, Hawthorne's characterization of Miriam is perhaps intended to stimulate his American readers' imaginations (Said 207). Likewise, by referring to the rumors of Miriam's "burning" Afro-American blood, the narrative constructs her, like Donatello, as passionate and emotional—outside the bounds of rational thought. As the narrator states, Miriam's Afro-American blood "so affected her with a sense of ignominy, that she relinquished all" (70). Thus, Miriam's racialized characterization is laden with sexuality, passion, sensuality, and eroticism.

Miriam's sexual transgressions, however, have dire consequences, for the narrator accuses her of "great error" and "fatal weakness" (34). Here the narrative voice presents Miriam as concealing a "dark sin" that evokes "mystery and terror" in Donatello (41). Miriam is aware of her "doom," and she feels great guilt regarding the "unwholesome acts" of her life. Upon hearing Donatello's declaration of love, for instance, she states:

> [F]or your own sake, leave me! It is not such a happy thing as you imagine it, to wander in the woods with me, a girl from another land, burdened with a doom that she tells to none. I might make you dread me—perhaps hate me—if I chose; and I must choose, if I find you loving me too well! (65)

By framing Miriam in mysterious "dark sin," we are reminded of Hawthorne's anxious reactions to the eroticism of Roman art and the sexually charged Italian lifestyle recorded in his travel notebooks. Miriam's unidentified dark sin speaks to Hawthorne's anxiety about unrestrained sensuality; dark sins are framed as the inevitable products of an inability to control one's sensual nature. Ironically, though, the lack of specificity regarding Miriam's sins contributes to her appeal as an erotic character, for they are left to the reader's imagination.

Miriam's dark eroticism is further enhanced through her textual juxtaposition with "the most feminine and kindly" Hilda (50). Hawthorne's characterization of Hilda is significant because she represents the femininity of "native New England": she is described as delicate, pure, sensitive, and intelligent (50). This moral purity is embodied in "her light brown ringlets, [and] her delicately tinged, but kindly face," all of which constitute a dovelike complexion that the text contrasts with Miriam's dark features. This juxtaposition corresponds with Hilda's and Miriam's unique dispositions: while Miriam is purely sensual and emotional, Hilda is "of pleasant deportment, endowed with a mild cheerfulness of temper, not overflowing with animal spirits, but never long despondent" (51). Hilda, then, is represented in terms of ideal Victorian womanhood (a woman distanced from her "animal spirits"), and as such she complies with the nineteenth-century American "myth of feminine purity" (Herbert, "Erotics" 115). By contrasting Miriam with Hilda, Hawthorne amplifies Miriam's erotic appeal, for her "impurity" places her outside the sexual boundaries of Victorian conventions.

The Roman Carnival

The final chapters of Hawthorne's novel are set during the Roman carnival, an eight-day festival that, in 1858, began on the sixth day of February (Hawthorne, *French* 62). According to his travel notebooks, Hawthorne experienced ambivalent sentiments regarding the Roman carnival: at times it is the "gayest and merriest" party, while at other times it is a very "shallow provocation" of which "there is very little to be said" (62, 67). Regardless of Hawthorne's reactions, the Roman carnival was an ancient tradition that attracted many tourists during the eighteenth and nineteenth centuries, for it provided an opportunity for travelers to abandon established social norms. Mikhail Bakhtin defines carnivals as inversions of the official social laws, whereby an authorized transgression of the usual norms creates a world parallel to that of the conventional culture (*Rabelais* 94–95). The carnival scene in *The Marble Faun*, then, displays a dissolving of the social order, a dissolving that profoundly affects Kenyon. Upon being submerged in the carnival, Kenyon experiences a vision of anarchy that generates in him anxiety and fear of the unknown. Part of Kenyon's anxiety derives from the lack of stable and fixed identity, a destabilization that is essential to the carnivalesque. To paraphrase Bakhtin, carnivals dismantle the formal distinctions between observer and observed, spectator and spectacle (*Rabelais* 96). The antirepressive moments of the carnival, therefore, dismantle the artificial structures that separate tourists (like Kenyon) from Italian citizens.

Kenyon responds to his anxious feelings about going native by attempting to diffuse and undermine the powerful forces of the carnival; he refers to the carnival as a "worn out festival" that is "traditionary, not actual" (347). In another passage he tries to dismiss the event as "the emptiest of mockeries," but he ultimately becomes engulfed in the "primitive antics" and is unable to retain the position of the touristic spectator that he has held to that point in the text (Bentley 933). Here, Kenyon becomes trapped among the participants of the carnival:

Fantastic figures, with bulbous heads, the circumference of a bushel, grin[ned] enormously in his [Kenyon's] face. Harlequins struck him with their wooden swords, and appeared to expect his immediate transformation into some jollier shape. A little, long-tailed, horned fiend sidled up to him, and suddenly blew at him through a tube, enveloping our poor friend in a whole harvest of winged seeds. (352)

The "enveloping" of Kenyon, then, means that he loses his powerful position as the spectator—the American tourist—and his identity becomes fluid rather than fixed, for the artificial structures that distanced him from Italian culture are lost amid the "riotous interchange" of the carnival (351). As a result, Kenyon becomes overwhelmed by the primitive characteristics that had heretofore been attributed to the Italians: "absurd figures surrounded him. . . orang-outangs; bear-headed, bull-headed, and dog-headed individuals" and they make him one of them (353). The carnival scene thus threatens to disrupt Kenyon's identity as the foreign observer, a threat that undermines the text's earlier idealization of Italian eroticism and sensuality.

The lack of fixed identity inherent to the Roman carnival likewise provokes transgressions of gender. According to his travel notebooks, Hawthorne experienced disorienting configurations of gender during the Roman carnival, when he was confronted with "some queer shapes [such as] . . . young men in feminine guise, and vice versa" (*French* 69–70). On another page Hawthorne records his reactions to the disguises that he saw at the festival:

a multitude of masks, set to an eternal grin, or with monstrous noses, or made in the guise of monkeys, bears, dogs, or whatever beast the wearer chooses to be akin to; a great many men in petticoats, and almost as many girls and women, no doubt, in breeches. (500)

This passage is significant because it combines the primitive, animal-like qualities of Hawthorne's Italians with a lack of gender fixity. Thus, the anxiety experienced by the gendered and racial images in this scene forces Hawthorne to admit that he does not have the ability to write about the disorienting aspects of the scene: "the whole humor of the thing . . . vanishes the moment I try to grasp one and describe it" (500). The primitivism and the gender fluidity of the carnival, then, remains unspeakable, for its "humor" must be experienced rather than represented. In other words, to grasp the experience one must be "caught up" in the carnival and lose one's identity; once one has returned to the stability of Victorian life, the humor of the experience becomes moot.

Echoing the British travel narratives of the eighteenth century, Hawthorne infuses discourses of eroticism and sexual promiscuity into his depictions of the carnival. Kenyon, for instance, experiences the sexually charged energy of the carnival when he is surrounded by cross-dressing men:

> Five strapping damsels (so, at least, their petticoats bespoke them, in spite of an awful freedom in the flourish of their legs) joined hands and danced around him, inviting him, by their gestures, to perform a horn-pipe in the midst. (352–53)

The erotic possibilities produced by these "strapping damsels" are powerful and alluring for Kenyon, but he successfully maintains his distance. This erotic image is followed by another sexually charged vision. A "gigantic female figure" who is attracted to Kenyon "[s]ingl[ed] out the sculptor, [and] began to make a ponderous assault upon his heart, throwing amorous glances at him" (353). When Kenyon rejects her, "the revengeful damsel" acts out a mock execution as rebuttal. Hawthorne uses this woman as a symbol of the sexual promiscuity inherent to the carnival—sexual possibilities that Kenyon rejects, resulting in his symbolic execution. Where Kenyon had been a controlling observer up to this point in the text, the carnival reduces him to an object of scrutiny and ridicule; in short, he becomes absurd. Thus, his control vanishes, and he becomes an object to be teased and pitied. In other words, while the earlier chapters had represented Rome through the lens of the American tourist, the text now describes Rome as being able to punctuate those representations by mocking Kenyon, thus questioning his preceding observations of the city.

It follows, then, that the disordering principles of the carnivalesque partially account for Hawthorne's inability to represent the Roman carnival in his travel notebooks. By deconstructing stable identities and the Victorian concepts of sexual purity, the carnival ruptures the stabilizing characteristics that would have helped Hawthorne capture the secrets of Rome. As a result, the erotic images of the young damsels fill the void left by that which Hawthorne finds impossible to represent—exotic and erotic images that he borrows from the eighteenth-century discourses of travel in Europe.

While these erotic images function as an attempt to restore stable identities by depicting the Italian women as sexual objects and the Americans
as sexually pure, Hawthorne is also able to retain the structures of
national-racial difference by sending his American tourists home. In the
penultimate chapter, for example, Kenyon insists that "Hilda guide [him]
home" (364). By returning to America, Hilda and Kenyon not only reinscribe the structure of difference between the Americans and the Italians,
but they also adhere to the nineteenth-century American ideologies of
race, gender, and sexuality by rejecting the Roman alternatives. Victorian
domesticity, for example, is maintained through the marriage of the
American characters, and Miriam's matrimonial gift of the bracelet
serves as a safe reminder of their Roman holiday. The American characters are thus left with a nonthreatening souvenir of their journey, and the
reader is left with an exotic gaze into a foreign culture.

CHAPTER 5

Savage America, Civilized England: Counterdiscourses and Fluid Identities in William Wells Brown's *Sketches of Places and People Abroad*

Clotel now urged Horatio to remove to France or England,

where both her and her child would be free,

and where colour was not a crime.

(Brown, *Clotel* 138)

Shifting Identities

In 1862, Nathaniel Hawthorne made a trip to Washington. The travel essay that chronicles this wartime journey compares a group of fugitive slaves with the same mythic fauns that found their way into his final novel. He notes that a group of Black men walking north on a Virginia road "were unlike the [other] specimens of their race," for they were "not altogether human, but . . . akin to the fauns and rustic deities of olden times" ("Chiefly" 362). By transforming these African American men into mythic fauns, Hawthorne depoliticizes them at a time of heightened political anxiety about race and the future of the nation. Hawthorne's African American fauns, in other words, are stripped of their political currency and seen not in terms of racial conflict but in those of mythic fantasy.[1]

Always concerned with politics, William Wells Brown would have had an ambiguous response to Hawthorne's comments. On the one hand, Brown's European travel text, *The American Fugitive in Europe: Sketches of Places and People Abroad* (1854),[2] condemns those who universalize particular historical and political circumstances. Regarding the 1849 Paris Peace Congress, for instance, Brown criticized those speakers who "dwell[ed] on the blessings of peace" as an abstract concept but did not mention that the "French army had invaded Rome and put down the friends of political and religious freedom" (117). On the other hand, because much of Brown's European travel writing is concerned with potential shifts in African American identity through disparate times and places, he may have partially approved of the fluid identities inherent to Hawthorne's sketch, in which an African American slave can transform into a rustic faun.

Brown's interest in shifting identities arises out of his own experience of displacement: his *Sketches* move from discussions of his oppressive "southern home" to discussions of the northern states where "color is [still] considered a crime," to discussions of his arrival in England where he was "received with great enthusiasm" (119, 101). Such an examination of displacement is explicitly political, for Brown claims that only in rejecting America and traveling to Europe can an African American gain freedom from the constant reminder of his or her racial "inferiority."[3] Thus, Brown is able to assert England's moral and ethical superiority over American culture; England, he states, has abolished slavery and "the oppressed and the oppressor have long since lain down together in the peaceful grave" (145). Here abolition is linked to moral and social progress: "on British soil . . . I was recognized as a man and an equal . . . [which caused me] to think of myself in a new world instead of an old" (98).[4] These discourses of British liberation, social progress, and moral superiority run counter to the rhetoric frequently disseminated in European travel narratives by white Americans, narratives that privileged American over European culture. While many white Americans (such as Hawthorne) recognized the potential cultural capital to be gained by taking the European tour, they also discursively maintained America's freedom and liberation from what they characterized as an oppressive monarchy, as well as America's advancements in social reform and, most of all, America's moral superiority.

In this chapter, I examine Brown's discourses regarding the conventional European tour, which often contradict the ideologies established by white Americans traveling through nineteenth-century Europe. I would like to suggest that Brown's sketches demonstrate a profound attraction to English moral and cultural "superiority" (an attraction that goes beyond touristic curiosity) that can best be characterized as anglophilia.[5] Brown's idealizations of England's literary and artistic history, for example, pervade *Sketches of Places and People Abroad,* and through comparisons of these accomplishments to American culture, Brown portrays England as a "civilized nation" in contrast to "wild America" (130). Within this binary of civilized England and savage America, Brown attempts to negotiate a complicated position: while he recognizes America as his home, he refers to England as his "father-land" and announces that Englishmen are his "brethren" (147, 164). Brown thus constructs himself as intimately affiliated with British culture by placing himself within an imagined English brotherhood. This alliance has a profound effect on the content and form of his text: in order to express his idealizations of English art and history, he rejects African American dialect in favor of traditional English grammar and syntax for his British sketches, a narrative voice that rhetorically mirrors the shifts in African American identity that occur throughout his travel writing.

A Fugitive in Europe

When *Sketches of Places and People Abroad* first appeared in the United States, Brown was well known; his 1848 *Narrative of William Wells Brown, a Fugitive Slave* had been widely circulated. As a result, his nineteenth-century American audience would have placed his texts within the fugitive slave tradition. It is thus important to note here that the slave narrative and travel writing are not mutually exclusive genres, for they are both first-person retrospective prose forms that reveal the development of the author's distinctive voice and point of view as he or she fashions differently managed accounts of successive stages in his or her life. Slave narratives are thus as much concerned with mapping changes in spiritual and physical geography as any conventional travel text. Brown's *Narrative,* for instance, begins by chronicling his bondage and suffering in slavery and then proceeds to chart his "pilgrim's progress north to freedom" (P. Jefferson 6).

Furthermore, while there are generic conventions unique to both literary forms, the travel text and the slave narrative share autobiographical strategies in that they portray acts of self-creation.[6] The act of recounting experience that is common to both genres, in other words, participates in the construction of a self in narrative form. In the fugitive slave narrative, for instance, the self that is invented in the escape from slavery is paralleled with the recreation of the self through the process of constructing a narrative. But such a re-creation of the self does not necessarily occur in Brown's European travel sketches. Instead, he plays his persona as fugitive slave off against his achieved self, particularly in his meetings with English writers and intellectuals. Thus, his European travel sketches present a self that is split to include a man of letters and an antislavery lecturer, as well as a self-educated fugitive slave. Such an anomalous identity functions as a political strategy whereby Brown demonstrates the absurdity of racist assumptions that posit the African American as intellectually inferior. As William Farrison points out, the writing of such a book "in a style and with an ability evincing much cultivation of mind and unusual intellectual development . . . was in itself a forceful argument against the 'peculiar institution'" (209).

Unlike the European travel writings of Hawthorne and his white contemporaries, Brown's *Sketches* were self-consciously political. Hawthorne, who occasionally commented on Euro-American politics, ordered his European sketches around the acquisition of cultural capital and the more picturesque elements of the Grand Tour. Brown's relationship to Europe and travel writing, as a fugitive slave and coming out of the political tradition of the slave narrative, differs significantly from Hawthorne's. Rather than simply taking the Grand Tour, Brown's initial journey to Europe arose out of the political act of attending the Paris Peace Congress of 1849. Politics, however, did not dominate Brown's European trip, for the five years he spent in Europe were marked by a number of personal and historical developments.[7] According to Farrison, during his abolitionist lecture tour of England, Brown "did a considerable amount of sightseeing" by "follow[ing] a guidebook" (153). Politics and tourism, therefore, became intimately connected during Brown's journey until September 1850, when the Fugitive Slave Law was passed. At this time, Brown's more picturesque journeys were interrupted by feelings of exile and expatriation; he knew that if he returned to the United States he would be captured, tortured, and sent back into slavery (Brown, *Sketches* 178). In contrast to Hawthorne's experiences in Europe, then, Brown's Grand Tour came to denote something very different: exile, emancipation, employment, political participation—these were just a few of the attributes that defined Europe for the African American traveler. Europe, for Brown, thus signified various meanings at various times; likewise, his presentation of Europe as a shifting signifier enabled him to exploit fluid identities so that he could move from abolitionist politician to American tourist to exiled slave as fluidly as he moved from England to France.

Discourse, Counterdiscourse

If, as Michel Foucault suggests, a discourse is a "group of statements that belong to a single system of formation," it is possible to conceive of American discourses regarding European travel as intimately connected to the eighteenth-century Grand Tour (*Archaeology* 107). However, while white Americans allied themselves with the discursive strategies of the Grand Tour, African Americans of the mid-nineteenth century departed from the travel texts by white Americans and established discourses about European travel that ran counter to those of their white contemporaries. Because Foucault stresses the connection between power and discursive systems, African American counterdiscourses may be read for their attempts to disrupt the powerful "mythologized narrativizations" of travel by questioning the assumption of white American superiority over blacks and Europeans (Kaplan 2). Nancy Prince, for example, resists the traditional American discourses of European corruption through her assertions of European moral superiority: she states that it is in America, not Europe, where whites are "permitted to take the . . . children of black women" (118). Furthermore, David Dorr's *Colored Man round the World* (1858) borrows from Brown's counterdiscursive technique when he tells of the freedom and "manhood" he gained from traveling to Europe: after traveling in Europe, Dorr recognizes that these two characteristics were denied him by the "immorality of American racists" (192).

Central to Brown's *Sketches,* moreover, is a radical counterdiscourse regarding the dominant racial ideologies that worked to oppress African Americans. A review in the *Morning Advertiser* of September 10, 1852, for instance, predicted that Brown's "doings and sayings . . . [would be]

among the means of destruction of the hideous abomination of slavery"
(qtd. in P. Jefferson 12). In his opening chapter, Brown reminds us of the
"oppressive laws" of his "home," a nation that inflicts the "democratic
instrument[s] of torture" upon its slaves (97). His ironic references to
American democratic ideals function as attempts to counter the rhetoric
of democracy used by a nation that profits from slavery: "What was to be
thought of a people boasting of their liberty, their humanity, their Christianity, their love of justice, and at the same time keeping in slavery nearly
four millions of God's children" (180). Brown's *Sketches,* in addition,
contradict the popular mid-nineteenth-century discourses disseminated
by white Americans who exempted the northern states from complicity
in slavery and racial injustice:

> In America I had been bought and sold as a slave in the Southern States. In
> the so-called Free States, I had been treated as one born to occupy an infe-
> rior position,—in steamers, compelled to take my fare on the deck; in ho-
> tels, to take my meals in the kitchen; in coaches, to ride on the outside; in
> railways, to ride in the "negro car"; and in churches to sit in the "negro
> pew." (98)

By placing *all* Americans within the category of the "slave-holding,
woman-whipping, [and] negro-hating people," Brown accuses the "so-
called Free States" of participating in slavery—an institution that north-
erners often dismissed as a southern practice prior to the passing of the
Fugitive Slave Law in 1850. Following his condemnation of the northern
states, Brown refutes the American claim that "the English laborer is no
better off than the American slave," for "the law will . . . guard and pro-
tect" the British laborer but not the American slave (126). Although he is
unable to recognize that hierarchies of race and class alike are culturally
produced and might at times be usefully analyzed together, Brown's
counterdiscursive project successfully contradicts established American
myths and powerful discursive systems that contributed the enslavement
of Americans of African descent (Gruesser 6).

Brown, in addition to refuting powerful American rhetoric, confounds the conventional American discourses of the Grand Tour. While
many American travelers (including Hawthorne) believed European
tours to provide freedom from the Victorian restraints of nineteenth-
century America, Brown takes the trope of liberation one step further by
describing his "absolute freedom." "But no sooner was I on British

soil," he states, "than I was recognized as . . . completely free" (98). Brown's freedom here is congruent with the European moral freedom experienced by white Americans. Yet the liberation experienced by white American travelers in Europe differed from Brown's sense of freedom in that Brown did not fear a potential transgression of Victorian sexual purity. Brown thus disrupts the discursive strategy of American moral superiority by heralding his feelings of liberation on "British soil" as proof of Europe's elevated principles: as he sets foot on a land that has "abolished slavery" he recognizes that "England has set a noble example to America" (179). Such inconsistencies with contemporaneous white American travel narratives contribute to Brown's construction of a binary that characterizes the United States as savage and Europe as civilized (221, 108). After quoting George Dawson's comments that "Americans are a nation, with no language, no creed, no grave-yards . . . [and] no literature," Brown compares the "uneducated" America man with the "enlightened" Englishman:

> When we contrast the ignorance, the rudeness, and the helplessness of the savage [American], with the knowledge, the refinement and the resources of the civilized [European] man, the difference between them appears so wide, that they can scarcely be regarded as of the same species. (186)

Here, Brown uses the term *savage* to refer to white slave-holding Americans—a term that he juxtaposes to "civilized" Europeans. Thus, where Hawthorne attributes primitive characteristics to Donatello and his other Southern European characters, Brown reserves such primitive images for Anglo-Saxon Americans. Conventional iconographies of the primitive, then, are displaced from their discursive status as attributes of non-Anglo-Saxon, nonwhite peoples: Brown appropriates the colonizing rhetoric traditionally used to describe the childlike primitive and applies it to the "uneducated" and "new" American nation. America, for him, is thus personified as both an "infant" and a "slender youth," the progeny of England (185). Importing such primitivist tropes suggests that American savagery is born out of the torturing of African Americans and subjugating them to slavery; this institution, Brown implies, must be abolished if America is to mature and move toward a civilized society.

Furthermore, the gendering of Britain as the mother to the American child-savage contributes to an antidemocratic counterdiscourse that establishes Brown's approval of the English monarchy. Once again calling

American democracy into question, Brown points out that American fugitive slaves "had not fled from a monarchical [nation], but from a so-called republican government" (179). Using this as confirmation that monarchies permit greater freedom than the so-called American republic, Brown goes on to pay homage to Queen Victoria as a great woman who is "loved by her subjects" (102). Such sentiments contradict dominant American discourses that are symbolized by the joke told by the newspaper boy in Horatio Alger's *Ragged Dick* (1867), who tries to cash in on the British monarchy's lack of popularity in the United States by exclaiming: "GREAT NEWS! QUEEN VICTORIA ASSASSINATED!" (86).[8] Such anti-monarchical comments are not present in Brown's narrative; in fact, his tour of England develops his appreciation for the British political system, an appreciation that inspires his nostalgia for prerevolutionary America when "the mother country" ruled the United States (179).

Anglophilia and Curiosity

Brown's belief that "the separation of the United States from the mother country was (to say the least) a great misfortune" is just one aspect of his infatuation with British culture. Throughout the sketches he consistently champions the great English literary tradition of Shakespeare, Milton, and Byron, a sentiment that leads him to the monument of Sir Walter Scott and the Poets' Corner of Westminster Abbey. Brown also marvels at the Crystal Palace—the great "Glass House," as he calls it—and goes on to claim that "no metropolis in the world presents such faculties as London" (163). Brown continues these loving descriptions of England by saying that "England stands preeminently the first government in the world for freedom of speech and of the press" (139). Here, Brown's anglophilia is undoubtedly the product of the rights and privileges that he enjoys in Britain, a position that inspires in him a profound curiosity regarding English culture. This counterdiscursive privileging of England signals an anti-American sentiment as well as a political and emotional investment in British culture. Such gestures directed against Americanness, though, work toward a voice that not only prioritizes English culture but constructs Britain as a fetishized site. Brown, upon meeting the landlady of a small inn, for instance, brings his anglophilia into the orbit of desire, for he states: "her magnificent red face [and] garnished curls" make her "the finest specimen of an English lady that I had ever seen"

(189). This "never-to-be-forgotten face" is said to be symbolic of "English beauty," and she thus becomes synecdochic of his more generalized erotic experiences in England.

The Freudian theory of fetishism can shed some light on Brown's attraction to British culture. In his 1927 essay on the fetish, Freud maintains that a fetish always reveals itself upon analysis to be "a substitute for the woman's (the mother's) penis that the little boy once believed in and—for reasons familiar to us—does not want to give up" (153). Thus, Freud uses the term *fetishism* to denote a consequence of castration anxiety in which the fetish object acts as a sign substituted for the thing thought to be missing. This substitution also functions to cover and disavow the traumatic site of absence. Freud asserts that the psyche then constructs a phantasmic topography to substitute the ugliness and anxiety of castration with beauty and desire. The fetish object thus becomes a sign left by the original moment of castration anxiety as well as a mark of mourning for the lost object. Freud's theory enables us to understand Brown's repeated statements about his symbolic Afro-American castration by white Americans, as well as about his so-called regained masculinity bestowed upon arriving in England, where he is immediately "recognized as a man" (98). Such restored manhood infers Brown's feelings of castration as an American slave, which, in turn, according to the Freudian model, result in a displacement of desire onto Britain as a way of disavowing the traumatic site of absence.

Kaja Silverman and other feminist theorists have critiqued Freud's theory and revealed its problematic assumptions. How, they ask, does an object acquire sexual value as the substitute for something else? And how is the maternal penis, which never existed in the first place, perceived as missing, as an absence? In one case, the sign of value fails to inscribe itself on an actual object; in the other, value is overinscribed on a site of imagined lack through a substitute object (Silverman 45). The Freudian figuration of fetishism is, moreover, problematic in relation to Brown's text because of his gendering of England as "the mother nation." Complications in such a reading arise when a displacement of desire is grafted onto the maternal image, for it is the mother's lack that inspires the displacement, not the object upon which desire is projected.

If, as Laura Mulvey suggests, fetishism and curiosity are not "irreconcilably polarized" but exist in a "dialectical relation" to each other, Brown's fetishized view of England may be refigured as "a desire to know" (59). Mulvey asserts that a fetishized space can manifest itself in a desire to know rather than an urge to see or possess the fetishized object, as in the Freudian model. Curiosity, then, appears as a desire to uncover the secret of everything within the forbidden space; thus, because American law frames England as a space forbidden to the escaped Brown, he experiences a desire to uncover its secrets, while simultaneously identifying himself as a "fugitive in Europe." Forbidden space is, according to Mulvey, essential for reconciling fetishism and curiosity, for it is always a prohibition that stimulates and provokes the desire to know, "the epistemophilia" (60).[9] Space and curiosity come together to form the epistemophilia for Brown during his trip to the British Museum, where he "linger[s] . . . for hours with interest" (131). Here, Brown is overwhelmed by a desire to know everything in the museum, so much so, that he becomes lost in inquisitive thought: "the officer [had to] remind . . . me that it was time to close and I was ushered out" (132). Early the next morning he returns to the museum in an attempt to examine everything in "the great building" (132). This desire to know every item in the British Museum stands in for his more general desire to know everything about English culture: the museum, Brown states, has a "wealth of precious artifacts" that have the potential to uncover the secrets of Britain (133).

Brown's profound curiosity and attraction to Britain is also expressed in his sketch of a "dark day in London" (135). Here he describes a dark, foggy afternoon in the city when his "sight could not penetrate through the dark veil that hung" in the air (134). The use of the term *penetrate* suggests the coupling of sexual imagery with his desire to know England. But rather than feeling frustrated by this impenetrability, Brown embraces the surrounding atmosphere:

> A London fog cannot be described. To be appreciated, it must be seen, or, rather, felt, for it is altogether impossible to be clear and lucid on such a subject. It is the only thing which gives you an idea of what Milton meant when he talked of darkness visible. (134)

The physical darkness experienced in this passage engenders a representational darkness; like Hawthorne's difficulties representing Rome, Brown expresses the impossibility of signifying the darkness of London's streets. Yet he is able to appreciate London's darkness, for his representational failure does not negate his desire to know; instead, he gains an epistemological understanding of the darkness that stands before him.

The symbolic nature of the darkness is made clear when, as if born out of the dark surroundings, a fellow African American man is seen "standing close to a lampost" (134). The narrative then symbolically connects the darkness of the city with the dark skin of the African American, a connection that is made clear when Brown realizes that this man is also a fugitive slave who has adopted "dark London" for his home (133).

As Brown begins to gain knowledge about England, questions of home and belonging move into the foreground. Following this "dark day in London," Brown refers to himself as an American "stranger in a strange land"; later in the text, however, he states that he had "begun to fancy [him]self an Englishman by habit, if not by birth" (136, 221). And in the final chapter, when he believes he "knows" Britain, he asserts that in England he felt "at home" wherever he went (221). At the thought of returning to America, Brown states:

> I commenced with palpitating heart the preparation to return to my *native land*. Native land! How harshly that word sounds to my ears! True, America was the land of my birth; my grandfather had taken part in her Revolution, had enriched the soil with his blood, yet upon this soil I had been worked as a slave. (221)

Placed in the context of the antebellum slave narrative, Brown's ambiguous relationship to questions of home is not surprising. That is, the travel writing of a fugitive slave constitutes, by definition, the slave-narrator's effort to displace himself or herself from what Brown calls his "Southern Home." As a result, the story of the fugitive slave is the story of a person attempting to find ground that he or she can call home. A central paradox thus arises: the slave must cross a boundary and become dislocated from his place of birth if he is to find the belonging that is often associated with freedom.

Passing Voices

Brown's paradoxical relations to a place called "home," coupled with his anglophilia, are intimately connected to his interest in fluid identities. As John Ernest argues in his reading of *The Escape; or, A Leap for Freedom,* Brown's political drama "challenged the terms by which identity is defined and maintained" (1109). Ernest goes on to suggest that Brown's identity performances "expose[d] cultural fictions" by "refiguring the reciprocal relation between white and black" (1110). Likewise, in Brown's travels, the crossing of boundaries from South to North and from America to England is caught up in the crossing of other boundaries, of the limits wherein identity is conventionally fixed. Such shifts in identity, accompanied by displacement, are necessary, for, as James Olney points out, the movement of the slave-narrator from bondage to emancipation is also a movement from "non-being" to "being" (157). The movement north and the writing of the journey, in other words, constitute freedom, as well as an assertion of an identity that was denied under the conditions of slavery. The antebellum African American travel text, then, is a "struggl[e] to locate identity . . . on which to effect . . . [a] transformation from legal nonbeing to being" (Weinauer 39). This process of locating an identity is played out in Brown's chapter on Joseph Jenkins, who was once "the victim of a slave-trader" but who escaped to London and became a street sweeper, a bill distributor, a singer, an actor, and a preacher (206). Jenkins's freedom through displacement results in his search for an identity that can ground him in his new home; rather than grounding him, though, this search exposes the artificiality of identities by presenting them as fluid and unfixed by conventional boundaries. Just as Brown is able to assert his brotherhood with the British nation, Jenkins can adopt a series of identities to suit all occasions.

A similar depiction of unstable identities arises out of Brown's lecture tour with William and Ellen Craft. Here, Brown writes of the abolitionist speeches he gave throughout England, Scotland, and Ireland, in which he introduced the Crafts, a couple who escaped American slavery when Ellen disguised herself as a white man traveling north with his slave, William. Bounded categories of identity are confounded by the Crafts' story: Ellen's ability to pass for a white man unsettles the smooth surface of conventional notions of discrete identities, notions that work on a single line of analysis and that view identity as one-dimensional. Brown thus used this story in his lectures to destabilize fixed notions of race and gender, notions that were used as powerful identificatory systems for justifying African American subjugation.

Brown, in his deconstructions of racial and gender boundaries, explores the spaces in which the link between appearance and reality seems to vanish. When Brown caricatures the Southern racist who asks him for an introduction to Victor Hugo, for instance, he invokes a question that lies at the heart of his text: what do racial categories really mean? Such a question underlies the preface to *Sketches* when he asserts that his motivation for writing the text is to prove that a fugitive slave has both the intelligence and the ability to write a narrative of his European travels (72). Here, Brown wants not only to complicate assumptions that African Americans are intellectually inferior to white Americans but also to challenge the boundaries of identity that separate black slave from white master. This rhetoric complicates the very idea of "reality" in antebellum America, for, by inquiring into the ontological status of racial categories, Brown is able to contest slavery's assumption of "natural" racial binary difference and to suggest that such difference is itself a mere construct.

Brown's desire to write "as well as a white man" forges a bridge between Ellen Craft's flight from slavery and his own writing practice (Craft 55). Brown's authorial motivation, that is, may be read as a kind of textual passing in which he adopts a white writing style and, at times, a white narrative voice. He often, for example, digresses from the counterdiscursive elements of his narrative to comment on the high points of European art and aesthetics. "Venus, seated, and smelling a lotus-flower which she held in her hand, and attended by three graces," Brown tells his reader, "[was] really one of the most precious productions of art I had ever seen" (131). Accompanying these moments of aesthetic appreciation are quotes from Shakespeare, Pope, and Byron. Upon visiting the British Museum, for instance, he quotes Pope's comment that "to be wise . . . is but to know how little can be known" (132). During such sections of the text, the African American voice that critiques American racial policies and disseminates counterdiscourses becomes blurred, and the narrative voice takes on the qualities associated with the white American traveler in Europe. Brown, moreover, chooses to reject the black vernacular that he uses sporadically in *Clotel* (1853); instead, he writes his *Sketches* in the standard English associated with the conventional white travel text. If, as Henry Louis Gates suggests, "black vernacular has assumed the single role as the black person's ultimate sign of difference," Brown's use of standard English functions as a mark of identification with the white tradition (92). Such identification, though, cannot be simply dismissed as an internalization of white aesthetics and form; rather, his use of standard English enables Brown to display his ability to "write as well as a white man"—an ability that, like the passing of Ellen Craft, confounds racial categories inherent to American justifications of slavery.

Brown's textual passing complicates racial identities but does not disturb gender fixity, as is done in the narrative of William and Ellen Craft.

Yet, while Brown's narrative voice remains masculine, gender fluidity is present in his depictions of British nationhood. Although he begins his text by calling attention to England's matriarchal status, Brown soon destabilizes the gender fixity of this claim by referring to his English journey as an "arrival in the father-land" (147). This shift in gender identification is complicated by a narrative voice that identifies England as its progenitor. Who is making this claim? Is Brown speaking as a disenfranchised African American slave? Is he passing as an American loyalist who believes England to be his homeland? Or is he simply being consistent with his other assertions of British superiority over America? Whatever the case may be, the subject position of the narrative voice remains unclear and unfixed.

Such ambiguity is echoed in Brown's declaration of a "brotherhood" with the British people (119). Images of brotherhood and "brethren" are repeated throughout the narrative, and Brown even defines his European trip as "flying to the embrace of our British brothers" (97). Here, brotherly affection comes to symbolize (and gender) his relationship to England; the shift from a maternal connection to a brotherlike one is consistent with nationalist rhetoric, a rhetoric that also foregrounds the masculinity he was denied on American soil. This movement from matriarch to fatherland (and brotherhood) enables Brown to form an intimate bond between his narrative voice and the "white gentlemen" of the English nation (210). By defining his relationship to England in "familial" terms, whether as son or brother, Brown attempts to pass for white, and he thereby reconstitutes his anglophilic attraction to the nation by inserting himself in a culture that recognizes his freedom.

Although his textual passing exposes discrete racial identities as social constructions, Brown's use of the generic conventions of the European travel narrative at times implicates him in dominant discourses that reinscribe categories of racial and cultural difference. His insight, in other words, is sometimes accompanied by blindness. While describing a visit to the House of Commons, for instance, Brown exposes his admiration for the landowning aristocracy, and celebrates "this assembly of senators" who participate in the expansion of the British Empire (212). But these "good-looking blond men" who were "educated at Oxford University" are contrasted with the "thin dark hair" and "Jewish face" of future prime minister Benjamin Disraeli (213). Brown describes "the Jew," as he calls Disraeli, in terms that are juxtaposed with the "delicate" Anglo-Saxon members of the House: he focuses on Disraeli's "cat-like" countenance, his "stealthy step," and his "unmerciful" persona (214). The most disturbing comment that Brown makes about Disraeli appears in his damning critique of Disraeli's rhetorical style, when he claims that Disraeli is a self-serving sophist who cares nothing for justice or truth (214).

Brown's anti-Semitic references to Disraeli highlight an aspect of conventionality in his narrative, a conventionality that is at odds with the counterdiscursive sections of the text. That is, the stereotyping and the juxtaposition of "the Jew" with the Anglo-Saxon members of the House of Commons revives the model of racial and cultural difference that much of the narrative attempts to deconstruct. Anglophilic tendencies thus engender Brown's mimicry of anti-Semitic English attitudes toward Disraeli, attitudes that were often used to justify nineteenth-century colonial projects. William Stowe reads Brown's anti-Semitic passages as an example of how Brown's counterdiscursive subject position fades away as he succumbs to the dominant ideologies of British imperialism (72–73). But Stowe fails to recognize that Brown is participating in the mimicry of colonial discourse. Such mimicry appeals to colonial subjects as it simultaneously reveals the ambivalence at the source of traditional discourses on authority. Rather than underwriting his counterdiscursive project, Brown's mimicry and his affiliation with the landowning aristocracy "speaks with a tongue that is forked" and thus produces an "ironic compromise" that is "constructed around ambivalence" (Bhabha 85–86). Indeed, it is the insistent presentation of counterdiscourses within a framework established by the white European travel genre that serves as a resonant and haunting emblem for the different ways that concepts of freedom, home, and displacement are negotiated through shifting identities—identities that present a vexed and fluid relationship between race and gender in the American journey toward emancipation.

CHAPTER 6

"Harems and Ceremonies":
Edith Wharton, *In Morocco*

> Everything that the reader of
> the Arabian Nights expects to find is here.
>
> (*In Morocco* 24)

Writing Morocco

"There is no guide-book to Morocco" says Edith Wharton on the opening page of *In Morocco* (1919), a narrative that recounts her travels through Morocco in 1917 (3). Wharton continues by suggesting that this lack of tourist information "rouse[s] the hunger of the repletest sight-seer" (3). Such comments establish Morocco as "unknown Africa," a space that is "remote," "exotic," and "untouched" by the European tourist industry (3). Thus, Wharton's initial Moroccan images depict North Africa as a place that is veiled in mystery—a mystery that has remained unsolved by Baedeker or Glossam.[1] For Wharton, then, Morocco is a clean slate, upon which she can inscribe her impressions and insights without the hindrance of a tradition of travel writing about this country. While this absence is in some sense liberating, it also signals a representational difficulty; the lack of textual tradition means that Wharton is left to compose her own form and style to uncover the "vast unknown just beyond Tangier" (4). Like Hawthorne in his representation of Rome, therefore, Wharton is faced with the difficulty of bridging the gap between her travels in North Africa and the signifiers that she must use to "write Morocco" and disclose its secrets.

Bridging this gap was problematic, for the Moroccan secrets that Wharton sought to reveal often remained out of reach. *In Morocco,* for instance, consistently returns to the trope of mystery: the text refers to North Africa as an "ancient mystery," a "world of mystery" and "secret beauty." Thus, in confronting this elusive country, Wharton is repeatedly confounded by its contradictions (6–7). She claims that she is inevitably brought

> back to the central riddle of the mysterious North African civilization: the perpetual flux and the immovable stability, the barbarous customs and sensuous refinements, the absence of artistic originality and the gift for regrouping borrowed motives, the patient and exquisite workmanship and the immediate neglect and degradation of the thing once made. (157)

In this passage, using rhetoric that reminds us of Homi Bhabha's theory of colonial ambivalence, Wharton posits Morocco as a paradoxical "riddle" that cannot be solved by Euro-American gazes. She thus foregrounds the impenetrability of Moroccan culture as well as the impossibility of describing its secrets to a Western audience. The text's title, then, might be read as ironic, for Wharton always remains culturally outside North Africa and is unable to position herself *in* Morocco.

Perhaps it is the lack of guidebooks that accounts for the unique style of this particular travel narrative. By the time of its publication in 1919, Wharton had written numerous travel texts: *The Cruise of the Vanadis* (1888), *Italian Backgrounds* (1905), *A Motor-Flight through France* (1915), *Fighting France: From Dunquerque to Belfort* (1915). According to Shirley Foster, these narratives are unified by the "feminine complexities of travel discourse," in which Wharton emphasizes "atmosphere" rather than "fact" (131). The "female voice" of Wharton's European travel narratives, for instance, place an emphasis on flowing and merging rather than unification and development, a voice that resonates with the Kristevan notion of "woman's time" and its rejection of finite progression and teleological development (Foster 132). *In Morocco* can be distinguished from these other travel writings because here, as Mary Suzanne Schriber suggests, Wharton "did not lay claim to 'womanly' subject matter . . . [instead] Wharton insisted on the right of women to write about such presumably masculine subjects as science, politics, and history" ("Dog-Eared" 149–50). Likewise, the form of *In Morocco* does nothing to subvert the predominantly masculine discourses of imperialism that had been established by European travel writers in North Africa (André Gide, for example). Wharton borrowed freely from such colonial rhetoric; in fact, imperial discourse became a representational access route into that which she considered inaccessible and mysterious, not only because of the lack of guidebooks but also because of Morocco's overwhelming impenetrability for the Western visitor. But Wharton's gender position places her in an ambiguous relationship to imperial rhetoric; as Sara Mills points out, "women travel writers were unable to adopt the imperialist voice with the ease with which male writers did" (*Difference* 3). *In Morocco* thus treads on an unstable ground where gender and imperialism are sometimes in conflict and at other times reconciled.

Gender and Imperialism

Although Morocco remained unwritten for (and thus inaccessible to) Wharton, North Africa was a space where late-nineteenth- and early-twentieth-century women could escape the constraints of domestic life in America and Europe. Marianna Torgovnick suggests that North Africa became a trope for women who wanted to liberate themselves from "the limitations of middle- and upper-class European life which dictated that women define themselves through family, not work" (*Primitive Passions* 64). Mary Kingsley's *Travels in West Africa* (1897) and *West African Studies* (1899), for example, present Africa as a place where women can actively seek out vocations and self-fulfillment, rebelling against the constraints of Victorian society.[2] However, Gayatri Spivak reminds us that it is necessary to "wrench oneself away from the mesmerising focus of the 'subject-constitution' of the female individualist" when it comes to examining imperial subject positions (177). In other words, we must recognize that women's travel narratives are often similar to those by men in that they are about the colonial situation, even though their relation to dominant imperial discourses may differ.

The gendering of colonial discourse as a masculine trope has been disseminated by postcolonial critics such as Edward Said.[3] Said even goes as far as stating that Orientalist discourse is a male conception of the world:

"Orientalism . . . was an exclusively male province; like so many professional guilds during the modern period, it viewed itself and its subject matter with sexist blinders. This is especially evident in the writings of travelers" (207). While Said's critique is useful and insightful, he ignores the participation of women in colonial projects; he thus, at times, entangles himself in the same male imperialist view that he criticizes. Such a lack of gender sensitivity is symptomatic of a much larger insensitivity within the Saidian model of Orientalism, for his theory gestures toward ahistoricism in that he refuses to distinguish between texts of different historical moments. Orientalist representation, as Said sees it, transcends historical specificity and can be imposed upon a diverse number of texts from distinct periods or genres; Said's notion of Orientalism runs the risk of becoming a broad and monolithic category (Reina Lewis 16). Rather than focusing on the individual ambiguities and tensions that form potential conflicts and paradoxes at different historical moments, this homogeneous Orientalist vision forces dominant readings of texts.

For the purposes of examining Wharton's travel writing, it is much more productive to use the concept of Orientalism in the way that Eva-Marie Kröller does in her reading of Isabella Bird's *Unbeaten Tracks in Japan* (1880). Kröller, without referring specifically to the Saidian conception of Orientalism, studies the paradoxes and contradictions inherent in Bird's Orientalist discourses: Bird fluctuates between depictions of Japanese men and women as partially "civilised" and completely "barbaric" (Kröller 92). More interesting, though, is that Kröller contradicts Said by analyzing Bird's use of masculine imperial rhetoric. For instance, Kröller describes Bird's arrival in Japan "as a form of penetration," which corroborates the masculine "trope[s] of arrival in a foreign land as an act of sexual penetration (and subsequent domination)" (91). While Wharton forgoes these images of penetration in her account of arriving in Morocco (perhaps because of its overwhelming otherness), many of her images of North Africa conform to the historically specific and gendered discourses of Orientalism that she appropriated from such writers (and friends) as André Gide.

Wharton and Gide

In 1915, while working on the Franco-American General Committee of World War I, Wharton developed a friendship with André Gide.[4] Although their literary collaborations failed, Gide introduced Wharton to his ideas about North Africa and the "exotic east" by giving her a copy of his *Prétextes* (1917). Upon reading it, Wharton was particularly taken with Gide's comments on Arabic culture, and she wrote to him saying: "What you have written about the *Thousand and One Nights* . . . have enchanted me . . . [and given] me a very lively and particular pleasure" (qtd. in R. W. B. Lewis 400). This section of *Prétextes* is notable, not only for its erotic depictions of Arabic culture but also for its appreciation of and fascination with ancient traditions and ceremonies. In reference to North Africa, for instance, Gide condemns the transformation of "ancient Arabic tradition" that has risen out of the "advent of the French colonial administration" (qtd. in Lucey 61). Gide's attraction to "ancient" North Africa is shared by Michel, the protagonist of *L'Immoraliste* (1902), who is drawn to such ruins of antiquity as Carthage and Timgad, the mosaics of Sousse, and the amphitheatre of El Djem, all of which become represented as Michel's symbolic retreats from civilization. Gide's own travels, however, were motivated by an attraction not only to antiquity but also to North Afica's sexual possibilities, possibilities that were free of the sexual prohibitions that he experienced in France. As Jonathan C. Lang notes, North Africa permitted Gide "access to the twin pleasures of idleness and deviancy" and sanctioned "values directly counter to those of the metropolitan culture where discipline and monogamatic sexuality rule workaday life" (85).

Wharton adopts Gide's discourses of North Africa in the reconstruction of her Moroccan travels. I would suggest, in fact, that Gide provided a vocabulary in which she could write a travel narrative about the country without guidebooks. In the summer of 1917, for example, when Wharton was preparing to visit Morocco, Gide sent her a copy of the English translation of *L'Immoraliste*. After reading the novel, Wharton wrote to Gide saying: "Your beautiful evocation of the desert I have so loved, far from awakening my nostalgia, gives me a taste in advance of what is waiting for me there" (qtd. in R. W. B. Lewis 404). This letter suggests that Wharton's initial impressions of North Africa were marked by the images that Gide had created in *L'Immoraliste*. Unlike Gide, however, Wharton did not consider Morocco as a space for sexual tourism; rather, she was attracted to Gide's descriptions of North Africa as a "semi-primitive and pastoral" release from the pressures of World War I Paris—a place where she could live "like a lady again" (404). In fact, Wharton considered this three-week trip to be a form of liberation, for this journey, according to *A Backward Glance* (1934), was her "only real holiday" during "those terrible years" of 1914–1918 (357). Echoing Gide, she describes Morocco as a timeless pastoral landscape where one could "escape civilisation for nature" (Lang 84).

Wharton's images of North Africa are also imbued with Gide's fondness for antiquity. For instance, she states that in North Africa "there is no break in the links" to ancient Rome, and she longs to see the settlements that were established when "the Romans pushed their outposts across the Atlas" (*In Morocco* 10). Wharton consistently returns to the images of the "unbroken contact" between North Africa and ancient European history, and I would suggest that her interest in "the Orient" claims her attention only insofar as it reveals the history of Western civilization (13). This interest continues in the final section of *In Morocco*, where the "Sketch of Moroccan History" focuses more on the Roman settlements and the European ties to North Africa than on other aspects of Moroccan history. Here, Wharton maintains a Eurocentric subject position. Even her description of Meknez meditates on

a colossal red ruin, something like the lower stories of a Roman amphitheatre that should stretch out indefinitely instead of forming a circle, or like a series of Roman aqueducts built side by side and joined into one structure. . . . But though the sun-baked clay of which the impatient Sultan built his pleasure-houses will not suffer comparison with the firm stones of Rome, 'the high Roman fashion' is visible in the shape and outline of these ruins. What they are no one knows. (65–66)

By comparing ancient Moroccan ruins to Roman amphitheaters and aqueducts, Wharton was undoubtedly attempting to convey images that her Euro-American reader would recognize. But such comparisons serve another purpose: they become a way of textually inscribing a space that has remained unwritten and shedding light on the "darkness and mystery" of North Africa (89). Points of comparison, in other words, help her to construct images that are meant to capture Morocco. Even this rhetorical strategy, however, is undermined by the last sentence of this quote—a sentence that conveys the impossibility of ever "knowing" Morocco.

Wharton also inscribes *In Morocco* with a representational tension that she inherits from Gide's images of North Africa. While Gide refers to Algeria as an essential place for uncovering the ruins of antiquity and discovering another chapter in the history of Western civilization, he also posits North Africa as an "uncivilised" space where he can experience "a leisurely life far from the hustle [and] bustle . . . of Europe" (Lang 87). *In Morocco* includes similar images, for Wharton's descriptions of ancient civilizations are disrupted by her images of the so-called uncivilized Moroccans. When describing Morocco's small communities, for instance, she states:

> One of these villages seemed to be inhabited entirely by blacks, big friendly creatures. . . . They were handsome blue-bronze creatures, bare to the waist, with tight black astrakhan curls and firmly sculptured legs and ankles; and all around them, like a swarm of gnats, danced countless jolly pickaninnies, naked as lizards. (43)

The repetition of the animal-like word *creatures,* coupled with her depiction of the North Africans as "gnats" and "lizards," echo Gide's images of "uncivilized" Algeria. Such representations force a tension between past and present: North Africa is, on the one hand, an important space for understanding the development of Western civilization; on the other hand, it is inhabited by uncivilized and even animal-like people. Wharton attempts to overcome this structural tension by focusing on Morocco's connection to antiquity to the exclusion of contemporary Morocco. The past, that is, governs the present moment of Wharton's travels, and it largely obliterates the contemporary scene. Soon after arriving in Morocco, for instance, Wharton calls it a

> rich and stagnant civilization. Buildings, people, customs, seem all about to crumble and fall of their own weight: the present is a perpetually prolonged past. To touch the past with one's hands is realized only in dreams; and in Morocco the dream-feeling envelops one at every step. (85)

These comments fit into the Saidian framework of Orientalism, for, as Said states, those who thought they traveled in present time to contemporaneous foreign lands can be said to have traveled to an idea of the past (*Orientalism* 12). The discourses of the foreign, in other words, no longer exist simply as lore but become substituted for the actual. Observation, then, is not vision but revision, which is filtered through the lenses provided by artists and books written in (or about) the past. Monuments and other tourist sights not only commemorate the past but are also part of a narrative about a world that is already past at the time of being written.

Wharton's Orientalism

Within this version of travel and travel writing, images are imported from other texts, and Morocco remains old through references to the past. In a country decribed by no guidebook, however, Wharton must fill in a textual void by importing Western discourses about other North African countries. As such, the rhetoric of Gide's Algeria and his writing in *Prétextes* form discursive models; thus, his historically specific Orientalist representations are repeated. Echoing Gide's comments on the *Thousand and One Nights,* for example, Wharton describes the military car that carries her throughout Morocco as a "Djinn's carpet" that makes her feel like a "medieval adventurer" (13). She continues this theme by returning to the image of the "seventeenth-century traveler" who "toiled across the desert to see [wonders], and . . . came back dazzled and almost incredulous, as if half-suspecting that some djinn had deluded them with the vision of a phantom city" (63–64). In addition to reinscribing Eastern eroticism, such discourses freeze Morocco in the past and frame North Africa as a space that does not change. The Moroccan soil, then, becomes an "unrolled frieze of a white Etruscan vase patterned with black vine garlands," and the marketplaces are presented as ancient "Oriental . . . gaiety" (48, 108). Depictions of this kind divorce Morocco from the materialist conditions of twentieth-century imperialism, casting it more as a timeless *objet d'art* rather than a modern political state. As James Buzard notes in *The Beaten Track* (1993), this form of picturesque travel writing supports the cultural activity of tourism by evading actual historical and political injustices (210). Wharton's image of Morocco as a timeless work of art, then, complies with those travel discourses that silence imperial rule; attractive ornaments and picturesque scenes come to stand in for the voices of anger and rage of a colonized nation.

Wharton's spectatorial and romantic tropes of North Africa accumulate throughout her text and position her as an outsider in relation to Moroccan life. She thus stands outside space and time and her gazes at the incomprehensible scenes inspire "dream-like feeling[s]," so her trip becomes a travel back into time rather than a geographical excursion in the present (85). Wharton's foreign gaze is illustrated clearly when she is confronted with Moroccan ceremonies. She describes the "feasts of the Hamadchas," for instance, in the following way:

The spectacle unrolling itself below us took on a blessed air of unreality. Any normal person who has seen a dance of the Aïssaouas and watched them swallow thorns and hot coals, slash themselves with knives, and roll on the floor in epilepsy must have privately longed, after the first excitement was over to fly from the repulsive scene. The Hamadchas are much more savage . . . and, knowing this, I had wondered how long I should be able to stand the sight of what was going on below our terrace. But the beauty of the setting redeemed the bestial horror. In that unreal golden light the scene became merely symbolical: it was like one of those strange animal masks which the Middle Ages brought down from antiquity by way of the satyr-plays of Greece, and of which the half-human protagonists still grin and contort themselves among the Christian symbols of Gothic cathedrals. (52–53)

Wharton goes on to describe the Hamadchas' dance as forming pools of blood "from [the] great gashes which the dancers hacked in their own skulls and breasts with hatchets and sharpened stones" (54). Her vantage point "from above the crowd" contributes to the voyeuristic distancing in which she gazes upon the festival "unrolling below" (52). Moreover, words and expressions like *savage* and *bestial* form a structure of difference between the observer and the participants. This differentiation between observer and participant enables Wharton to establish herself as an outsider and calls attention to her position as a tourist who stands outside looking in. Such a position accounts for her images of Morocco as "a dream-feeling" that is never materially graspable or comprehensible to the gaze of the outsider. Likewise, Wharton's rhetorical reaction once again engenders references to European traditions: The "Middle Ages," the "satyr-plays of Greece," and the "Christian symbols of Gothic cathedrals"—all of these things come to stand in for the incomprehensible actions of the Hamadchas' dance.

Wharton's reconstruction of her travels in *In Morocco* dematerializes the North African scenes of the twentieth century and participates in the Saidian tissue of intertexts by filling in the textual void with imaginative projections. Moreover, as an experienced travel writer, she makes comments on antiquity, landscapes, festivals, buildings, and ruins that are part of well-established generic conventions. Such responses to the cultural artifacts of a foreign community are a generic means of codifying and transmitting values that support imperial projects. Descriptions of the "rich and beautiful" ceremonies of the Moroccans, for instance,

construct her text according to the aesthetic conventions of the picturesque. These eyewitness reports arise out of her continual querying of
the appropriateness of such conventions: would "normal people," the
narrative seems to inquire, participate in the Moroccan ceremonies of
self-sacrifice and physical mutilation? At the same time, though, one
senses an attraction to the ceremony that is unfolding, for, during the
Hamadchas' dance, "the beauty" of the scene redeems the "bestial horror," and Wharton's comparison of the dance to European traditions
serves as a circumlocution of her attraction to the "barbaric actions" of
the dancers (53).

Simultaneous attraction and repulsion, combined with other ambiguities, characterize Wharton's unique voice as a travel writer. A unique
voice is also present in Wharton's departure from other women's travel
writing about Africa (such as Mary Kingsley's) in that she does not depict
her relationship to North Africa in terms of a "Being-ness with the material Africa" (Torgovnick, *Primitive Passions* 64). That is, Wharton's writing differs from Kingsley's because she refuses to present Africa as a space
where "spirituality and landscape" come together to capture "the Natural life"—a life in which the writer becomes one with the land (67). Instead, Wharton portrays the North African landscape as the "dirt and di-
lapidation" of a "featureless wild land" whose "fatalistic smile" is
always threatening and never serene; therefore, like Moroccan culture,
the landscape itself is resistant and impenetrable (12, 40).

It is not long, though, before Wharton becomes familiar with this
same landscape and contradicts those bleak images by using the feminine
pronoun to describe her surroundings. Wharton refers to the picturesque
scenes in terms of "her [Morocco's] little languishing bazaars" and "her
[Morocco's] animosity against the intruder" (109). Such gendering is
congruent with Gide's identification of the vast African landscape as female, a gendering that conforms with the feminine trope of Africa established by Rider Haggard and Joseph Conrad.[5] This gender-specific language was used by colonizing male writers to determine Africa's
inferiority and penetrability, and Wharton's appropriation of it forms a
structural ambiguity in her initial descriptions of the African landscape.
By reconstructing the landscape as accessible and passive, the gendering
of Africa in the feminine (in the rhetorical tradition of male travelers)
undermines Wharton's earlier descriptions of Africa as impenetrable and
threatening. This ambiguity in the gendering of North Africa resurfaces
in Wharton's comments on the Moroccan harems.

The Dread of the Harem

R. W. B. Lewis reads Wharton's comments on the Moroccan harems in a less ambiguous frame than my analysis of her comments on North African ceremonies and landscapes (405). Lewis asserts that although Wharton was not a proto-feminist, she was shocked by the oppressive confinement of Moroccan women within the harems. During her three-week vacation, however, Wharton visited numerous harems, and each experience inspired distinct responses, both negative and positive. If we are to understand her visits to the harems, in fact, we must register her responses both as a woman, since her gender gains her entry, and as Western, since her presence is represented always as spectator and never as participant. As a result, the transformation of personalities that such expeditions provoke are complex and often produce contradictory reactions.

Wharton begins her discussion of North African harems by asserting that "as a rule no women are admitted" who are not themselves part of the harem. Ambiguity is woven into this brief statement by its inaccuracy; according to Reina Lewis, harems were "relatively easy for Western women to visit," and they even became popular tourist attractions during the late nineteenth and early twentieth centuries (149).[6] Wharton's erroneous statement works to disseminate the myth of the isolated and forbidden harem, thus implying that the reader will have a privileged gaze into an exotic and erotic world that is generally inaccessible to Western subjects. The trope of mystery established throughout the text, then, continues in her descriptions of the harems; and tropes of this kind construct harems in terms of the two most common themes of the Orientalist fantasy: sex and idleness. Wharton's thematic structure recalls literary representations of the West's vision of the harem as a space devoted to indolence and passion. The harem, through Wharton's eyes, is an "atmosphere of sensuality without seduction" and a place that never loses its ties to sex and eroticism (195). Upon arriving in the sultan's harem at Rabat, for example, Wharton focuses on the countless number of beautiful women who are sexually accessible to the sultan:

> The door of the *mirador* was always opening to let in another fairy-tale figure, till at last we were surrounded by a dozen houris, laughing, babbling, taking us by the hand, and putting shy questions while they looked at us with caressing eyes. They were all (our interpretess whispered) the Sultan's

"favorites," round-faced apricot-tinted girls in their teens, with high cheek-bones, full red lips, surprised brown eyes between curved-up Asiatic lids, and little brown hands fluttering out like birds from their brocaded sleeves. (173)

Here, Wharton's illustration of the "houris"—the mythic nymphs of a Muslim paradise—places her frame of reference outside her material surroundings by transforming the scene into the voluptuous and beautiful images of fantastic legend. Images of beautiful, young, and sexually accessible women permeate Wharton's sketches of the harem—images that express the same discourses established by Western men's sexual fantasies of the Orient. As Irvin Cemil Schick points out, the theme of sexual accessibility evoked the impression of "unbridled sexuality" in the harem and became a traditional "orientalist [representation] . . . of women [that] served to define 'otherness'; to express Western men's sexual fantasies in socially acceptable . . . ways; and to justify colonialism by conjuring the backwardness and depravity, the timelessness and availability, of the Middle Easterners" (347).

Idleness, according to Wharton, was a prominent feature of life in the Moroccan harem, and *In Morocco* lingers on the "lazy" and "indolent" women of the harems (190). During a visit to a harem in Old Fez, for instance, Wharton describes "a languor . . . [that] lay on . . . the household," and she uses such words as *passive* and *apathy* to describe the women (191, 192, 193). Such rhetoric distinguishes the passivity of the women of the harem from the leisure experienced by upper-class Europeans and Americans, including Wharton herself. Wharton implies that although European women of the upper classes were encouraged to live a life of leisure, this leisure was registered as productive because it permitted the acquisition of cultural capital. Therefore, the activities of travel, philanthropy, and cultural appreciation posit the leisure of European women as qualitatively different from the perceived idleness of the harem women.

Instead of drawing a connection between the "idleness of the harem" and the leisure of upper-class Western women, Wharton's distinction becomes yet another structure of difference separating her from Moroccan culture. Wharton does, however, attempt to form an alliance with North African women by blaming the "harem's idleness" on what she considers the oppressive "patriarchal system" that "imprisons and enslaves" the women of Morocco (165). When visiting a harem in Fez, for instance, Wharton comments on its prisonlike quality and laments that there are few points of contact between the open-air occidental mind and beings imprisoned in a conception of sexual and domestic life based on slave-service and incessant espionage. These languid women on their muslin cushions toil not, neither do they spin. The Moroccan lady knows little of cooking, needlework or any house-hold arts. . . . And all these colourless eventless lives depend on the favor of one fat tyrannical man, bloated with good living and authority, himself almost as inert and sedentary as his women, and accustomed to impose his whims on them. (193)

According to R. W. B. Lewis, this passage illustrates how the harems inspired "all her feminism [to] rise up in futile anger and helpless compassion" (405). Sarah Bird Wright agrees with Lewis by stating that the "plight of women in Moroccan harems recalls and throws into relief the ideal of the 'New Frenchwoman,'" a liberating model of gender that Wharton explores in her 1919 *French Ways and Their Meaning* (103). And Elizabeth Ammons even goes as far as stating that, in Morocco, Wharton sees the "patriarchal sex pushed to its logical, primitive . . . and very depressing extreme" (49).

While such analyses of Wharton's descriptions are fruitful, they ignore the fact that, by framing the harem as a prison, Wharton is drawing on certain social conventions, for, as Malek Alloula argues, the theme of the imprisoned harem women is a common image in early-twentieth-century Western representations of harems. Alloula suggests that this theme became part of a "sexual phantasm, not the phantasm of an individual . . . but a collective phantasm, proper to colonialism and produced by it" (28). Thus, by describing the harems as prisons, Wharton uses a vocabulary of male eroticism that constitutes the harem as a space where women are enslaved and objectified.

Wharton's portrait of the North African harem differs from the images to which Alloula refers in that she condemns, rather than idealizes, this space. Yet such a condemnation also may be read as supporting Western colonial projects; that is, her critique of harem life does nothing to destabilize the lavish fantasies projected onto Oriental women. Rather, her accounts of the prisonlike harem utilize the same discourses that judged North African (and Islamic) society by the treatment of its women, a judgment that was usually polarized by characterizing Islamic culture as either cruelly repressive or wantonly promiscuous. Thus, instead of drawing parallels between the positions held by North African women and the female world of Euro-American domesticity, Wharton's critique

assumes the prominence of Western domestic structures, so the subjugation and exploitation suffered in the harem reinforces an image of Western moral superiority.[7] Such a hierarchical position implicitly justifies the
Western *mission civilisatrice* in North Africa, defined as the "white man's
burden," and casts the colonial project into a benign and paternalistic
light. The subtext of Wharton's critique, therefore, is a vindication of the
"superior" French protectorate that is supposedly attempting to save
Morocco from its uncivilized traditions.

Although she chooses to reject the view of the harem as a social space
marked by positive relations between the female figures, Wharton complicates her condemnation of harem life by describing her encounter with
an "old Empress" in the imperial harem of Rabat (178).[8] Wharton is
overwhelmed with her "inexplicable majesty," an attribute that breaks
the "vacuum of the harem" and inspires admiration:

> Here at last was a woman beyond the trivial dissimulations, the childish
> cunning, the idle cruelties of the harem. It was not a surprise to be told that
> she was her son's most trusted advisor, and the chief authority in the pal-
> ace. If such a woman deceived and intrigued it would be for great purposes
> and for ends she believed in: the depth of her soul had air and daylight in it,
> and she would never willingly shut them out. (178)

The empress does not exhibit the negative features of harem life; rather,
Wharton is greatly impressed by her knowledge of international politics
and world affairs. More important, though, is that Wharton disrupts the
stereotype of the powerless North African woman and offers an alternative reading of relations of power, kinship, and life in the harem. The empress is described as the "trusted advisor" and the "chief authority" in the
palace, thus casting a shadow of doubt over the tropes of idleness and isolation that Wharton turns to in her earlier presentation of harem life.
While it is true that as an empress she has access to power that may not be
shared by the other women in the harem, Wharton's description suggests
that the harem cannot simply be dismissed as a structure of oppression.

Such ambiguous responses to North African women denote how
Wharton's literary representations are not necessarily homogeneous. As
Rana Kabbani points out, "Europe's feelings about Oriental women
were always ambivalent ones. They fluctuate between desire, pity, con-
tempt and outrage" (26). And given Wharton's positive depiction of the
empress, one might add the feeling of admiration to this list. Wharton's

ambivalent responses illustrate her ultimate departure from travel writers like Gide. Although Wharton reiterates many of the discourses that Gide disseminates regarding the exoticism and eroticism of North Africa, her paradoxical presentations of Morocco serve as examples of the rhetoric of ambivalence that threatens to expose the tenuous constructions of imperial discourse. Similar to her impressions of the country itself, Wharton's disclosures and critiques of Morocco's harems and ceremonies exist in perpetual flux.

PART 3
Travels at Home; or, Mapping the Modern City

Mapping the City

It is commonly noted that travel writing from the eighteenth century to the present took two major forms: the exploratory narratives that were designed for the purpose of fact gathering and the leisurely travel sketches that were designed for an audience's pleasure. Although similar techniques and strategies were used in both of these textual forms, the former was meant to be "scientific" and the latter "ornamental" and "recreational" (Stafford 33).

In the mid-nineteenth-century United States, however, another form of travel writing developed in America's urban areas. Unlike earlier travel narratives, these texts were written by Americans who chose to stay at home rather than travel abroad. Authors of travel texts now turned to what Alan Trachtenberg has called the "mysteries of the modern city" as sources for "foreign" exploration and/or pleasure (*Incorporation* 103). Urban "exposés" such as George Foster's *New York in Slices* (1849), *Fifteen Minutes around New York* (1854), and *New York Naked* (1850) depicted an urban explorer who toured the city, gathering various fragments and scenes of everyday life. David S. Reynolds argues that this trend was influenced by the urban realism of texts such as George Lippard's *New York: Its Upper Ten and Lower Million* (1842) and George Thompson's *New-York Life* (1849), both of which depicted illicit sexuality, crime, and the "actual" life of a large city (Reynolds 221, 316). While some of these texts were published as fiction and others as urban reportage, the narrator always played the role of the explorer who journeyed through the bustling crowds to describe the "burly workers, squalid prostitutes, [and] dandyish theatergoers" (Thompson 317). As this quotation suggests, many urban travel texts focused on the gender and sexuality of city life. Perhaps one reason for this is that the cityscape is, as Mary P. Ryan asserts, a public space that "defies exact boundaries between male and female spheres" (59). That is, because the city provides a public space where men and women can mix with a multiplicity of people, urban zones question gender distinctions and become a place of erotic possibility. In *Letters from New York* (1844), for example, Lydia Maria Child comments on the beauty of the working men on Broadway, as well as the men she meets in the "less genteel Bowery" (167). The spatial axis of urban life gives Child the freedom to walk the public streets and gaze at the men of New York, wondering about the erotic possibilities that await her on every corner.

During the 1860s, a number of flaneurs-cum-journalists made careers out of defining the boundaries of the cityscape. Junius Browne was one such writer who attempted to penetrate the mysteries of the city through what Lyn Lofland has called "categorical knowledge" (19). Browne, that is, tried to order New York by drafting textual maps of the city; if the city was known, he thought, the threatening areas of the urban terrain could be controlled and restrained (28). This rhetoric resonates with the language used by the cartographers of imperialism who wrote travel literature to chart the boundaries of alien spaces so that the empire could conceptualize and control foreign lands. Browne thus traveled the city streets, writing about the various neighborhoods of the wealthy and poor, immigrants and natives, men and women. His writing "categorized places as well as people" in order to compose "mental maps" for "reading the city" and deciphering its various districts (M. P. Ryan 61). His decoding of New York was also inspired by a desire to discern gender boundaries within the public realm. In certain areas, Browne states, men and women mix so freely that it is difficult to differentiate between the genders: "Old and young of both sexes are mingled everywhere. You hardly know the men from the women but for their beards and dress" (507). New York provokes an anxiety in Browne concerning gender ambiguity; his mental maps of the city attempt to contain this anxiety by revealing the areas where proper rules of conduct based on gender difference are not maintained.

In the late nineteenth and early twentieth centuries, writers such as Jacob A. Riis, Stephen Crane, Fanny Fern, and Henry James continued this textual form; they traveled to depressed areas of the city and attempted to capture the other sides of urban life—sides that differed from that of the middle-class readership of their books and articles (Edwards 66).[1] While the political intentions of these authors were undeniably progressive and often resulted in improvements in the material conditions of urban slums, these urban travel texts participated in many of the same colonizing discourses found in traditional travel narratives. Like Melville's *Typee* and Edith Wharton's *In Morocco*, the urban travel narrative brought "foreign" objects in the writer's/reader's field of vision under conceptual control. In other words, because the urban travel text attempted to reclaim slums and poverty-stricken areas for middle-class understanding, they took on the techniques of the traditional travel text by setting up an artificial dichotomy between "norm" and "other," center and margin.

Techniques that were employed in urban travel writing can also be found in American novels of the nineteenth century. For instance, Melville's *Pierre* (1852), one of the earliest examples of a literary urban travel text, presents a character who enters a city and is overwhelmed by the mysteries that he finds; his tour of the city thus functions as an attempt at decoding the signifiers of urban life. Horatio Alger's *Ragged Dick: or, Street Life in New York* (1867) serves as another example of this urban American form of travel literature. In this novel, Dick initiates Frank into city life by modifying his speech and providing him with an urbane fashion sense. Frank's transformation from country bumpkin into urban man begins with an extended tour of Manhattan for which Dick serves as the tour guide, demystifying the system of streets, signs, and sounds.[2] The urban milieu, therefore, is used by both Melville and Alger as a space that has to be explored, implying that only a guided tour can uncover the mysteries of the metropolis.

New York! New York!

Texts decoding the mysteries of the modern city were largely inspired by urban shifts in ethnic and racial demography. Between 1880 and 1930 the United States received its greatest number of immigrants; roughly twenty-eight million people arrived in those years. According to Ann Douglas, this population increase changed the face of modern New York:

> Three-quarters of the nation's immigrants in the late nineteenth century came to New York; a census report of the day revealed that in its sixth ward there were 812 Irish, 218 Germans, 189 Poles, 186 Italians, 39 blacks, 10 native-born white Americans. . . . [And] by 1920, only 1 million of the city's 6 million residents were white native-born Protestants. (304)

Because so many of the immigrants who arrived between 1880 and 1930 were not Northern European—in fact, during this period, 2.5 million Jews arrived from Russia and Eastern Europe—urban areas became increasingly populated by citizens who were visibly different from America's older white population (305). These new immigrants, moreover, tended to settle in New York, no longer dispersing themselves throughout the nation but choosing instead to live in the enclaves of the city. The visible and cultural differences associated with these men and women had dire social implications: social Darwinists and eugenicists began to develop theories of racial difference based not only on color but on ethnicity and nationality, and these doctrines soon found their way into popular discourse.[3] The popular discourses that grafted cultural and racial differences onto recent immigrants motivated modern writers such as Henry James and Djuna Barnes to unveil the so-called mysteries that accompanied cultural variations by employing textual analyses of the emerging "ghettos."

The years 1880 to 1930 witnessed another population redistribution: southern blacks began to move to the northern cities in search of employment and greater freedom, and by World War I, the Great Migration had significantly altered the appearance of New York. In *Black Manhattan* (1930), James Weldon Johnson stated that 1.5 million blacks moved from the South to the North between 1910 and 1930 (17). In fact, during this time, 1,203,000 African Americans moved to the urban areas of the North (Osofsky 23). New York, particularly Harlem, was the final destination of many southern blacks; in 1880 one in seventy people in Manhattan was black; by 1930 this ratio had changed to one in every nine (Douglas 73). As well as developing thriving African American communities in New York, black life throughout the United States shifted from a rural, agrarian existence to an urbane and sophisticated culture. African American culture, though, was still considered primitive by many whites, and thus black neighborhoods frequently became playgrounds for white pleasure seekers.

Because early-twentieth-century representations of modern American cities are numerous, I have chosen to limit my discussion to those urban travel texts that focus on New York. In my reading, New York not only came to stand in for a more generalized American urban experience but was also a model of American ingenuity, strength, progress, and modernity. New York, then, can be read as symbolic of a specifically modern experience of urban space as uncontrollably vast and spectacularly unknowable; it is therefore a space that needs to be explored, to have its mysteries uncovered.

Furthermore, the vastness of the modern cities like New York, according to Raymond Williams, was responsible for the "liberating diversity and mobility of the city," which produced a new way of seeing and experiencing the world: a sense of isolation, of being lost in the crowd, created a desire to know and explore the topography of urban space as well as the new psychology created by this anonymity (37). Georg Simmel points out that the explosion in size and complexity of early-twentieth-century cities such as New York began to reshape the mental life of the modern city dweller, whose psyche responded to the city's myriad stimuli with increased feelings of freedom and mobility that often found an outlet in touring various areas of the metropolis (39).

One important aspect of this new psyche of modern citizens of New York arose out of the city's mass immigration of people from overseas between 1890 and 1920. During this period, areas of New York's urban grid resulted in what Rosalind Krauss refers to as the creation of "pockets," where cultural difference was not only encouraged by the individual communities but, in its containment, became advantageous to those located both inside and outside its parameters (9). Such pockets, of course, were a source of anxiety for many middle-class citizens, and Anglo-Americans feared a loss of cultural and political power as a result of the shifts in New York's racial and ethnic demography. At the same time, however, middle-class Americans were often fascinated and intrigued by areas such as Chinatown, the Tenderloin district, and Harlem; these neighborhoods were thought to sanction liberatory possibilities while maintaining a sense of anonymity and privacy. Articles and books thus attempted to capture these pockets of the city in order to satisfy the appetites of middle-class readers; William Dean Howells's *Hazard of New Fortunes,* for instance, divides New York into a number of distinct sections based on the diverse racial and ethnic areas of the city. Stephen Crane, moreover, published an article in 1896, entitled "Opium's Varied Dreams," in which he describes his journey to New York's Tenderloin area to visit an opium den.

Racial, ethnic, and class differences are not the only themes to be found in the urban travel text: issues of gender and sexuality are also common topics taken up by urban explorers. For example, Fanny Fern's 1858 article, "A Law More Nice Than Just," begins by recounting the story of Emma Wilson, a New Yorker who was arrested for "wearing man's apparel" (825). Fern attacks the "prudes" and "Miss Nancys" who support such laws, furthering her protest by putting on a suit of her husband's clothes, parting her hair on one side, and taking to the streets. In this early example of the female flaneur in drag, Fern meditates on the "delicious freedom of her walk," a walk in which she is not "stifled" by long dresses, veils, or umbrellas. And she urges other women to visit a tailor and to dismiss the conventions that force women into debilitating attire. Fern's concern for the status and treatment of women in the city builds upon Margaret Fuller's flaneurie depicted in her travel letter on the working-class women of Manchester. Here, Fuller takes on the role of the urban traveler: she walks "by night in the streets of Manchester," talking to the "girls from the Mills," who are "strolling . . . through the streets . . . or seated drinking" in the gin palaces (*At Home* 47). Fuller expresses outrage that the deplorable living conditions of these women can coexist with the wealth and opulence of the English upper classes. Likewise, Fanny Fern's 1868 newspaper article, "The Working-Girls of New York," describes the women of the Bowery and the other "Celtic" districts of New York in order to call attention to the "squalor . . . that ails the working-girls" of the city (1955). During her walks through these areas, Fern meditates on the tenement houses, the poor working conditions of young women, and the various hardships of working-class life.

However, as well as providing exotic neighborhoods inhabited by working-class and immigrant communities, the topological spaces carved out by such pockets in the modern city often created areas where "forgotten" or "invisible" subcultures took root and thrived (Boone, *Libidinal* 213). This conception brings the city into the orbit of desire by sanctioning areas, such as Greenwich Village and Harlem, where gay and lesbian subcultures could flourish. The texts that I examine by Djuna Barnes, Carl Van Vechten, and Claude McKay all represent interventions in the connections between racial or ethnic difference and the dissident sexual identities that can be accessed within the various pockets of the modern city.

CHAPTER 7

"Why Go Abroad?":
Djuna Barnes Explores New York

The rear of the tenement-houses showed him the picturesqueness
of the clothes-lines fluttering far aloft, as in Florence; and the
new apartment-houses, breaking the old sky-line with their
towering stories, implied a life as alien to the American manner
as anything in continental Europe. In fact, foreign faces and foreign
tongues prevailed in Greenwich Village.

(Howells 255)

There's no subject so fascinating to the general average of people
throughout the country as life in New York City.

(Howells 124)

In her December 7, 1913, article, "Why Go Abroad?—See Europe in
Brooklyn," a piece published in the *Brooklyn Daily Eagle*, Djuna Barnes
informs her readers that the European Grand Tour is no longer "three
thousand miles away" but can be experienced in the "atmosphere" of
Brooklyn's Little Italy (131). In Brooklyn, Barnes claims, the pedestrian
will find the "life," "bustle," "color," "music," "smells," "food," and
"hucksters" of Europe: "no trip to the foreign land is needed" (135).
Barnes goes on to reflect upon the tremendous acceleration of early-

twentieth-century immigration, which resulted in the substantial expansion of New York's "ethnic districts" such as Little Italy and Chinatown.
The growth of these communities meant that, by the turn of the century,
New York—with a population of approximately two million—was divided
into "villages" based on income and ethnicity. Although these neighborhoods were geographically continuous because of their physical penetrability, the socioeconomic and cultural distances between them were
enormous. The uniqueness of these zones engendered shifts in American
cultural self-identification and provided spaces that influenced and transformed American discourses of travel. Thus, Walter Benjamin's theory
that "the story-teller" is a "seafarer," bringing tales from distant lands,
can be amended in that the urban travel sketches written by New Yorkers
such as Djuna Barnes incorporated a diversity of urban experience that
functioned to "bring intelligence from a distant land" ("Storyteller" 89).

Using Benjamin's terms, we may describe Barnes's sketches as the
work of a seafarer-storyteller. Benjamin wrote that the seafarer conveyed
tales over great distances, telling his audience about lands they would
never visit. Barnes's New York articles were, for the most part, read by
inhabitants of that city. Yet in writing about New York's different neighborhoods—Little Italy, Chinatown, Greenwich Village—Barnes was, in
effect, providing information about regions that were "foreign" to her
readers but were nevertheless within the city limits of New York. In this
chapter, I want to explore Barnes's use of these seemingly foreign spaces
and the so-called mysterious customs that she encountered in New York's
immigrant communities. My analysis will foreground what she saw as
the city's strange and "exotic" areas, many of which she depicts by using
the same rhetoric and generic conventions as in conventional travel narratives. The stereotypical exotic and mysterious world of Chinatown, the
eroticism expressed in Barnes's descriptions of working-class Irish immigrants, the primitivist tropes she uses to describe her visit to the circus,
the liberatory space of Greenwich Village (with its alternative expressions
of gender and sexuality) all come together to echo the defining qualities
of travel discourse.

Urban Travel Writing

Rather than conflating Barnes's urban sketches with the travel literature
of Melville to Wharton, I prefer to consider Barnes's work as a context to

which alternative patterns of experience can be compared. In short, I would like to suggest that the early-twentieth-century shifts in urbanization and immigration inspired anxiety in many Anglo-American New Yorkers and that travel discourses provided a forum in which these fears could be purged. With this in mind, it is important to note that travel writing, as Terry Caesar points out, was often considered a "non-literary genre" because it was generally produced for mass consumption. And Caesar goes on to say that the popularity of these "mass-market" texts "increased dramatically after the Civil War," so "there were an enormous amount of them by the century's end" (97). American travel narratives, then, combine a multiplicity of representational modes and thus "constitute a species of literary production very difficult either to differentiate or to classify" (97). One of the reasons that travel writing is awkward to define is that it occupies a textual space between objective descriptions of touristic areas and the subjective responses of the author. Because of this merger of objective observation and subjective response, this textual mode fit well into the new forms of journalism that were being established by Joseph Pulitzer, who encouraged journalists to explore the odd and unique elements of urban American life (Mott 112).[1]

Exploration of the Other and the foreign became important subjects for white American journalists, and many of them traveled through New York looking for new and strange cultures. Jacob Riis, for instance, left his middle-class environs and traveled through New York's slums, recording and photographing them for his uptown audience. While many of Riis's articles can be characterized as vertical movements in that they breach only barriers of class, his descriptions of "Jewtown" and "Chinatown" in *How the Other Half Lives* (1890) also present the horizontal movement involved in charting "alien" environments. This same movement is seen in Stephen Crane's urban experiments; in "Opium's Varied Dreams" (1896), for example, the author visits a Chinese opium den in New York's Tenderloin district so that he may experience the drug before writing about it for the McClure newspaper syndicate.[2] Urban experiments, as they were developed by Riis and Crane, became a significant form of city reporting in which the journalist would disguise himself as one of the residents of the neighborhood he was visiting. On a number of occasions, Stephen Crane disguised himself as a vagrant in order to gather information about New York's underprivileged citizens; in effect, Crane was "going native" for a brief period of time.

Such vertical and horizontal movements are also present in Djuna

Barnes's New York sketches; she moves across the physical boundaries that separate white Anglo-Americans from "ethnic" New Yorkers and at the same time crosses the psychological boundaries separating the economically secure middle class of New York from the poverty and misery of the city's slums. It is fair to assume that most white middle-class New Yorkers were, for the most part, oblivious to the inner workings of the poverty-stricken areas and ethnic communities that Barnes visited. Barnes may thus be read as an explorer, an urban traveler, who enters environments unknown to most of her peers; her sketches, then, place her in the group of early-twentieth-century writers who explored the "frontiers of civilization."

Engendering Urban Travel Writing

This new form of travel writing was genealogically tied to the journalistic culture of letters that developed during the turn of the century, a culture that reinforced masculine identities. Prior to World War II, few women worked for newspapers, and the meaning of newspaper work for most journalists of the era was tied to issues of male identity.[3] Journalist and travel writer William Dean Howells attempted, according to Michael Davitt Bell, to use realist literary modes to reassure writers that they were "real men" in a culture that regarded writers and artists as feminized (131). Bell argues that Howells was driven by his gender anxieties and, like journalists such as Jacob Riis and Stephen Crane, sought out homosocial bonds and aggressively masculine relationships. Such fraternal kinship among city reporters was common, and as Michael Robertson points out, this kinship was "marked by male bonding, misogyny, and homophobia" (5). Urban reporting, then, fell under the influence of these gender constructions and more often than not was intended to pronounce the authenticity of a writer's masculinity.

The gendering of urban reporting was translated into the formal characteristics of urban realism, which writers like Howells attempted to develop and promote. In fact, the city, as it is reported by Riis and Crane, is partially allied with the urban spaces that were used as both setting and subject of American urban realism. The images of poverty, corruption, crime, and addiction captured by these writers echo Howells's novels, which treat the seamy side of urban life as a touchstone of "the real" itself.[4] This tradition established the "realistic" city as degenerate, corrupt, and mysterious, a threatening space that needed to be exposed to the scrutiny of middle-class, suburban readers. Realist modes of representation assumed that the more depictions of slums, poverty, crime, and corruption that existed in a text, the more realistic that text was. However, as Amy Kaplan notes, late-nineteenth-century American realism also presented an alternate image of the mysterious and "unreal" qualities of urban space:

> [In] late nineteenth-century writing . . ."the city" often signifies "the unreal," the alien, or that which has not yet been realized. Represented by what it might become—by its potential, its threat, its promise—"the city" figures as a spatial metonymy for the elusive process of social change. (*Social Construction* 44)

For urban journalists, then, representations of the city were fueled by a desire to combat the mysteries and otherness of this elusive "spatial metonymy" by fixing its protean changes within the confines of a coherent textual form. Journalists like Riis and Crane, using their "masculine" vigor, confronted the city's otherness—the site and sign of social change—by presenting an urban topography in which different districts of the "unreal" city are classified and categorized in an attempt to control and undermine their threatening features. As Mary P. Ryan puts it, the "mental maps" used to control the city were "drafted by masculine hands" (63). But such cartographic techniques were also used by Barnes; as Carl Herzig correctly suggests, her fears, which were inspired by the city's mysteries, were accompanied by a desire to explore urban space and "judge it critically and philosophically" from a distance (257). These seemingly contradictory impulses exist simultaneously, pulling Barnes in different directions and enabling her to stake out a middle ground where she could enter into an alien community without running the risk of "going native" (Kannenstine 32).

Conceptions of the modern city as a dangerous space, combined with the homosocial nature of journalism, made women writers "unfit explorers" of the cityscape (Schriber, *Writing Home* 6). Walter Benjamin, in his study of the nineteenth-century city, implies that women were unfit urban documenters because they lacked the privilege or freedom to stroll and observe the city in an unacknowledged state (*Baudelaire* 37). Georg Simmel's writing on the twentieth-century city agrees with Benjamin: Simmel claims that the metropolis is a "locale of freedom" only for those who can move about unobserved in the crowd (419). As the objects of male gazes, though, women were rarely able to pass unnoticed in urban settings (Nord 351).[5] Such comments are particularly significant in light of the genre of the urban experiment, for the success of a piece of urban writing frequently depended upon an erasure of one's status as object. Urban experiments, that is, were written by individuals who could go undercover to explore strange locales; such individuals were almost exclusively men.

Barnes, of course, chose to reject these gendered discourses of city writing by taking assignments that drew her to the "unexpected" and "bizarre" mysteries of urban life (Nancy Levine 28). She thus conceived of herself as a "newspaperman" (her term) and adopted a masculine voice and persona in the form of Reginald Delancey, a fictional dandy man-about-town whom Barnes guided through the dance halls and fashionable clubs of New York.[6] This masculine persona and the adoption of a male textual perspective expose gender identity as a mere performance in which Barnes is able to play a masculine role on the stage of the city's topography. Such an act contradicts the traditional gendering of urban geography, the urban experiment and the city travel sketch: Barnes refuses to be confined to specific spaces in New York or to be restricted by the gendering of particular literary conventions.

In the context of early modernist writing, Barnes's urban sketches contest and redefine women's space by moving outside the domestic realm and into the mysterious pockets of New York. But this regendering of urban space also transforms the urban experiment; Barnes wrote numerous sketches about New York's suffragettes, and one of her protofeminist urban experiments chronicles her experience of being force-fed while mimicking a hunger strike in support of the suffrage movement.[7] By focusing on this subject matter, Barnes distinguishes her work from men's by striking a pose and constructing women-centered urban travel texts for public consumption. These suffrage articles, unlike her "Reginald Delancey" sketches, refuse to conceal her gender but directly introduce it as a subject to be discussed and debated. Thus, they effect transformations crucial to the study of urban travel writing: she turns a male generic literary practice into a vehicle for visions of the modern woman's city. These transformations and revisions provided a forum in which to rewrite accepted understandings of the cityscape and its relationship to American social order. At the same time, the gendering of urban space in Barnes's accounts made visible the previously unrecognized gendering of the world in men's urban travel writing. Men's constructions of the modern metropolis, taken to be normative, became visible as merely one set of possibilities.

However, while Barnes set the stage for diverse urban possibilities, she also at times reinscribed accepted understandings of American urban space as they were established by her male counterparts. Before examining the new directions in which Barnes takes urban travel writing, it is necessary to outline the conventions she borrows from traditional urban travel writers.

The Other Half

One such example arises out of her journey to "Pigtown," a Brooklyn slum that Barnes describes in a 1913 sketch, "Who's the Last Squatter?"[8] Here, Barnes visits squatters who live "on the other side of the divide" that separates the middle-class families of Washington Avenue from the poverty-stricken inhabitants of Pigtown. This dividing line, made up of railroad tracks and "rank bushes," calls attention to the construction of a narrative that echoes the "other half" of Jacob Riis's New York (119). Barnes's image of the city thus gestures toward discourses that construct particular urban pockets as unwieldy spaces that must be brought under conceptual control; by crossing the divide of Washington Street, Barnes moves away from the relative safety of the middle-class district and into the threatening and mysterious world of the squatters. Meditating on this dividing line, Barnes states that these squatters "stand outside" the rest of New York, "watching the city . . . [from their] leantos, with their broken panes stuffed with rags, their doors sagging on the lock, their patches of tin like the patches on a beggar's knee" (119–20). Pigtown residents are presented by Barnes as outsiders who live as spectators, gazing at the rest of the city from the other side of the dividing line. This spatial configuration speaks to the conceptual pockets that exist throughout textual presentations of the city: the line functions as a guiding principle that steers Barnes through Brooklyn and allows her to distinguish between threatening and nonthreatening neighborhoods. Divisive strategies of this kind frame a coherent picture of a city that attempts to combine the mysterious and threatening aspects of otherness to a specific geographic area. The power of the dividing line thus relegates Pigtown to a peripheral district that cannot threaten the surrounding middle-class realms.

The foreignness of Pigtown is, however, attractive to Barnes. Although she states that this area is "deplored by society" and that she cannot "sympathize" with the inhabitants, Barnes sentimentalizes the squatters. "Watch the hurry of people who work for their rent," she states, "and somehow there creeps into your heart a mad desire to place your foot on the earth and claim it as yours by the inalienable right of birth" (119). Such sentimental depictions turn into a desire to penetrate urban borders in search of "the real Brooklyn squatter" who, she believes, lives in the "house[s] across the divide" (120). Part of this attraction originates in Barnes's desire to "get to the bottom of the mystery" of Brooklyn's slums; but these mysteries ultimately remain unsolved, for the squatters she meets all claim to own the "shacks" in which they live. Finally, Barnes decides that she will abandon the slums of Pigtown and "get back to civilization" (122).

Echoing Riis and Crane, Barnes's acceptance of these borders implies that she or any other urban dweller can step over a line that separates "us" from "them," affluence from poverty. By moving across such a line, Barnes looks for the action and adventure associated with an "uncivilized" region. For her, as for Riis and Crane, navigating the course between civilized and uncivilized urban spaces becomes a central strategy for manipulating urban images and undermining the potentially threatening mysteries of the city. The drawing of boundaries, in other words, offers the urban travel writer a narrative solution to the ideological question of how to represent and control the social conflicts inherent to the urban milieu. The border between Pigtown and the rest of Brooklyn divides the city map into two separate but unequal camps and veils the antagonism between them so that the social nature of the division fades from view. Such a maneuver undermines the city's mystique and also provides Barnes with the agency to choose which side of the line she wishes to explore.

Yet Barnes's exploration of Pigtown differs from Riis's and Crane's depictions of New York in that she focuses on the women of the area. Men are, in fact, completely absent from her account, for she chooses to structure her narrative around her conversations with two women squatters. One of these women, Winnie McGraw, is described as a "buxom woman" who denies that she is a squatter and complains that Pigtown is "a sad place to be" (120). Barnes's portrait of Winnie McGraw is seen through a sympathetic light; she presents Winnie as a strong woman who supports an injured husband without much income. Similarly, Barnes paints a compassionate picture of a nameless woman who claims to be the "caretaker" of the land, a woman who struggles to care for her brother and nephew.

By focusing on these women, Barnes contributed to early-twentieth-century representations of gender, in which women's presences and voices came to include a more public role. Like her sketches of the suffrage movement, Barnes's article on Pigtown depicts women (including Barnes herself, as an urban travel writer) as secure outside conventionally conceived domestic spaces—they are women who clearly express their place in and discontent with the city. These women are presented as moving through time and space as men have historically done: the women of Pigtown support their families, and Barnes does the cultural work that has been traditionally performed by men. From this perspective her urban travel writing offers encounters with women who, "in the act of freeing themselves physically from geographical constraints, free themselves from less tangible ideological boundaries hemming them in" (Schriber, *Writing* 8).

Less progressive is Barnes's depiction of her trip to Chinatown, a trip that she chronicles in a 1913 article entitled "Chinatown's Old Glories Crumbled to Dust." Barnes, writing a decade after the New York opium hysteria generated by the increase in Chinese immigration that occurred between 1890 and 1900, searches for the myths associated with the criminal and drug-induced mysteries of Chinatown.[9] Although many of the late-nineteenth-century fears and anxieties regarding Chinatown had been assuaged, Americans of 1913 still conceived of this space as torn apart by the bloody underground societies called tongs. And New Yorkers generally associated these tongs with news of gambling raids, opium smuggling, murder, and prostitution (Latimer and Goldberg 215). As a result, Barnes chose to enter Chinatown with two "brave" and "courageous" men; still, her sense of adventure is tinged with anxieties based on stereotypes: "fear tagged behind and goaded us [upon entering Chinatown] with a sense of danger and of pitifully wicked things, which we must see and might not enter into" (123). Here, Barnes identifies herself as the typical adventurer whose gaze possesses the sites that surround her. But she rejects "enter[ing] into" or becoming entwined with the gazed-at culture; she merely wants to observe and experience "the war whoop of a Chinaman" (124). Likewise, Barnes tells us that she intends to "discover Chinatown" and disclose its mysteries for her readers; she thus describes the "narrow alleyways" and "a shot [that is] fired in the night," as well as the "girls who grew old in a year and men who laughed at death" (124).

By reinscribing stereotypes of Chinatown, Barnes searches for the outcasts and criminals that could contribute to a depiction of urban mystery. To satisfy middle-class curiosity and reinstate structures of difference, she divides the city in terms of ethnicity and of social order and disorder. Chinatown's spatial barriers, here based on ethnic difference, echo the line that separates the threats of Pigtown from the rest of Brooklyn, thus confirming the conventional trope of the divided city: a fragmented urban landscape with borders that can be penetrated by the adventurous urban tourist.

Instead of repeating Riis's moral formulations of Chinatown, though, "Chinatown's Old Glories" grieves the loss of the danger and threats associated with the district's past. "China has given up serving the devil," she laments, "and is serving America. . . . Oh the departed glory . . . China is now walking the straight and narrow path" (125). The slippage whereby "Chinatown" transforms into "China" echoes typical urban sketches by foregrounding the foreignness of the area.

But Barnes uses the generic conventions of the urban travel text to puncture some of the urban myths about Chinatown. Upon visiting an opium den, for example, she observes that these rooms are not pervasive in the neighborhood and that opium addicts are, in fact, "rare birds" in Chinatown (128). Such comments, which debunk established myths and stereotypes, undercut the reader's fears about this area; Chinatown, Barnes concludes, is simply a place to eat chop suey and drink tea without the threat of tong wars or the evil Chinamen of popular stories (128). Nostalgia, in turn, takes over this sketch: Barnes yearns for the danger of Chinatown's past, for it is no longer an unwieldy or threatening space that must be brought under conceptual control by the travel writer.

Chinatown, which Barnes presents as an exotic (but not erotic) district, lies in sharp contrast to the Irish communities of working-class New York, which Barnes presents in sexually charged language. In a series of interviews that she conducted in the fall of 1913, Barnes profiles a number of elderly Irish workers, many of whom had arrived in New York with the great wave of immigration that occurred during the late nineteenth century. These men are—like postman Joseph Dowling—described as "masculine" and "virile" workers who are "lusty and gruff" (79). Barnes's picturesque portraits of their "gleeful Celtic style" are marked with sexual currency; Dan Sheen, for instance, is described as "a good lover" and the father of ten children (104). By characterizing the "merry Irish race" as "a virile one," Barnes analyzes the Irish community through an erotic lens, examining their masculinity and sexuality as if they were a newly discovered society or culture (113). Her references to these men in terms of "lust" and "manliness" signals an interest in them that lies beyond camaraderie and is rooted in an erotic appeal derived from Irish stereotypes.

Interestingly, while her comments on the Irishmen do not depart from the colonizing gazes used in standard travel literature, Barnes's use of the discourses of primitivism do not infantalize or idealize non-Western cultures. "Humanity!, humanity! What is it all," says one working Irishman during an interview; "we are animals . . . our people are animals—we are all animals now" (115). These comments made by the interviewee gesture toward primitivist ideologies, but the self-reflexive nature of the words place them outside the bonds of colonizing rhetoric.

Furthermore, in a 1914 article titled "The Girl and the Gorilla," in which she jokingly "interviews Dinah the Gorilla," Barnes uses primitive posturing to question conventional gender roles (180). By anthropomorphizing Dinah as "the gorilla woman," Barnes inquires into "the different kinds of femininity in the world" (180). "Dinah the bushgirl," Barnes says, dismisses "fads, fancies and fashions"; nor is she interested in the "virtues" or "discretions" of the "civilized" American woman (180). Although this sketch is clearly satirical, it includes an idealization of "primitive" gender constructions that are "neither very feminine nor very fragile," while it also questions "a life called civilized" (180). Disrupting conventional femininity connects this piece to the much more serious sketches about the suffrage movement, as well as to her own intervention in the "non-feminine" world of urban travel writing. In effect, Barnes entangles Dinah with her textual practices and her presentations of suffragettes in that Dinah is "the newest womankind in the world," a "new woman" who dismisses the "advantages of civilization" (182).

The Village in the City

Barnes's inquiry into the nature of conventional gender roles is continued in articles she wrote about the bohemian subculture of Greenwich Village.[10] In these texts the Village is presented as a pocket of the city that sanctions alternative configurations of gender and sexual desire. Barnes's explorations thus construct it as a liberating space where one can avoid the constraints of bourgeois moralities. For example, in "The Last Souper (Greenwich Village in the Air—Ahem!)" she observes three "characters of the Village" as they walk through the district and meet in a "favorite cafe for tea" (218). She gives these three men effeminate names—"Vermouth, Absinthe, and Yvette"—and tells us that they do not "transmit" any "masculine impulses" (219). Vermouth, with his long "blond cane" and "yellow gloves," is, in fact, compared with a gentle "sparrow" whose favorite pastime is sipping a "lovely cup of French coffee" (219). Likewise, Yvette is a "feminine" man who wears a "neatly shaped" and "genteel" coat that looks convincingly like a "skirt" as he swings his legs "imperially" and "acts girlish" (220–21).

Such gender performances provide a spotlight from which we see the "odd ones" of the Village; the audience thus peers vicariously at a world beyond the middle-class realms of the city (221). Barnes even goes so far as to refer to these men as symbols, as "summ[ing] up all those little alien things" that exist in the subculture of the Village (221). Indeed, although they inhabit the Village, these men are referred to as "foreign," and set against the backdrop of other areas of the city, they are framed as "outcasts" who have come together to form an exotic community. While Barnes examines their posturing and posing through a satiric (and at times sardonic) lens, she chooses not to condemn these men on moral grounds. Rather, she uses such words as "genteel," "special," "gentle," and "dilettante" in her descriptions of them. More interesting, though, is her statement that these feminine men are "special children of nature" (220). Here, as in Stoddard's depictions of feminine Polynesian men, Absinthe and his companions are infantilized and characterized as "closer to nature" than other men (220). Although this gesture is, at times, patronizing, Barnes's presentation of these feminine men works to naturalize them during a historical moment when many effeminate and sexually othered men would have been considered "unnatural." These men are not, Barnes asserts, mentally deficient, perverse individuals who need to be cured.

Fluid gender identities and the emerging gay subculture that Barnes captures in the Village of 1916 are intimately linked to the other aspects of bohemian life she found there.[11] Greenwich Village of this period, as George Chauncey points out, gained a reputation for its "long-haired men" and "short-haired women," many of whom generated "accusations of perversity . . . since the gender reversal implied by such images directly evoked the semiotic codes that denoted sexual perversion" (229).

Moreover, the Village's developing avant-garde movement (1910–1920) was spawned by many homosexual or bisexual artists, such as Marsden Hartley, Charles Demuth, Hart Crane, Charles Henri Ford, Parker Tyler, Carl Van Vechten, Claude McKay, Margaret Anderson, and Jane Heap.[12]

It is important to recognize that the bohemianism of these "queer" artists in the enclave of the Village is partially akin to the forms of cultural rebellion and free love that Melville and Stoddard sought in the South Seas. That is, the geography of the ambiguously gendered and homosexual community that Barnes maps during her exploration of Greenwich Village is closely tied to the production of urban space according to the distinct pockets on the grid of New York City. A city grid, which provides the complex layering needed to conceptualize the city in terms of multiple and diverse microcosms, is seen by Barnes to sustain an island (or sanctuary) for those individuals who identify themselves as living beyond the boundaries of conventional constructions of gender and sexuality. Barnes's Greenwich Village is, in other words, a space where "naturally queer" individuals can exist without fear of rejection, alienation, or scandal (Boone, *Libidinal* 252). This "island," then, may be read as a liberating district for New Yorkers who wish to explore alternative configurations of gender and sexuality.

Furthermore, Barnes's intervention in the conceptual space of the "Bohemian Village" is continued in "Greenwich Village As It Is." In this 1916, article, Barnes presents the Village's "long hair[ed] men" and "short hair[ed] women" alongside the multicultural immigrants that seek the affordable living conditions that this area has to offer (225). Barnes's "beatific vision" of Greenwich Village includes

> dark-eyed Italian children shrieking now with Yankee-cockney accent, a moment later whispering to their deep-bosomed mothers in the Tuscan of Dante. Here a bunch of Jewish girls like a nosegay, there a pair of Norwegian emigrants, strong of figure and sparing of speech; a colored girl on the sidewalk jostles a Japanese servant and wonders whether he, too, is colored or if he is thought to be white. (226)

This multicultural "vision" constitutes an important aspect of the "wild exotics" that Barnes sees as central to life in the Village (234). The coming together of New York's immigrant communities with the Village bohemians, that is, provides a "spicy" lifestyle that speaks to her "preference for foreign make" (234). And as Lillian Faderman points out,

"Greenwich Village bohemians . . . prided themselves on being on the side of the underdog and the minority" (83).

On the one hand, Barnes's Village writing paints a sympathetic image of the coexistence of marginalized groups wherein the bohemians, estranged from the conventional gender and sexual roles of New York, live harmoniously with other "foreign" groups. On the other hand, however, Barnes neglects to comment on the extreme poverty that plagued immigrant life; instead, her portraits emphasize the "spice" and "beatific" aspects of their presence in the city. This rhetorical strategy borders on the conventions of traditional travel discourses that use the processes of idealization and abstraction to bring "foreign" cultures into the reader's field of vision. Barnes, in other words, works to bring the city's immigrants under conceptual control by providing an exotic and nonthreatening image of them. Exotic images, not the realist material conditions of these communities, are mapped onto the unfamiliar and potentially menacing sites of the Village.

These provocative glimpses of Village life also functioned as exotic drawing cards that helped to lure uptown tourists to the area. In her 1916 articles, "Becoming Intimate with the Bohemians" and "How the Villagers Amuse Themselves," Barnes captures the uptown tourists who travel to the Village for the purposes of "slumming" and viewing the "spicy foreign" communities (250). Barnes, for instance, describes "Madam Bronx," a "fur-trimmed woman, heavily laden with jewels," who is disappointed that she does not find "odd women and men who sit on the curbs" of the Village "quoting poetry" (237). Returning to her sardonic lens, Barnes derides those tourists who search for the mythic Village where "women smoke and men make love" (238). These "slummers," Barnes suggests, flee their conventional lives to break taboos in the afternoon, only to return to their cozy bourgeois lives in the evening. In contrast to the Village bohemians, they are criticized as creatures of fashion, victims of rules and customs.

This social critique of the uptown "slum-ites," though, is tempered by Barnes's own participation in the tourist industry; that is, just as *Nigger Heaven* (1926) and *Home to Harlem* (1928) promoted 1920s Harlem as a tourist site, Barnes's exotic portraits of Village life were partially responsible for stimulating the vogue that led "uptowners" to Greenwich Village.

Barnes's oversight here reverberates with her inability to revoke completely the colonizing discourses of the masculine urban travel text.

Structures of difference, an insensitivity to material conditions and a reinscription of stereotypes implicate her in the conventions of travel rhetoric. But Barnes intervenes in and transforms the genre of the urban experiment by inserting women's voices and subject positions that were previously neglected and undervalued. Her treatments of Chinatown and her uses of primitivism, moreover, attempt to debunk established myths and complicate our conceptions of their presence in the twentieth-century metropolis.

CHAPTER 8
Carl Van Vechten's
Sexual Tourism in Jazz Age Harlem

Ain't gonna hush. Gonna tell him what I think. Gonna say what I think
'bout all these meddlin' whites. They oughta stay outa Harlem.

(Thurman 137)

This quote from Wallace Thurman's 1932 novel *Infants of the Spring* expresses an opinion that was shared by many African Americans in 1920s
Harlem. Such sentiments, which echo Djuna Barnes's comments about
the uptown tourists in Greenwich Village, arose from resentment directed
not only toward the white patronage of Harlem Renaissance artists but
also toward the Harlem tourist industry that thrived between 1919 and
1929. One of the most visible figures in this tourist trade was the writer,
photographer, editor, critic, and Harlem Renaissance patron Carl Van
Vechten. Widely considered the most prominent "ofay" of 1920s Harlem, he holds a place in American literary and cultural history that is
fraught with multiple tensions. On the one hand, Van Vechten helped
countless black writers publish their work and made a substantial contri-
bution to the advancement of black scholarship by founding the James
Weldon Johnson Memorial Collection of Negro Arts. On the other hand,
however, he exploited the vibrant culture of Jazz Age Harlem by taking
his white friends on "exotic tours" of the area, tours that culminated in
the publication of his 1926 novel, *Nigger Heaven,* a text based on these

forays. Publication of this touristic novel, combined with his regular excursions through Harlem's nightlife, place Van Vechten in the foreground of white Americans who were attracted to Harlem. I would even suggest that Van Vechten was synecdochic of the many white Americans who migrated to 1920s Harlem in search of exotic and erotic adventures that were inaccessible in most white American communities.

Jazz Age Harlem can be compared to the erotic spaces depicted in Melville's and Stoddard's South Pacific islands in that it appealed to Americans who wanted to indulge in rebellious sexuality. Harlem of this period, as Lillian Faderman correctly notes, gained a reputation as a "free-for-all party" and "a synonym for naughtiness" as well as "free love" (68). These predominantly white American notions of black Harlem are also consistent with South Sea travel narratives to the extent that they gesture toward sexual colonization through the commodification of an exotic space. As in many colonized nations, in fact, tourism became a lucrative industry in Harlem, for many of the nightclubs and speakeasies catered to a white clientele. As Nathan Huggins ironically suggests, a white American seeking forbidden adventures with blacks need not go on a "safari . . . [or to a] tropical jungle. There was thrill [in Harlem] without danger. For these black savages were civilized—not head-hunters or cannibals—they could not run amok" (90). Moreover, Huggins notes that popular stereotypes of the period—disseminated by texts like Carl Van Vechten's *Nigger Heaven* (1926) and Claude McKay's *Home to Harlem* (1928)—maintained that African American men and women were more likely to engage in illicit sexual activity. George Chauncey confirms this observation, remarking that the pervasive policing of sexual desire throughout 1920s New York had not infiltrated Harlem's largely white-controlled "vice industry" (247). Consequently, many white men and women cruised the speakeasies, nightclubs, and parties searching for anonymous sexual liaisons with African American patrons. Wallace Thurman's *Infants of the Spring* captures this interracial coupling and "free love." Stephen Jorgenson, the text's central white character, has multiple sexual relations with the black women and men of Harlem. And this theme continues when, during a wild party, the white "ex-wife of a famed American playwright" (182) dances seductively with numerous black men, while "whites and blacks cling passionately together as if trying to effect a permanent merger" (186).

Thurman's depiction of Stephen Jorgenson must be contextualized within contemporary discourses alleging that "forbidden fruits" could be tasted within Harlem's polysexual boundaries. As Lillian Faderman and Eric Garber have shown, an extensive bisexual and homosexual community developed in this complex cultural context, a community that attracted many African American gays and lesbians from small southern towns. For white Americans, Harlem provided not only a space of interracial sexual opportunity but also a place where homosexuals could be open about their sexual orientation. It thus became a district where white homosexuals could interact with a similarly dispossessed culture. Furthermore, given that Jazz Age Harlem was 80 percent black, most white homosexuals did not need to conceal their identities on Harlem's streets; there was little chance that white gays and lesbians would encounter their homophobic peers. This liberating space for gay whites is depicted on the opening pages of Van Vechten's 1930 novel, *Parties*. Here, David and Hamish awake in bed together and discuss their rendezvous in a Harlem speakeasy on the previous evening. Although their relationship (and sexual identities) are never clearly stated, Hamish and David often share a bed, and David goes as far as saying that he feels more comfortable in Harlem than anywhere else in New York. It is Harlem, moreover, that erases the inhibitions of Dick Savage, the bisexual protagonist of John Dos Passos's *Big Money* (1936); for it is only in an African American gay bar that Dick can openly dance with, and kiss, another man. Depictions of Harlem as a gay-friendly space are also presented in Blair Niles's *Strange Brother* (1931): Mark Thornton, the text's openly gay character, states that Harlem offers him "a temporary and comforting refuge from the alienation of his 'shadow world'" (13). Such texts suggest that homosexual whites of this period came to see themselves as minorities who were allied with the racial minorities of 1920s Harlem.

Exotic Journeys

Brought up in Maple Valley, Iowa, Carl Van Vechten moved to New York City in 1906 to free himself from the small-minded ideals of his hometown, a town that he comically depicted in *The Tattooed Countess* (1924). But it was in 1922, after the publication of his novel *Peter Whiffle*, that he "became violently interested in Negroes . . . [almost to the point of] an addiction" (qtd. in Huggins 99). At this time Alfred Knopf introduced Van Vechten to Walter White, who began taking Van Vechten to all of the parties, dinners, speakeasies, cabarets, and nightclubs, where

Van Vechten met many of Harlem's important artists and intellectuals. Van Vechten's initiation into this "new black world" led him on a decadent two-week tour of Harlem, after which he claimed that he "knew every educated person in Harlem" (*Letters* 100). According to his letters of the period, Van Vechten was overcome by this unique community, and he repeatedly told his friends that he had never seen anything like it in Chicago and certainly never in Cedar Rapids. Partially responsible for this overwhelming experience was Harlem's nightlife, in which Van Vechten began to participate actively: "I frequented night clubs a great deal. They were very popular at the time in New York—at least they were popular after I started going because I used to get other people to go and it became quite a rage for a year or two, to go to the clubs in Harlem" (*Letters* 88). Although married to the actress Fania Marinoff, Van Vechten was often accompanied on these soirées by gay African Americans, and, according to Bruce Kellner, was known to spend much of his time and money "on [the] handsome black call boys" of the neighborhood (Kellner, "Black" 27).

By the end of 1922, Van Vechten had become the so-called white authority on Harlem, and he had made a name for himself as the renowned tour guide of Harlem's clubs and cabarets (Cooley 13). Men and women from Greenwich Village sought out Van Vechten for information about the latest speakeasies and the most "authentic" places to drink. Visitors from other American and European cities considered themselves privileged when Van Vechten gave them tours of Harlem at night, for he prided himself on steering tourists away from the fake glitter of the white-owned Cotton Club by taking them to the gay and lesbian bars, which featured drag shows and unconventional sexual opportunities. The French journalist Paul Morand, for instance, remembers being ushered past the Cotton Club and taken to the "African Room" of the Harlem Club, a gay and lesbian bar that featured female impersonators (269).[1]

Van Vechten's exotic tours eventually carried over into his textual practices. As well as writing extensively on Harlem life and culture, he wrote critical works about nineteenth-century texts that explored the erotics of foreign locales. In a collection of papers published by Knopf, entitled *Excavations* (1926), Van Vechten included essays on his favorite literary figures. One of the more noted authors that he praised was Herman Melville, who began to be recognized as an important man of American letters only during the early 1920s. By 1926, *Moby-Dick* had been rediscovered and accorded a higher station than it had enjoyed during the author's life. But Van Vechten's critical writing on Melville is significant in that it acknowledges *Typee, Pierre, The Confidence Man,* and *Israel Potter* as major literary accomplishments. In a 1921 letter to Mabel Dodge, Van Vechten expressed his admiration of Melville's texts: "I wish you could read . . . Pierre!! [*sic*] Such a book for 1851. It has never been republished. Moby Dick [*sic*] will give you thrills, but not quite such good ones. . . . The past is always so amusing in terms of the present" (*Letters* 42). Although contemporary literary critics had dismissed these texts as ineffectual, Van Vechten claimed that all of Melville's novels were worthy of canonization. What could have motivated Van Vechten's profound attraction to Melville's writing? Perhaps one explanation lies in their shared interests: both men were drawn to exploring and disseminating the tropes of primitivism, exoticization, eroticization and same-sexuality in exotic places.

Modern Primitives

It is also important to recognize that Van Vechten's interest in *Typee* and *Pierre* came at a time when Melville was being rediscovered and reevaluated by Lewis Mumford and Raymond Weaver, both of whom hailed him as an archetype of the American writer and a forerunner to Freud. The connections between Melville and Freud are convincingly outlined by Ann Douglas, who shows how *Typee* and *Moby-Dick* intervene in themes that reverberate with Freud's work on primitivism during the 1920s and 1930s (21, 209). While Freud's influence on Van Vechten remains undocumented, New York publishers of the 1920s were "quickly translating Freud's major works," and Freudian analysts were rapidly taking over the city's psychiatric practice so that "American culture was being visibly refashion[ed] . . . along Freudian lines" (21).

Van Vechten's attraction to the exotic world of 1920s Harlem was compatible with a shift in American culture wherein artists and intellectuals who considered themselves alienated from conventional lifestyles sought out the primitive, the savage id of Freud's new psychoanalytic discourse. In fact, Freud's writing on primitive cultures in *Totem and Taboo* (1913) and *Civilization and its Discontents* (1930) outlines a binary model of savage and civilizing principles that sheds light on the relationship between modernism and primitivism. In both texts Freud turns to premodern communities to consider the conquering of the primitive id by the civilizing influences of the conscience-charged superego. However, civilization is, in Freud's view, not an entirely stable category. By the time of *Civilization and Its Discontents*, for instance, he gestures toward a critique of the subordination of primitive impulses by the traditional Western paradigms of civilization. "Civilization behaves towards sexuality," Freud states, "as a people or a stratum of its population does which has subjected another one to its exploitation" (57). While he ultimately rejects the "oceanic" impetus in favor of civilizing principles, Freud uses the imagery of imperialism to question the subjugation of man's primitive urges. Interestingly, similar to modernists like Van Vechten who delved into primitivist aesthetics, Freud's concern with the primitive can be traced to his disillusionment with Western society in light of World War I. In the 1915 article, "Thoughts for the Times on Life and Death," for example, Freud suggests that civilized man could, under pressures like war, lose touch with his superego by giving way to the impulses of primitive man.

Inspired by Freud's work on primitivism, modernist writers began to impose primitivist ideologies on African American culture. Modernists as diverse as Eugene O'Neill, e.e. cummings, Waldo Frank, Sherwood Anderson, and Gertrude Stein idealized black American communities as alternatives to white lifestyles. Eugene O'Neill's successful play *The Emperor Jones* (1920), for example, broke new ground in American theater by employing both black and white actors and by hiring an African American man for the title role of the play (Cooley 15). Most influential for Van Vechten's writing, though, was the publication of Gertrude Stein's *Three Lives* (1909), which includes "Melanctha," a story about the life of a young African American woman. While texts such as Stein's and O'Neill's attempted to assert progressive racial politics by representing African Americans free from common stereotypes and prejudices, the discourses found in these texts were sometimes ambivalent. Stein's "Melanctha," for instance, at times resorts to racist ideologies by referring to "the simple, promiscuous unmorality of the black people" (86). Thus, while white modernist writers claimed to "champion . . . civil rights and human decency," their portraits of black culture approached insensitivity and maladroitness, perpetuating pejorative images of African American life (Cooley 15).

As Marianna Torgovnick points out, primitive cultures were "defined and valued" in the early twentieth century as "precapitalist utopias" where sexuality was "promiscuous and undiscriminating" (*Gone Primitive* 8–9). Such tropes were grafted onto Harlem and became a form of racial essentialism that framed Harlem as an exotic extension of mind-cure tactics—a place that was thought to provide therapeutic healing for whites. White Americans, then, began to regard Harlem as a place that offered more than just jazz music; Harlem provided an entirely different way of life. While a handful of whites were attracted to the artistic developments of the Harlem Renaissance, the majority of white Americans were inspired by the sensuality of Harlem by night. Racially mixed parties, sexual opportunities, overt homosexuality, and disavowal of prohibition laws—these were a number of the attributes often unavailable in other neighborhoods. Popular conceptions held by whites traveling to Harlem assumed that such a trip would strip away the artifice of civilization and provide freedom from the restrictions of Western rationalism.[2] Thus, the liberation that Melville sought during his textual trips to the South Seas was now considered to be available north of Manhattan's 110th Street. Individuals in search of exotic adventures no longer needed to travel across the Atlantic or Pacific oceans for excitement, they simply had to "take the 'A' train" uptown.

Ofay Heaven

Van Vechten imports primitive ideologies into *Nigger Heaven* by guiding the narrator, "a careful observer," through Harlem's exotic streets (151). Using the same travel techniques found in the urban experiments of Riis, Crane, and Barnes, Van Vechten's narrator/observer is motivated by the didactic imperative to convey a comprehensive and informed view of African American life in 1920s Harlem. Such rhetorical strategies, combined with the fictional necessities of the story, work to record Harlem's cabaret landscapes. In addition, the narrator explores the topology, as well as the topography, of Harlem as a way of appropriating them for his readers by bringing the conceptual and material spaces of Harlem into the audience's field of vision.

White appropriation of Harlem's black renaissance is, in fact, an important theme of *Nigger Heaven*. Gareth Johns, the white novelist who represents the autobiographical voice of the author, tells Mary Love, the African American protagonist of the text, that he would "like to write a Negro novel" (104). This theme is further developed when Russett

Durwood, the white editor of a prominent literary magazine, advises Byron Kasson, a young African American writer, that "if you young Negro intellectuals don't get busy, a new crop of Nordics is going to spring up who will take the trouble to become better informed [about Harlem] and will exploit this material before the Negro gets around to it" (223). Indeed, this metafictional statement seems apt in light of the fact that the "Nordic" Van Vechten exploits this same material throughout *Nigger Heaven*. But neither Gareth Johns nor Russett Durwood realize the controversy that would ensue because of the white exploitation of this African American culture.

The dispute over the publication of *Nigger Heaven* has been thoroughly documented: the majority of America's black critics were outraged, while many white Americans praised the text's authenticity and immediately made the novel a financial success. W. E. B. DuBois considered the book a "blow in the face" and an "affront to the hospitality of black folk and the intelligence of white [people]" (qtd. in Ikonné 26). Alain Locke and Countee Cullen despised the novel, though neither expressed this opinion in print. Because of the controversy, African Americans petitioned the mayor of New York City to prohibit distribution of the book, and the management of Smalls's Paradise banned Van Vechten from his favorite Harlem night spot (D. Lewis 181). Much of the criticism was provoked by the text's title. But not all African Americans despised the book, and three of its supporters—Langston Hughes, Wallace Thurman, and James Weldon Johnson—publicly defended it by claiming that Van Vechten had painted a realistic portrait of contemporary Harlem. Edward Lueders, Van Vechten's biographer, insisted that the novel's strength lay in its realism, its "restraint from propaganda," and its ability to make "sociological points" (125). At the heart of this controversy, then, was the question of authenticity: had Van Vechten created a realistic representation of 1920s Harlem, or had he merely confirmed white stereotypes and mythologies about Harlem's decadent culture?

In a letter to Gertrude Stein dated June 30, 1925, a few months before the publication of *Nigger Heaven,* Van Vechten wrote: "It [*Nigger Heaven*] will be about NEGROES, as they live now in the new city of Harlem. . . . About 400,000 of them live there now, rich and poor, fast and slow, intelligent and ignorant. I hope it will be a good book" (*Letters* 80). His desire for authenticity led him to do research and immerse himself in black culture. This immersion is expressed in a 1925 letter to Knopf: "I have during the past year written countless articles on Negro subjects . . .

and I have seen to it that so many outoftowners [*sic*] as possible saw enough of the life themselves" (87). By researching and writing on various African American topics, as well as by serving as Harlem's white tour guide, Van Vechten undoubtedly accumulated the information he needed to create a realistic textual representation of life in Harlem. Nevertheless, his concern with verisimilitude motivated him to seek out the advice of Langston Hughes, James Weldon Johnson, and Walter White, all of whom read the manuscript of *Nigger Heaven* and endorsed its authenticity.

Charles Scruggs correctly points out that Van Vechten's attempt to capture authenticity in *Nigger Heaven* meant that the author "was functioning as a cultural anthropologist" ("Crab" 152). This statement is supported by a letter that Van Vechten wrote to H. L. Mencken in November 1925: "Ain't it hell to be a Nordic when you're struggling with Ethiopian psychology?" (*Letters,* 84). This remark strikes us as blatantly racist, but for Van Vechten an understanding of "Ethiopian psychology" was essential to making his project seem authentic; if he captured authenticity, Van Vechten believed, he would avoid repeating racist ideologies and white stereotypes of African American culture. As a result, he dismissed the camplike style of his earlier novels and turned to the pseudo-anthropological techniques that were employed by Melville in *Typee.*

Van Vechten's anthropological lens is clearly derived from his interest in travel literature. The generic conventions of a travel text like *Typee* (a text that Melville published as "an authentic narrative of his adventures") often highlight anthropological posturing to convey authenticity (Woodcock 8). Van Vechten's claim of authenticity, like Melville's, works to justify his voyeuristic "peep" into a culture that was supposedly unrestricted by Nordic rationalism. One of the techniques Van Vechten uses in his specter of authenticity is a "Glossary of Negro Words and Phrases," which appears on the final pages of *Nigger Heaven.* This brief dictionary enabled Van Vechten to use words and phrases from African American culture that may have been unfamiliar to his white readership. These terms, taken from the streets of Harlem and combined with Van Vechten's infamous reputation as Harlem's white tour guide, would have encouraged his readers to treat this novel as a representation of *real* life in *real* Harlem. Thus, the presumed authenticity of *Nigger Heaven* meant that "it soon became a guidebook, and visitors carried it in their pockets as they went to Harlem" (Ikonné 29).

While *Nigger Heaven* differs from conventional travel narratives in that it does not trace the journey of an individual subject through a foreign nation, the white characters of the text journey to Harlem as a way of escaping the "repressive restrictions" imposed by white American culture. Gareth Johns, for instance, travels to Harlem to experience the "other side" of America for a book he is writing. During his stay, Johns, accompanied by Campaspe Lorillard, frequents the parties and clubs of Harlem; in fact, he first enters the novel during a Harlem dinner party, where he meets Mary Love. The reader soon becomes aware of Gareth Johns's attraction to the primitive when he becomes excited by Mary's exhibit of African wood carvings at the local public library. Such attractions to the primitive are also evident in the other white characters who frequent the Harlem nightclubs in search of gin, jazz, and sexual opportunities. For example, Rusk Baldwin, a white columnist who has come to Harlem looking for a good time, exclaims: "Well, it's wonderful up here. . . . It's as wild as a jungle" (209). These patronizing views are shared by his companion, Roy McKain, who says to his black host, Byron: "I think you are a wonderful people. . . . Such verve and vivacity! Such dancing! Such singing! And I've always thought coloured people were lazy! I suppose . . . that it's because you're all so happy" (210). Although Van Vechten's ironic narrator pokes fun at McKain's racist assumptions, the irony is effective only because McKain's comments reflect an opinion that many white Americans expressed regarding Harlem's nightlife.

A more overt reference to white sexual tourism and homosexual opportunities in Harlem's nightclubs occurs when Dick (who is passing for white) and Byron are engaged in an enthusiastic conversation about passing and the issues confronted by the New Negro. Assuming that Dick is white, two unidentified black men watch him speaking with the obviously African American Byron and remark: "Look at duh spaging-spagade talkin' wid duh fagingy- fagade, Byron heard a voice behind him say. Out fo' a little hootchie-pap, Ah *pre*-sume, another voice commented" (208). According to the text's glossary of black terms, these homophobic remarks imply that the black patrons assume Dick is a white man who is out to cruise a black man. Although no signs appear to suggest that Dick is looking for sexual opportunities among the black clientele of this club, the simple fact that a white man is conversing with an African American is enough to imply that—like so many other white men in Harlem—Dick is engaged in sexual tourism.

While *Nigger Heaven* exploits Harlem's speakeasies and nightclubs for its literary material, it is also the first American novel by a white writer to attempt representations of black middle-class characters. The central protagonists of the text are the young writer, Byron Kasson, and Mary Love, an assistant librarian, both of whom are well educated and from middle-class families. The prim and proper Mary falls deeply in love with Byron, who has just graduated from the University of Pennsylvania and moved to Harlem. Much of the text focuses on Mary's prudish sexuality and self-restraint compared with the passionate and lusty women who surround her. Byron, however, lacks control over his passions and is filled with petulance and self-doubt. Two-thirds of the novel depicts the relationship between these two characters: Mary and Byron meet at a party and fall in love; Byron is not much of a writer and must take a working-class job to pay his rent; their relationship deteriorates when Byron feels pressured and smothered by Mary; and Byron seeks sympathy in the arms of a wealthy, self-indulgent entertainer, who soon disposes of Byron when she tires of him.

Even though the novel focuses on these middle-class characters, the text is framed by the stereotypical Harlemite, Anatole Longfellow, who is otherwise known as the Scarlet Creeper. Opening on a Harlem street scene, the novel introduces the reader to "the Creeper," who displays his "tight-fitting suit of shepherd's plaid which thoroughly reveal[s] his lithe, sinewy figure." His outfit is complete with a "great diamond, or some less valuable stone which aped diamond, glisten[ing] on his fuchsia cravat" (3). As Nathan Huggins points out, the reader is not informed how the Scarlet Creeper makes his living, but it is implied that his occupations include pimping, running numbers, bootlegging, male prostitution, and selling narcotics. The opening pages of the novel, then, unveil the world of Harlem's decadent tourist trade. As well as seeing the Scarlet Creeper prospering from his criminal activities, we glimpse a black prostitute discussing her encounters with white men; she tells the Creeper: "Oh, Ah been full o' prosperity dis evenin. Ah met an ofay wanted to change his luck. He gimme a tenner" (11). Such representations undermine Van Vechten's claim to reject white myths of black culture; instead, we are exposed to the white discourses that defined Harlem as a site of decadence.

The conclusion of Nigger Heaven echoes the text's sensational introduction. Byron's despair over racial discrimination and the realization that he is not much of a writer leads him to indulge in a self-effacing affair with Lasca Sartoris. Van Vechten, by depicting Byron as a character who seeks comfort in orgiastic pleasure, returns to the racist assumptions that construct African Americans as essentially promiscuous and primitive; even middle-class blacks, the narrative suggests, are ruled by their physical desires. Furthermore, Byron's humiliation is compounded once Lasca has disposed of him, which leads him to the Black Venus Club to murder Randolph Pettijohn, Lasca's most recent lover. The Scarlet Creeper, however, robs Byron of his vengeance by shooting Pettijohn first, and Byron is reduced to emptying his pistol into the corpse. Once again, Van Vechten's conclusion depicts all blacks—the middle-class Byron as well as the criminal, Anatole Longfellow—as rejecting reason and being motivated only by the emotions that lead to sex and violence. Thus, Van Vechten's "conscious effort to serve the interest of the Negro" (Ikonné 34) by presenting African Americans of all classes in order to destroy the idea that all black men and women are alike and to abolish the myth that skin color can be equated with moral and intellectual power is betrayed by the conclusion.

The text fails in part because the most enduring scenes in *Nigger Heaven* are those containing the Scarlet Creeper and Lasca Sartoris. Unfortunately, the sections of the novel that focus on the middle-class lifestyles of Mary Love, Byron Kasson, Olive Hamilton and Howard Allison fail because they seem trite, banal, and overdetermined. Mary, for example, is too good, and her middle-class values are too overstated to be readily believed: she has read every book in the public library where she works; her knowledge of both the French language and modern art is impeccable; she is able to recite long passages from Gertrude Stein and Wallace Stevens without difficulty; and her prudish personality seems more characteristic of Jane Austen's England than Van Vechten's America. As a result, the textual framing of Harlem's licentious lifestyle and assumed racial stereotypes undermine Van Vechten's intention to present blacks devoid of white misconceptions.

Van Vechten's use of sensational scenes to entice his reader into the text signals his participation in the devices of standard travel narratives. Just as Melville presents sexualized portraits of Polynesians in *Typee,* Van Vechten showcases the exotic and erotic scenes of Harlem for the voyeuristic pleasure of his audience. Such scenes establish Harlem as seductive and sensual, implicating Van Vechten in representations that are colonizing rather than empowering to African American culture. That is, Van Vechten, writing from a white subject position, etches *Nigger Heaven* with what he believes to be exotic within presumably authentic images of Harlem. This occurs, however, without consideration that what may seem exotic from his vantage point might strike African Americans as peculiar or even deeply offensive. The result is that Van Vechten, under the guise of authenticity, presents Harlem's mythical hedonistic culture in order to engender voyeuristic pleasure. Indeed, voyeurism was even used to market the novel: Knopf promoted *Nigger Heaven* in a number of popular white periodicals by asserting that it "analyzes the fascinating and inscrutable drama that takes place in the vast theatre of New York— from which the white world below can be seen, but which it cannot see" (Scruggs, "Crab" 150). While this blurb explains "nigger heaven" as black slang for the balcony in a theater and equates this image with the geographical position of uptown Harlem, it also implies that the novel's white readers will be given a privileged view of a "fascinating" milieu—a world that white Americans usually "cannot see."

Such gazes into Harlem imply that "primitive" life there possesses more cultural currency than the "civilized" areas of white New York, an implication that is more congruent with Rousseau's colonizing myth of the noble savage than with the realism and authenticity that Van Vechten wished to convey. By claiming that African Americans exist in opposition to the conventions of white America, Van Vechten gestures toward the discourses established by Rousseau that equate particular racial features with "natural-ness." Black Harlemites, then, become fixed in Romantic nostalgia, for white Americans can escape the ethos of industrial capitalism for the brief period of time that they spend on Harlem's streets and in nightclubs.

Such primitivist depictions differ from those of *Typee*, however. Whereas the space represented in *Typee* offers an inversion of American capitalism to be admired in the abstract, Harlem's tourist trade cannot be divorced from the forces of industry and capital. Thus, as an exotic space, Harlem can be distinguished from the South Pacific islands in that the bizarre and potentially threatening aspects of the cultural Other as it exists in Harlem remain domesticated and commodified within the structures of tourism and capitalism.

What draws me to *Nigger Heaven* (and what connects it to *Typee*) is the way Van Vechten uses rationalist rhetoric alongside the most heightened idealization of Harlem's nightlife. As mentioned earlier, Van Vechten rationalizes his depictions of Harlem life by stating that he intended to capture "*real* life in *real* Harlem." But at the same time that he recognizes the strategic value of capturing a cross-section of Harlem life, he celebrates what he perceives to be the rarefied primitivism of African American culture. This rationalization resonates with Melville's anticolonial discourse in *Typee*. Melville justifies his exotic presentations of the

Typees as an anti-imperial gesture—a rebellion against the social and political configurations of nineteenth-century America—while implicating himself in colonial discourses.

By choosing to use these textual devices associated with the genre of the travel narrative, Van Vechten is unable to avoid the discursive strategies of eroticization, voyeurism, and taxonomy—all of which contradict his claims of authenticity in favor of contemporary stereotypes. Light can be shed, then, on Nathan Huggins's criticism of *Nigger Heaven* that "what is missing . . . is a clear moral or intellectual perspective that might engage the reader in the dramatic issues of Negro life" (107). Huggins is indeed correct in his assertion that the novel's racial content is problematic; however, he overlooks the fact that Van Vechten's use of the generic conventions of travel literature contaminates the very structure of *Nigger Heaven*. By depicting Harlem as a space that needs to be explored by the white world, Van Vechten, like other American travel writers who came before him, employs discourses that construct African American culture as primal and exotic.

Having said this, however, I must note that *Nigger Heaven* is significant as an historical document of the discourses that sensationalized Harlem's Jazz Age. In addition, Van Vechten's exploitation of Harlem's provocative material influenced many black writers to do the same, thus opening up a space for alternative representations of the "Black Mecca." Claude McKay, Langston Hughes, Wallace Thurman—these were a few of the Harlem Renaissance writers who, in the wake of *Nigger Heaven,* turned to Jazz Age Harlem as the site of literary explorations. More important, however, is that *Nigger Heaven* marked a shift in American travel narratives whereby the conventions of nineteenth-century travel writing became refigured in order to investigate the so-called primitive spaces within the nation.

CHAPTER 9

Going Home?: Questions of Belonging and Sexualized Space in Claude McKay's *Home to Harlem*

> Again she had had that strange transforming experience, this time
> not so fleeting, that magic sense of having come home. Harlem,
> teeming black Harlem, had welcomed her and lulled her into
> something that was, she was certain, peace and contentment.
>
> (Larsen 43)

Van Vechtenism

In a 1928 review of Claude McKay's *Home to Harlem* (1928) for *The Crisis,* W. E. B. DuBois claimed that the "dirt" and "filth" of the novel made him feel ill (qtd. in Giles, 69). DuBois's disgust with *Home to Harlem* undoubtedly arose out of his belief that McKay was pandering to commercial tastes by presenting Harlem as a space inhabited by working-class African Americans and characters who ran counter to DuBois's conception of Harlem's "Talented Tenth." His critique goes on to couple McKay's novel with Van Vechten's *Nigger Heaven:* they both, DuBois claims, satisfy the white demand for texts depicting black primitivism, and they both read as textual tours of Harlem's nightclubs and cabarets. More recent critics have continued this condemnation of *Home to Harlem* for what they call McKay's "Van Vechtenism."[1] Nathan Huggins, for instance, asserts that McKay's novel "became a best seller precisely because it pandered to commercial tastes by conforming to the sensationalism demanded by the white vogue in black primitivism," a vogue that was presented and established in *Nigger Heaven* (126). James de Jongh, in his assertion that the "two sensational, best-selling novels were published at the height of the Harlem vogue," implies that both authors were motivated by opportunism (26). And James Giles states that "the belief persists that McKay, in an attempt to capitalize upon the *Nigger Heaven* vogue of the black man as an exotic primitive, labeled his race as untalented denizens of a world of vice and promiscuity" (70).

Van Vechtenism, though, was not the only defining quality of *Home to Harlem,* for McKay's writing style differs greatly from that of *Nigger Heaven.* As James de Jongh points out, whereas Van Vechten gave voice to the literal details of Harlem's landscape, McKay's black Harlem is "evoked lyrically and figuratively" (26). "Take me home to Harlem," Jake says in the opening chapter of the novel, "take me home to the brown gals . . . take me home" (9). For Jake, Harlem is not so much the "foreign" space of *Nigger Heaven*—a space that must be explored and recorded for the gaze of his white readership—as it is a figurative home where Jake can be himself within the liberating space of an African American community. Jake's sense of belonging does not arise out of an anticipated reacquaintance with family and friends or a return to a familiar domestic space. Rather, home as Harlem is McKay's figurative depiction of a black city, the home of Alain Locke's "New Negro," where the symbolic "chocolate-black and walnut-brown girls" call for Jake's return (8).

In this final chapter, I want to consider questions of belonging and the place of "home" in the erotics of American travel literature. Such questions, as well as providing closure to my own narrative, are central to all texts of travel, but I have chosen McKay's novel because it moves away from conventional conflations of home and domesticity. McKay chooses to present "home" as a sexualized space where all desires and appetites may be satisfied. For instance, McKay's Harlem is a haven that is defined by its "womens," "chocolate, chestnut, coffee, ebony, cream, yellow," all of which generate promises of erotic pleasure. This figurative rendering of a home genders Harlem as a consumable "chocolate brown gal" who will satisfy Jake's sexual desires—desires that are not satisfied abroad. In fact, upon returning to Harlem, Jake penetrates its nightlife by meeting and sleeping with a prostitute, Felice, who inspires his emphatic declaration: "Where else could I have all this life but Harlem? Good old Harlem! Chocolate Harlem! Sweet Harlem!" (14). Jake continues to use this conceit of Harlem as a sensual woman throughout the novel, for much of the text's action depicts Jake's travels through Harlem's streets in search of Felice.

This search for Felice, the symbolic spirit of Harlem, moves the perceptual foreground of the novel into the same cabarets and nightclubs that are recorded in *Nigger Heaven*. Once Jake penetrates Harlem, its figurative dimensions fade into the background and the Harlem setting is particularized in the style of Van Vechten's text. Jake's search is transformed into a gaze that narrates the pictorial descriptions of "the lowly of Harlem's Black Belt" (20). As in urban experiments by Jacob Riis, Stephen Crane, and Djuna Barnes, the narrator of McKay's text transforms into Van Vechten's "careful observer," who cruises the Harlem streets recording the sights he sees. The reader thus tours a variety of Harlem environments, a textual strategy that has inspired a number of critics to claim that Jake exists "mainly for the purpose of taking the reader on a tour of Harlem" ("Claude McKay" 982). Wayne F. Cooper, moreover, correctly characterizes *Home to Harlem* as a "picaresque journey through 'the semi-underworld' of black working-class America" (xxiii). Consequently, in the words of McKay's narrator, we are able to gaze at that "strange un-American world where colored meets and mingles freely and naturally with white in amusement basements, buffet flats [and] poker establishments" (106).

This tour of Harlem life, in which we are introduced to characters such as the singer Congo Rose, the "sweetman" Zeddy, and the intellectual Ray, surveys the topography of Harlem as home, complete with its own borders, boundaries, and characters. McKay, in fact, presents Harlem in terms of Robert Park's "little world" within a larger city, a district that is part of a greater mosaic and that serves as both refuge and home to a vibrant African American community (608). To use Park's words, McKay's Harlem is a pocket, a communal identity, that permits both stability and mobility; that is, while Harlem is the safe home of the New Negro, whites who seek an element of chance and adventure can penetrate its borders and experience all that this "pocket" has to offer. Such borders are fluid in McKay's text: his representation of Harlem echoes Park's theory that the city is similar to an organism that is constantly growing and changing shape like an ameba. "Harlem! Harlem!," Jake exclaims, "a little thicker, little darker and noisier and smellier, but Harlem just the same. The niggers done plowed through Hundred and Thirtieth Street. Heading straight foh One Hundred and Twenty-fifth. Spades beyond Eighth Avenue. . . . Oh Lawdy! Harlem bigger, Harlem better . . . and sweeter" (25–26).

Celebrating Harlem's overflowing boundaries, the narrative focuses on a growth that arises out of an increase in the number of citizens who conflate Harlem with home. These images of growth sustain the feminine gendering of Harlem, for such images present the "black metropolis" as a maternal entity that unfailingly reproduces citizens to expand the internal network of the community. These reproductive impressions are coupled with references to Harlem as "sweet," an adjective that is also used throughout the text in reference to Felice. McKay, by imagining Harlem as a woman, depicts a complex network within "the pocket," a network that does not so much foreground the feminine comfort of traditionally conceived domestic space as it illustrates a sexually exciting locale that is reproductive, erotic, and sexually alluring to Jake. For McKay's narrator, then, Harlem as home is presented as a symbolic woman who comes to stand in for the multiplicity of human contacts and sexual possibilities within the urban milieu.

Home (W)here?

McKay's vision of Harlem as home was shared by other African American artists and intellectuals of the Harlem Renaissance. In his 1925 anthology, *The New Negro*, for example, Alain Locke presents a synthetic utopian image of Harlem as the home of the modern African American. The modern city is, according to Locke, a space that exists as the home for the displaced African, a home that will restore the "common consciousness" lost in the diaspora (7). This conception of the city as a homeland, a social ideal, arises out of Robert Park's theory that the city allows the human possibility of expanding, developing, and finding a sense of belonging, which would be impossible within the spatial and moral confines of rural life (608). Borrowing from Park, then, Locke disturbs standard notions of the American home by locating belonging and community in an urban center;

no longer lodging home in the rural cottage or the suburban ring around the city. Locke rejects the nonurban spaces that define a purely white notion of belonging and kinship. By embracing Harlem as home, Locke conceptualizes an appropriate space of belonging for the African American experience in the wake of the Great Migration.[2] Moreover, his grounding of Harlem in a sense of black community presents the city as both a physical home and a symbolic home, an imagined "capital of Black America" (Jones 87).

Questions of home and belonging in Harlem are explored by other writers of the Harlem Renaissance: Langston Hughes, Countee Cullen, Jessie Fauset, Nella Larsen, and Rudolph Fisher all conflate images of Harlem with home. These writers differ, however, on what Harlem-as-home signifies.[3] Alain Locke, for example, conceives of the "mecca of the New Negro" as a space that would produce great African American art that would be both "classical" and "masculine" (Scruggs, *Sweet* 57). For Rudolph Fisher, Harlem-as-home means a refuge from the American racism that threatens African American life. And Nella Larsen's depiction of Harlem presents it more as a temporary abode in the never-ending search for identity and belonging. Such diverse visions of home in Harlem suggest that the central mythology of Harlem contains multiple versions of its function and importance, not simply a single unified space of community and fellowship.

This image of Harlem as both physical and mythic space, a space that is simultaneously there and not there, may best be expressed through Foucault's vision of the heterotopia. Heterotopic spaces, Foucault states, are "simultaneously mythic and real" districts that stand "outside of all places, even though it may be possible to indicate their location in reality" ("Other Spaces" 24). Such spaces, moreover, are "counter-sites" that, unlike utopias, are concurrently defined by physical presences and the ability to contest and invert other sites. Borrowing from Foucault's theory, we can replace Locke's utopic Harlem with a heterotopic Harlem; under this framework, the "real" and "mythic" Harlem—the city within the city—confounds those sites that we traditionally define under the categories of city, mecca, capital, and of course, home. Sexuality, moreover, finds its way into Foucault's descriptions of the heterotopia when he describes the "honeymoon trip" as a heterotopic space where "sexual virility" and "the woman's deflowering" take place "nowhere" ("Other Spaces" 24). Here, Foucault anticipates contemporary feminist and queer geographers who correctly assert that space is sexed and gendered, and sex and gender are "spaced" (Probyn 10).

Home Truths

Claude McKay's gendering and sexualizing of the organic, heterotopic site of Harlem is consistent with the broader gendering of New York City by modernist writers. F. Scott Fitzgerald's "My Lost City" (1926) serves as one example, for the narrative voice asserts that New York is "essentially cynical and heartless—save for one night when *she* made luminous the Ritz Roof" (143). Fitzgerald goes on to describe this experience with the "luminous" roof as his only "nocturnal *affair*" with the city, an affair that transforms the gendered space of the city into a site of erotic desire. Sue Best suggests that the gender and sexualized language imposed on New York is part of a more general characterizing of space as feminine: "In an extraordinary array of contexts, space is conceived as a woman. This is particularly noticeable in relation to the 'bounded' spatial entities which are seen as the context of, and for, human habitation: the world, the nation, regions, cities, and the home" (181). Locating the spaces of "city" and "home" under a gendered rubric speaks to the traditional sense of belonging and habitation that conflates domestic space with the feminine; as Sidney H. Bremer points out, America's mainstream culture has defined "home" as "a purely white, motherly wife" (47). This equation of the feminine with domesticity distinguishes urban experience from the rural (or suburban) notions of home. As a result, potentially threatening areas like Harlem of the 1920s come to be defined by white Americans as centers for drinking and dancing and elicit sexuality—centers that were established in opposition to the traditionally white notion of the safe and "blissful" rural or suburban home.

Contrary to pastoral conceptions, McKay positions home within the communal belonging of a sensual and erotic urban setting, which rejects the nostalgia, employed by writers such as Paul Laurence Dunbar, that located the African American home in the rural South of pre–Great Migration America. McKay thus uses his diasporic characters to bring powerful feelings of origin and belonging to bear on the "image of Harlem as an erotic place" (Osofsky 186). McKay's Harlem/home is not the intellectual center portrayed by Alain Locke, nor is it the domestic and familial space presented by Larsen; McKay's Harlem is an anthropomorphized site that his character Jake longs to merge with:

> Oh, to be in Harlem again after two years away. The deep-dyed colour, the thickness, the closeness of it. The noises of Harlem. The sugared laughter.

The honey talk on the streets. And all night long, ragtime and "blues" play-
ing everywhere . . . singing somewhere, dancing somewhere! Oh, the con-
tagious fever of Harlem. Burning everywhere in dark-eyed Harlem. . . .
Burning now in Jake's sweet blood. (286)

Here, Harlem is defined by its anthropomorphic and edible characteristics: sugared laughter, honey talk, feverish, dark eyes—all of these physical features come together to define the topography of Harlem through
Jake's eyes. Such visions call attention to the "sensory" and "fleshy" aspects of the city (Lee 71). The noises, the tastes, the erotic contagion of
this passage construct Harlem as a city of physical pleasures, a city that
LeRoi Jones similarly refers to as "the pleasure-happy center of the uni-
verse" (88). The physicality of this "city of senses" is also conveyed
through the constant references to food:

Dusk gathered in blue patches over the Black Belt. Lenox Avenue was
vivid. The saloons were bright and crowded with . . . liquor-rich porters,
banana-ripe laughter. . . . Women hurrying home from days' work to get
dinner ready for husbands. . . . On their arms brown bags and black containing a bit of meat, a head of lettuce, butter. . . . From the saloons came
the savory smell of corned beef and cabbage, spare-ribs, Hamburger steaks.
Out of the little cook-joints wedged in side streets, tripe, pigs' feet, hogs'
ears and snouts. Out of apartments, steak smothered with onions, liver and
bacon, fried chicken. (290)

Allusions to nourishment occur throughout the text. Like the "chocolate-
brown" and "walnut-brown girls," Harlem's sensual pleasures are irre-
sistibly presented for Jake's consumption (5). McKay's Harlem, then, is a
site where physical appetites and desires are immediately satisfied; no-
body, the text implies, will ever go hungry in Harlem, no matter what
tastes he or she may have or cultivate.

While Harlem and home are linked through the domestic images of
food and eating, McKay's gendering of Harlem and his images of women
as food suggest, as Sidney Bremer does, that McKay's narrative is in part a
masculinist fantasy of the African American neighborhood. That is, if we
read Harlem/home as a "unit of consumption," we cannot deny that
McKay writes a "male" Harlem, for the women exist only as consumable
commodities within the black city of the senses (Saunders and Williams
81). This male-centered vision is continued in McKay's complex depiction

of multiplicity and possession. The multiple appetites that the city stimulates in Jake forge a yearning for proprietorship of the surrounding
women and commodities. After sleeping with Felice, for instance, Jake
states: "she's a particularly sweet piece of business. . . . Me and her again
tonight. . . . Handful o'luck shot straight outa heaven. Oh, boy! Harlem
is mine!" (17). Jake's comments continue the earlier food/sex imagery by
expressing his sexual satisfaction with Felice in terms of an oral sensa-
tion, presenting her as a "sweet piece." These expressions of sexual satisfaction, moreover, lead Jake to claim ownership of Harlem; by stating
"Harlem is mine!" in this context, Jake interprets his sexual conquest as
an acquisition of the whole city. In Jake's terms, then, the sexual possession of Felice is equivalent to possessing the multiplicities of urban life.

Desire and Belonging

Possessing Harlem is central to Jake's notion of home, and the images of
possession even arise out of his characterization of Felice as representative of Harlem's "world of strangers" that has a "life space . . . and sexuality of its own" (Knopp 151). From Jake's perspective, Harlem takes on
the eroticized experiences of modern urban life: anonymity, voyeurism,
exhibitionism, consumption, and power. Such a sexualized space becomes home for Jake in that it provides access to the multiple possibilities
determined by the large, dense, and permanent cluster of heterogeneous
human beings. For Jake, these possibilities instil a sense of belonging; his
return to Harlem signifies a return to a place in which he feels "at home."
But Elspeth Probyn notes that notions of "home" and images of sexuality
are not mutually exclusive. She argues that desire or *longing* is central to
our notions of belonging, for it "expresses a desire for more than what
is" (6). By locating belonging in the realm of desire, we can grasp how
Jake's imagined home in Harlem can fluctuate from a place of belonging
to a sexualized space. Building on Robert Park's theory that a city's diversity provides a sense of belonging through its very openness and multiple
perspectives of experience, we see Jake, who is entwined in the complex
social dynamic of Harlem's grid, desiring to make connections with those
who surround him. Jake's desire for belonging, his desire to connect, fails
with Zeddy, Rose, and Ray and ultimately manifests itself in sexual terms
through the penetration of Felice and the subsequent gendering and sexualizing of the Harlem cityscape.

Peter Saunders defines the connections between home and belonging in his claim that "the home is where people are offstage, free from surveillance, in control of their immediate environment. . . . It is where they feel they belong" (184). These comments reflect the traditional conception of home that is articulated by James Duncan when he states that the home is a medium for the expression of individual identity, a space that serves as a symbol of the self (4). Identity is essential to notions of home; as Madan Sarup suggests, "The concept of home seems to be tied in some way with the notion of identity—the story we tell of ourselves and which is also the story others tell of us" (95). Home, as seen through these theoretical patterns, can be distinguished but not separated from belonging in that home represents a subjective site that is tied to an individual's identity. Belonging, though, must be recognized as more than simply subjective, for such notions depend upon a communal understanding. Thus, belonging, unlike traditional conceptions of the home, cannot be an isolated and individual affair. Home and belonging, however, merge in McKay's text through the placement of the communal site of Harlem under the rubric of home. That is, McKay's depiction of home is taken out of its private context—an individual's house or apartment—and located on the public stage of the city. Such a depiction not only complicates traditional notions of home by merging subjective and communal spaces but also confounds traditional conceptions of identity.

If, as Madan Sarup suggests, the concept of home is intimately connected to notions of identity, Harlem can be read as a place where Jake feels most alive and free to express what the text calls his "spontaneity," "instinct," "naturalness," and "primitive passion" (30, 62, 267, 44). Harlem, in other words, is a locale where Jake can "be himself" by expressing the story he tells of his life. This conception of Harlem thus departs from traditional notions of home because (outside of experiencing a racial sense of belonging in this neighborhood) Jake is not surrounded by those who share a common and unified identity. Harlem, instead, is presented as offering a multiplicity of identities: abundant sexual identities, a multiplicity of desires, as well as numerous and fluid representations of gender all characterize this space.

Although Jake's gender and sexual identities remain static, the characters who surround him are often presented as sexually ambiguous and engaged in elaborate gender performances. When Jake goes to the Congo nightclub, for instance, a woman cabaret singer with a "man's bass voice" appears in drag and sings a song entitled "I'm Crazy about a

Man" as she walks from table to table where "the dark dandies were loving up their pansies" (30–31). Congo Rose's gender identity, an identity that is displaced by her attire and the "wonderful drag 'blues'" song, is applauded by the "bulldycking women and faggotty men" of the club (36). Jake enjoys the song as well as the "pansies and dandies" who "stare and look him up and down," yet the narrator attempts to stabilize Jake's sexual identity by claiming that "he didn't seem aroused at all" by the advances of the gay men of the club (32). These gay men, however, are described in the same sensual and erotic terms as the women that Jake meets on Harlem's streets: "The pansies stared and tightened their grip on their dandies. The dandies tightened their hold on themselves. . . . Dandies and pansies, chocolate, chestnut, coffee, ebony, cream, yellow, everyone was teased up to the high point of excitement" (32). By describing these men in the same colorful and edible terms as Harlem's eroticized women, the narrative feminizes and sexualizes them as objects waiting to be possessed; they become food that is offered for the specific tastes of the Congo's patrons.

Jake's trip to the Congo leads to his relationship with Congo Rose, who refers to Jake as "mah brown" and a "sweet-loving papa" (39, 40). By transcribing the colorful and edible images back onto Jake, Congo Rose appropriates the same possessive and sensual terms that Jake projects onto the women and gay men of Harlem. Such appropriations of masculine posturing are congruent with Rose's drag show, a show that is reminiscent of those put on by the tuxedo-attired Gladys Bentley, who performed double-entendre songs at Harlem's Clam House. Unlike Bentley, though, Rose's masculine gender performance does not signal her identification as a lesbian; rather, her sexual attraction to Jake resonates with the fluid sexualities expressed by contemporary jazz singers such as Bessie Smith, Ma Rainey, and Ethel Waters.[4] Thus, by complicating the conventional codes of gender and sexuality that map the body as a category, Rose disturbs the illusory naturalness that is thought to conceal a stable gendered and sexual identity. In anticipation of Judith Butler's theory of performative genders and sexualities, Congo Rose's performance complicates the imagined conception of a unified subject and the epistemology of the hermetic body (Butler 225). Rose, that is, confounds traditional accounts of the body that assume its importance as a privileged site on which one reads the gendered and the sexual.

Questions of home and belonging are central to Rose's rupture of stable identities, in that conventional theories of home and belonging

depend upon a fixed "story we tell of ourselves and which . . . others tell
of us." If conceptions of home and belonging are tied to an individual
identity, what happens to such conceptions when identities are presented
as fluid and unstable? Rose's flexible identity is typical of modern urban
life as it is described in Robert Park's theory, for the city enables people to
"try on" and experiment with multiple personas that would remain impossible in rural communities. This situation is a result of the size of the
modern metropolis, which provides the anonymity necessary to those individuals who wish to make and remake themselves. A modern urban
space such as Harlem, therefore, is not limited by the intolerance of a
small town that stifles difference; in fact, according to Park, the twentieth-
century city actually rewards eccentricities and thus allows for potential
shifts in gender and sexuality (Park 608).

Redefinitions of seemingly stable identities emerge elsewhere in
McKay's novel. During his second visit to the Congo Club, for instance,
Jake is struck by a new entertainer whom he names "doll boy" (91). This
boy "was made up with high-brown powder, his eye-brows were elon-
gated and blackened up, his lips streaked with the dark rouge so popular
in Harlem, and his carefully-straightened hair lay plastered and glossy
under Madame Walker's absinthe-colored salve 'for milady of fashion
and color'" (91). Like Congo Rose, this "skirt-man" is representative of
the multiplicity of identities within the urban context. Subsequently, traditional notions of home that conflate belonging with stable identities (by
assuming that home is a site where one expresses his or her "true" identity) become ineffectual when the home is attributed to an urban space, a
space where identities are multiple and in constant flux. McKay's Harlem, then, attempts to reevaluate notions of home in order to articulate
feelings of belonging that can accommodate the fluid identities of characters such as Rose and the "doll boy." Home-in-Harlem, as it relates to issues of identity, thus functions as a space of convergence, for it is a site
that overcomes assumed divisions based on gender and sexuality; not
only are individual characters able to assume varied identities, but
hetero- and homosexual identities are not conceived as discrete categories. McKay's conception of home, therefore, displays a human geography that is hybrid: neat gender divisions and polarizations of sexual identity are absent here.

Interestingly, one of the many identificatory shifts in the text occurs
when Rose expresses a vision of home that stabilizes gender, sexuality,
and belonging. Rose's ideal home differs from that of Jake: she conceives

of it as lying not on the communal plain of the city but in a more private and domestic setting. Such a view speaks to Rose's search for a stable identity to which she can attach herself—an identity that depends upon a stable sexualized space. While singing a song, she turns to Jake and sings:

> If I had some one like you at home
> I wouldn't wanta go out, I wouldn't wanta go out. . . .
> If I had some one like you at home,
> I'd put a padlock on the door. . . . (39)

Although Rose relocates the region of home by divorcing it from a public setting and placing it in a private realm, she shares Jake's conception of home in terms of sexual possession. As a result, she implies that Jake's domestic presence would make her home complete: she would not need to go out for anything—all of her appetites and desires would be fulfilled within the boundaries of this imagined space. In addition, by claiming that she would padlock the door, Rose repeats Jake's desire to possess the objects of his affections. Both characters thus imply that sexual possession will forge a space of belonging that will satisfy their desires for a home.

While Rose's account of this domestic space may be read as a desire to construct a stable identity by moving her gender performance back into the field of standard constructions of femininity and domesticity, Jake reads it as a gesture that would undermine his masculinity. He views Rose's domestic assertions as a feminizing move, for he considers her offer as providing a space in which he will become possessed and economically dependent. "If you'll be mah man," Rose says to Jake, "you won't have to work . . . hard work's no good for a sweet-loving papa" (40). But Jake's response is a complete dismissal: "I've never been a sweetman yet. Never lived off no womens and never will. I always works" (40). Jake's fear of feminization through possession is shared by the other characters in the text: Miss Curdy, for instance, distrusts any man who "want[s] to be kept like women," and she defines dependent men as "a lazy and shiftless lot" (61). Zeddy, moreover, is called a "skirt-man" when he is economically supported by his girlfriend and subsequently attempts to perform a masculine role by asserting his "independence" in the Congo Club in order to "show the boys that he was a cocky sweetman and no skirt-man" (90). Jake's rejection of Rose's offer both stabilizes his conception of a home outside the domestic sphere and confirms his masculinity, for, although he enjoys the company of "pansies" and "bulldykers," he wishes to remain within the boundaries of conventional masculine codes and roles.

In Transit

While he is able to stabilize his own gender identity, Jake's formulation of Harlem as home ultimately proves to be inadequate. After his conflict with Rose, for instance, Jake takes a job on the railroad "just to break the hold that Harlem had upon him" (125). He explains that he needs to "get right out of the atmosphere of Harlem" before it "gets him" (125). Here Jake expresses a fear that Harlem's boundaries have the power to imprison him and make him succumb to living his entire existence inside its borders. Such comments seem to contradict his earlier descriptions of Harlem, descriptions that establish it as a home that provides food for all appetites, satisfactions for all desires. The narrative then moves to counter Jake's earlier exuberant expressions of Harlem; in an ironic reference to Van Vechten's *Nigger Heaven,* Susy states: "I should think the nigger heaven of a theater downtown is better than anything in this heah Harlem. . . . This here Harlem is a stinking sink of iniquity. Nigger hell! That's what it is" (98–99). These ambivalent presentations of Harlem are continued by the narrator when Ray decides to leave the city:

> Going away from Harlem. . . . Harlem! How terribly Ray could hate it sometimes. Its brutality, gang rowdyism, promiscuous thickness. Its hot desires. But, oh, the rich blood-red color of it! The warm accent of its composite voice, the fruitiness of its laughter. . . . He had known happiness, too, in Harlem, joy that glowed gloriously upon him like high-noon sunlight of his tropic island home. (267)

Here Harlem is an ambiguous space: on the one hand, it is a place of happiness and joy; on the other, it is to be hated for its insensitive brutality." As with Jake's radiant descriptions of Harlem, this ambivalent sketch focuses on the physical nature of the setting: Harlem is anthropomorphized by being endowed with "accent," "voice," "laughter," and "blood." Even the earlier edible, sensual images are invoked through the image of "fruitiness"; furthermore, the sexualized space that is established in the earlier depictions remain; its promiscuity is signaled by "hot desires." Such images are contained within the realm of home. But, for Ray,

Harlem is only "like" home—he locates his "real" home in the space outside of the city, the tropical island of his youth.

Jake's ultimate rejection of Harlem, like Ray's, comes in the final stages of the novel. Upon finding Felice, the symbolic "heart" of the city, Jake becomes "jest right down sick and tiahd of Harlem" (303). Part of Jake's sudden dislike of the city arises from his realization that it is no longer a purely African American space, for it has been infiltrated by "white pleasure-seekers from downtown" (317). Jake thus recognizes that his feelings of belonging have been ruptured by the "ofay's mixing in" (104). This rupture is once again similar to Park's formulation of the city as a space of distinct microcosms that can be penetrated by outsiders (in this case, whites who seek adventure in a black neighborhood). Harlem, like other modern cities, is a space of multiple borders, which make it possible for "individuals to pass quickly and easily from one moral milieu to another and encourages the fascinating but dangerous experiment of living at the same time in several different contiguous, perhaps, but widely separated worlds" (Park 608). Harlem is no longer a safe haven, and Jake experiences dangerous encounters through the city's brutality, a brutality that is experienced by Ray in earlier sections, when Zeddy threatens him with an open razor. While Jake is able to defend himself with his gun, he sees Zeddy's action as a symbolic destruction of his sense of belonging to Harlem. The symbolic power of this attack is explained by the narrator, who states that "he [Jake] was caught in the thing that he despised so thoroughly. . . . Brest, London, and his America. Their vivid brutality tortured his imagination. Oh, he was infinitely disgusted with himself to think that he had just been moved by . . . savage emotions" (328). In this passage, Brest, London, and some American cities are conflated with Harlem to suggest that the "black metropolis" does not make a sufficient home—it does not provide a relief from the "savage emotions" that Jake encounters elsewhere.

While somewhat paradoxical, Jake's shift from praising Harlem to disdaining it speaks to Park's theory that the city is an ameba-like entity that constantly changes space and character to define itself as a confusing terrain. Jake's change of heart also presents Harlem as a heterotopic space that not only lacks equilibrium and stability but also confounds all spaces through its resistance to distinct definition. Such lack of balance is emphasized when Jake's "brutal" and "savage" experiences result in his departure from Harlem. But his inability to find any sense of meaningful community in this city does not destroy his search, for, when Felice says that "Chicago [is a]. . . mahvelous place foh niggers," Jake envisions the South Side as a "promised land" that will satisfy his need for an ideal home (Priebe 24).

Jake's ongoing search for belonging, instigated by his feelings of displacement and dislocation is similar to the search for a stable community that McKay describes in his autobiographical travel text, *A Long Way from Home* (1937)—a search that, perhaps because of McKay's "lust to wander and wonder," is never fulfilled (*Long* 4). Throughout this travel text, McKay echoes many of Jake's negative responses to Harlem. Speaking of Harlem in 1937, for instance, McKay states that it has developed into "an all-white picnic ground . . . with no apparent gain to the blacks" (*Long* 133). Such sentiments further Jake's disillusioned image of Harlem, for, in the final analysis, the Mecca of the New Negro does not provide a comfortable home.

Conclusion

In this book, I chose to focus on the erotics of travel literature composed by American writers. The central reason for this choice was to limit a vast topic to a national tradition of travel writing by uniting the works discussed through their historical and cultural similarities. While this national congruence may be, in the words of Benedict Anderson, an "imagined" unity, my focus has engendered analyses that attempt to link texts to the historical discourses of gender, sexuality, race, and American expansionism. This emphasis runs the risk of implying that the erotic discourses found in American travel literature do not exist in other national literatures. Such an assertion would be misleading. Comparative work could, for example, connect the erotic images in Jack London's search for male kinship to Gilgamesh's journey and his subsequent relationship with Enkidu, the wild man of the woods in *The Epic of Gilgamesh*. Or comparative analyses would be fruitful in linking David Dorr's sexual exploits in France with those described by Laurence Sterne in *A Sentimental Journey* (1768). Readings of travel texts that traverse national traditions by comparing sites of eroticization by writers from various countries would result in many fascinating comparisons and parallels. Such comparative work, though, must be left for another journey.

Furthermore, due to the restrictions of time and space, I chose to confine my study to texts written between the mid-nineteenth century and the early twentieth century. By focusing on texts from this period, I was able to read the erotics of travel in traditional travel texts during the period of American expansion and a time when the United States was "becoming modern." Following these analyses, I wanted to turn to one of the central questions of my thesis: what happens to travel literature, particularly the erotics of travel, during the rise of twentieth-century modernism? By examining modernist texts about American travel, I was able to illustrate and examine the migration of travel discourse and eroticism to texts about the modern city. However, I would not want to give the false impression that eroticism and travel discourse are not present in postmodern travel literature. Although the Depression of the 1930s and World War II shifted the focus of American travel literature away from erotic imagery, the Beat writers of the 1950s returned to the erotics of travel with a vengeance. The writing of William Burroughs, for instance, explores the exotic and erotic splendors of Tangiers, and his *Queer* depicts his homosexual experiences in Mexico. Moreover, Jack Kerouac's *On the Road* (1955) and *The Subterraneans* (1958) both describe travels across the nation, travels that are peppered with miscegenation and other forms of sexual liberation. And finally, I see Norman Mailer's "White Negro"—the hipsters whom he calls "a new breed of adventurers, urban adventurers who drifted out at night looking for action with a black man's code"—as the heir to Van Vechten's adventures in Jazz-Age Harlem (2).

The continuation of this study to include the Beats and other postmodern travel writers is the next step in a larger and more comprehensive study of the erotics of American travel literature. The impetus for such work comes out of a need for an analysis of American travel literature within its social, regional, and historical contexts while studying American travel writing from a more global point of view—a perspective that would encompass American travel texts about Japan, China, Mexico, South America, Canada, and elsewhere. Such a study, in the age of globalization, would allow for a new, insightful, and more contemporary analysis of the relationship between American travel, eroticism, and expansionism.

NOTES

Introduction

1. See Irving's *Sketch Book* (1819), which is often read as a continuance of the conventions of British literary travel texts, and his *Alhambra* (1832), a travelogue that utilizes British travel discourses to describe Spain as mysterious, irrational, and premodern. For more on Irving's travel writing, see W. W. Stowe's *Going Abroad* (58–59).

2. I am indebted to William W. Stowe's reading of David Dorr's portrayal of himself as a "young bachelor" and "man about town" who wishes to assert independence in the wake of his experiences as an American slave (Stowe 63).

3. As we will see in pt. 3, urban travel writing became an increasingly popular form between 1840 and 1900, and a number of writers experimented with this form in order to profit from the "best-selling exposés" of modern city life (Reynolds 316–17).

4. For an in-depth analysis of Said's neglect of homosexual discourses within colonial projects, see Tom Hastings's "Said's Orientalism and the Discourse of (Hetero)sexuality," *Canadian Review of American Studies* 23 (1992): 127–46.

Part 1. Cruising the South Seas

1. For more on the history of American imperial expansion in Hawaii, see Thomas J. Osborne's *Annexation of Hawaii: Fighting American Imperialism* and Michael Dougherty's *To Steal a Kingdom: Probing Hawaiian History.*

1. Melville's Peep Show

1. For an interesting reading of racial ambivalence in *Benito Cereno,* see Dana D. Nelson's *Word in Black and White* (109–31) and Eric J. Sundquist's *To Wake the Nations* (135–210).

2. T. Walter Herbert's *Marquesan Encounters* is an excellent source for biographical information on Melville's Polynesian travels.

3. For more on the titillating aspects of the genre, see Robert K. Martin's "'Enviable Isles': Melville's South Seas."

4. Neil Rennie's *Far-Fetched Facts* (1995) discusses the structural influences of these texts on *Typee.*

2. Primitivism and Homosexuality

1. It is important to note that Stoddard's textual expressions of same-sex desire are, at times, contradictory and paradoxical. In fact, as Roger Austen notes, Stoddard's repeated assertions as to the "naturalness" of same-sex desire were undermined in his unfinished article, "The Confessions of an Unnaturalist" (Austen, *Genteel* 154).
2. David Spurr helpfully refers to this process as "the rhetoric of naturalization," a discursive strategy that he traces through a number of nineteenth-century texts (110).
3. According to Robert K. Martin, the Calamus poems inspired many nineteenth-century homosexuals to pressure Whitman to explain his position on adhesiveness and "the love of friends"; among those who wrote to Whitman were Bayard Taylor, John Addington Symonds, Edward Carpenter, D. H. Lawrence, and Stoddard (Martin, *Homosexual Tradition* 50).
4. A similarly authoritative character appears in "Kane-Aloha" (1904) in the image of "the chaperone," a figure who unsuccessfully attempts to police Stoddard's sexual desires (*Cruising* 72).
5. It is interesting to note that "Kane-Aloha" was based on Stoddard's 1864 trip to Hawaii, but it was not written until 1903. It seems possible, then, that it was influenced by John Addington Symonds's *Problem in Modern Ethics* (1891), a text that Stoddard read in 1901 (Austen, *Genteel* 154).
6. It is interesting to note that Paul Clitheroe, in *For the Pleasure of His Company*, does not return to America, but this scenario is not consistent with Stoddard's other travel writing.

3. "Closer than blood-brothership"

1. Stoddard and London were in fact acquaintances, and their brief correspondence is cited in *The Letters of Jack London*. It is also clear that London was familiar with Stoddard's travel sketches, for he borrowed the title of Stoddard's *Leper of Molokai* (1885) for a 1908 article that he published in *Woman's Home Companion* (London, *Letters* 186).
2. For more on homosexuality and homophobia in London's fiction, see Jonathan Auerbach's *Male Call: Becoming Jack London* and Joseph Boone's *Tradition Counter Tradition: Love and the Form of Fiction*. For more on gender roles in London's novels, see Clarice Stasz's "Androgyny in the Novels of Jack London" (*Western American Literature* 11 [August 1976]: 121-33) and Sam S. Baskett's "Sea Change in *The Sea-Wolf*" (*American Literary Realism* 24.2 [1992]: 5-22).
3. Earle Labor's "Jack London's Pacific World" summarizes London's imperial

stance but does not touch on representations of same-sexuality. Tietze and Riedl do a good job of discussing colonization and irony in "'Saints and Slime': The Ironic Use of Racism in Jack London's *South Sea Tales*," but they too fail to read the homoerotic nature of these texts. Moreland's "Violence in the South Sea Fiction of Jack London" provides an excellent postcolonial analysis of London's texts but issues of sexuality are not discussed.

4. In addition to his South Sea stories, London wrote about ideal male friendships in his novels: *The Sea-Wolf* (1904) and *The People of the Abyss* (1903) depict intimate relations between male characters that transgress traditional notions of masculinity and stereotypes of gender (Hedrick 66, 122)

5. Such interracial friendship had been represented in the relationship that develops between Ishmael and Queequeg in *Moby-Dick* (1851). It is important to note that London was a great admirer of Herman Melville's sea novels.

6. For more on the term *homosocial,* see Carroll Smith-Rosenberg's *Disorderly Conduct* (30–50), Eve K. Sedgwick's *Between Men* (1–20), and Robert K. Martin's *Hero, Captain, and Stranger* (13).

7. For more on London's voyage to Typee, see chapter 10 of *The Cruise of the Snark* (1911).

8. A similar idealization of the virile male body occurs in London's *Sea-Wolf,* when Van Weyden describes Wolf Larsen's naked body. Like Cudworth's aesthetic attraction to Lyte, Van Weyden's desire for Larsen is never physically expressed.

9. For more on the cultural discourses of hybridity during the nineteenth and twentieth centuries, see Robert Young's *Colonial Desire: Hybridity in Theory, Culture and Race,* 1–28.

10. McClintock's insightful reading of Rudyard Kipling's *Kim* shows how the "cultural hybrid" can be used to suggest a reformed colonial control in that the cultural hybrid can pass as Other in order to police and enforce colonial policies (70).

11. "The Heathen" was first published in *London Magazine,* September 1909, and has been reprinted in London's *South Sea Tales.*

12. According to Marianna Torgovnick, the central primitive trope is that "primitives are our *untamed* selves" (emphasis mine) (*Gone Primitive* 8).

13. This theme is explored in "The Inevitable White Man" (1909) and "The Seed of McCoy" (1909). Both of these stories depict the brutality that colonizers inflicted upon the Polynesian natives. As Earle Labor puts it, London's South Pacific stories explore how "[i]n the midst of ruthless savagery, the white man in Melanesia is reduced to like savagery" ("Pacific World" 213).

14. David A. Moreland correctly argues that "the primary source of Jack London's philosophy of race was Benjamin Kidd," whose text *The Control of the Tropics* (1893) was instrumental in developing London's racial theories (Moreland 8).

4. Roman Holiday

1. Hawthorne has left us with an invaluable record of his Roman holiday in the form of his *French and Italian Notebooks,* much of which include his impressions of Rome gathered between January 24, 1858, and May 24, 1859.
2. This case was widely publicized in the *London Journal.*
3. T. Walter Herbert's *Dearest Beloved: The Hawthornes and the Making of the Middle-Class Family* illustrates how the ideal of domesticity was central to the Hawthorne family. Herbert also convincingly argues that the ideology of domesticity functions as a means of redemption in a number of Hawthorne's novels.
4. For more on nineteenth-century American discourses of purity, see Herbert's *Dearest Beloved;* for more on nineteenth-century American gender roles, see Welter's "The Cult of True Womanhood: 1820–1860."
5. It is interesting to note that Hawthorne's description of the Faun of Praxiteles is similar to Melville's depiction of Marnoo in *Typee.*
6. Although Miriam's national and ethnic heritage is never clearly stated, she is described as having the same "dark" features as Donatello.

5. Savage America, Civilized England

1. For more on the connections between this travel sketch and *The Marble Faun,* see Nancy Bentley's "Slaves and Fauns: Hawthorne and the Uses of Primitivism."
2. For this chapter, I have chosen to use the American edition of Brown's European travel text, published in 1854 and generally referred to as *Sketches of Places and People Abroad.* This edition is an expanded version of a text that Brown published in England in 1852 under the title *Three Years in Europe; or, Places I Have Seen and People I Have Met.*
3. Nancy Prince, an African American woman who traveled to Russia in 1824, expresses similar sentiments concerning her feelings of liberation in light of the European attitudes toward race. Prince claims that she feels completely free in Eastern Europe, for here she does not experience any "prejudice against color" (114).
4. The British Parliament abolished slavery in the British Empire in 1834.
5. I am using this term as it is defined (as "anglomania") in the *Concise Oxford Dictionary:* a person who has an "excessive admiration of English customs."
6. For more on the structural elements and generic conventions of slave narratives and African American travel texts, see William L. Andrews's *To Tell a*

Free Story: The First Century of Afro-American Autobiography, 1760–1865.
Urbana: University of Illinois Press, 1988.

7. Brown was in Europe from July 1849 to September 1854. After attending the
Paris Peace Congress and following by a brief trip to Germany, he spent his
time traveling and lecturing in England, Scotland, and Ireland.

8. It should be noted that Queen Victoria was not unpopular in the United
States; however, the institution of the monachry was unpopular.

9. While Mulvey asserts that the coupling of fetishism and curiosity can be characterized as a "Woman's look," the motifs of space and curiosity persist
throughout Brown's *Sketches* (61).

6. "Harems and Ceremonies"

1. Wharton does cite a few French texts on Morocco, including Pierre Loti's *Au
Maroc* (1886), Marquis de Segonzac's *Voyages au Maroc* (1909), and Augus-
tin Bernard's *Le Maroc* (1916).

2. For more on Mary Kingsley's travel writing, see chapter 6 of Sara Mills's *Discourses of Difference: An Analysis of Women's Travel Writing and Colonialism.*

3. Trent Newmeyer examines the issues of gender and sexuality in relation to
Said's theory in his article entitled "Travel Literature and the Making of
'Orientalisms': The Cases of Flaubert and T. E. Lawrence," *HyperPhorum*
1.1 (winter 1997): 1–10.

4. For more on the Wharton and Gide relationship, see R. W. B. Lewis's *Edith
Wharton: A Biography* (370–400).

5. For more on Gide's construction of the African landscape as feminine, see
Torgovnick's *Primitive Passions* (20–30). Torgovnick also points out that
Rider Haggard's *King Solomon's Mines* (1885) refers to the African landscape as "Sheba's breasts" and that in *Heart of Darkness* (1899), Conrad uses
the image of the African woman to depict "the immense wilderness, the colossal body" of Africa (27).

6. For more on the harem as a tourist site, see Inderpal Grewal's *Home and
Harem: Nation, Gender, Empire, and the Cultures of Travel* (Durham: Duke
University Press, 1996).

7. Reina Lewis discusses a number of texts by European and Islamic women
who illustrate the connections between the constraints imposed on European
women within the Western domestic ideals of the nineteenth and early twentieth centuries and the status of women living in harems.

8. Some women writers, such as Sophia Poole in *The Englishwoman in Egypt*
(1844), celebrated the harem as a women's network of kinship rather than exploitation and subjugation.

Part 3. Travels at Home

1. For more on Stephen Crane's writings about New York slums, see Alan Trachtenberg's "Experiments in Another Country: Stephen Crane's City Sketches" and Michael Robertson's *Stephen Crane, Journalism, and the Making of Modern American Literature* (1997). For more on Henry James's travel writing about New York City, see my "Henry James's 'Alien' New York: Race and Gender in *The American Scene*.

2. For more on the city in Alger's novel, see Trachtenberg's *The Incorporation of America* (120–22).

3. In Henry James's *American Scene,* for instance, Italian and Jewish immigrants are called "aliens"; James goes on to describe them as *racially* othered within the American context.

7. "Why Go Abroad?"

1. Alan Trachtenberg's *Incorporation of America* makes important connections between Pulitzer's influence on journalism and its relation to the modern city (124–26).

2. For more on Stephen Crane's urban experiments, see Michael Robertson's *Stephen Crane, Journalism and the Making of Modern American Literature* and Alan Trachtenberg's "Experiments in Another Country: Stephen Crane's City Sketches."

3. In addition to Djuna Barnes, the notable exceptions to the male world of journalism before World War II were Willa Cather, Eudora Welty, and Katherine Anne Porter.

4. It is interesting to note that the narrative structure of Howells's *Hazard of New Fortunes* (1890) works to unveil the dangerous slums of New York while the main character, Basil March, writes "picturesque sketches" and "strange studies" of the urban poor (203, 211).

5. For more on women and the nineteenth-century city, see Deborah Epstein Nord's "The Urban Peripatetic: Spectator, Streetwalker, Woman Writer" and her *Walking the Victorian Streets: Women, Representation, and the City* (Ithaca, N.Y.: Cornell University Press, 1995).

6. Barnes uses the character Reginald Delancey in "You Can Tango—A Little—at Arcadia Dance Hall" and "Twingeless Twitchell and His Tantalizing Tweezers," both of which where originally published in the *Brooklyn Daily Eagle* in the summer of 1913. They have been reprinted in Djuna Barnes's *New York*.

7. The urban sketches in which Barnes describes the suffrage movement include

"Part Victory, Part Defeat at Suffrage Aviation Meet," "Seventy Trained Suf- fragists Turned Loose on City," and "How It Feels to Be Forcibly Fed."

8. In 1915 much of "Pigtown," an area in Flatbush, was demolished during the construction of Ebbets Field.

9. Such myths sparked fears and anxieties about the potential corruption of Americans; Jacob Riis, for example, states that "the Chinaman smokes opium as Caucasians smoke tobacco, and apparently with little worse effect upon himself. But woe unto the white victim upon which this pitiless drug gets its grip" (122).

10. It is important to note that these articles differ from her other urban sketches in that Barnes saw herself as part of this bohemian culture of the Village. In fact, she lived in Greenwich Village between 1913 and 1918 (Field 37). How- ever, although she positions herself as an "insider," her sketches are written for an "uptown" readership who are interested in learning about this exotic locale.

11. It is interesting to note that the connections between gender ambiguity, sexual fluidity, and bohemian culture are also explored in Barnes, *Nightwood* (1936).

12. For more on the gay subculture of Greenwich Village between 1910 and 1920, see George Chauncey's *Gay New York: Gender, Urban Culture, and the Making of the Gay Male World, 1890–1940* (228–33) and Joseph Boone's *Libidinal Currents: Sexuality and the Shaping of Modernism* (251–65).

8. Carl Van Vechten's Sexual Tourism in Jazz Age Harlem

1. Van Vechten also served as a Harlem tour guide for William Faulkner and Os- bert Sitwell (David Lewis 24).

2. Nathan Huggins notes that this general disillusionment with abstractions such as "Western rational thought," "civilization," and "high culture" had its roots in the disturbing realities of World War I (88).

9. Going Home?

1. Those critics who claim that McKay's novel is derivative of *Nigger Heaven* fail to note that McKay had begun work on *Home to Harlem* in 1923, three years before the publication of Van Vechten's text (Giles 73).

2. For more about the effects of the Great Migration on notions of home and community in Harlem, see Gilbert Osofsky's *Harlem: the Making of a Ghetto* (1963).

3. See Langston Hughes's short story "Home" in *The Ways of White Folks*

(1934), Jessie Fauset's "Home" section of *Plum Bun* (1929), Nella Larsen's conflation of home and Harlem in *Quicksand* (1928), and the presentation of Harlem in Rudolph Fisher's *City of Refuge* (1925).

4. For more on the indeterminate sexualities of these jazz singers, see Angela Davis's *Blues Legacies and Black Feminism: Gertrude "Ma" Rainey, Bessie Smith, and Billie Holiday* (1998). Davis correctly reads these women as representative of the first generation of postslavery African Americans who were able to freely choose the gender of their sexual partners.

WORKS CITED

Adams, Percy G. *Travel Literature and the Evolution of the Novel*. Lexington: University Press of Kentucky, 1983.

Alger, Horatio. *Ragged Dick*. 1867. *Ragged Dick and Mark, the Match Boy*. New York: Collier, 1971. 39–216.

Allen, Grant. *The European Tour*. New York: Dodd, Mead, 1908.

Alloula, Malek. *The Colonial Harem*. Minneapolis: University of Minnesota Press, 1986.

Ammons, Elizabeth. *Edith Wharton's Argument with America*. Athens: University of Georgia Press, 1980.

Anderson, Charles Roberts. *Melville in the South Seas*. 1939. New York: Dover, 1966.

Auerbach, Jonathan. *Male Call: Becoming Jack London*. Durham: Duke University Press, 1996.

Austen, Roger. *Genteel Pagan: The Double Life of Charles Warren Stoddard*. Ed. John W. Crowley. Amherst: University of Massachusetts Press, 1991.

———. Introduction. *Cruising the South Seas*. Charles Warren Stoddard. San Francisco: Gay Sunshine Press, 1987. 11–28.

Bailey, Brigette. "Travel Writing and the Metropolis: James, London, and the *English Hours*." *American Literature* 67 (June 1995): 201–32.

———. "Visual Subjection: The Italian Tour and the Making of the National Subject in Sedgwick's Travel Writing." Paper presented at the Snapshots from Abroad travel writing conference, University of Minnesota, Minneapolis, November 1997.

Baker, Paul R. *The Fortunate Pilgrims: Americans in Italy, 1800–1860*. Cambridge: Harvard University Press, 1964.

Bakhtin, Mikhail. "Forms of Time and of the Chronotope in the Novel." *The Dialogic Imagination*. Trans. Caryl Emerson and Michael Holquist. Austin: University of Texas Press, 1981. 78–89.

———. *Rabelais and His World*. Trans. Hélène Iswolsky. Cambridge: MIT Press, 1968.

Barnes, Djuna. "Becoming Intimate with Bohemians." 1916. *New York*. Ed. Alyce Barry. Los Angeles: Sun & Moon Press, 1989. 233–45.

———. "Chinatown's Old Glories Crumbled to Dust." 1913. *New York*. Ed. Alyce Barry. Los Angeles: Sun & Moon Press, 1989. 123–30.

———. "Daniel Sheen, Newsdealer Fifty-five Years Selling Papers." 1913. *New York*. Ed. Alyce Barry. Los Angeles: Sun & Moon Press, 1989. 104–9.

———. "The Girl and the Gorilla." 1914. *New York*. Ed. Alyce Barry. Los Angeles: Sun & Moon Press, 1989. 180–4.

———. "Greenwich Village As It Is." 1916. *New York*. Ed. Alyce Barry. Los Angeles: Sun & Moon Press, 1989. 223–32.

———. "How the Villagers Amuse Themselves." 1916. *New York*. Ed. Alyce Barry. Los Angeles: Sun & Moon Press, 1989. 246–52.

———. "The Last Souper (Greenwich Village in the Air—Ahem!)." 1916. *New York*. Ed. Alyce Barry. Los Angeles: Sun & Moon Press, 1989. 218–22.

———. *New York*. Ed. Alyce Barry. Los Angeles: Sun & Moon Press, 1989.

———. "Postman Joseph H. Dowling Forty-Two Years in Service." 1913. *New York*. Ed. Alyce Barry. Los Angeles: Sun & Moon Press, 1989. 78–81.

———. "Who's the Last Squatter?" 1913. *New York*. Ed. Alyce Barry. Los Angeles: Sun & Moon Press, 1989. 119–22.

———. "Why Go Abroad?—See Europe in Brooklyn." 1913. *New York*. Ed. Alyce Barry. Los Angeles: Sun & Moon Press, 1989. 131–35.

Bell, Michael Davitt. *The Problem of American Realism: Studies in the Cultural History of a Literary Idea*. Chicago: University of Chicago Press, 1993.

Benjamin, Walter. *Charles Baudelaire: A Lyric Poet in the Era of High Capitalism*. Trans. Harry Zohn. London: New Left Books, 1973.

———. "The Storyteller." *Illuminations*. New York: Schocken, 1969. 82–89.

Bentley, Nancy. "Slaves and Fauns: Hawthorne and the Uses of Primitivism." *ELH* 57 (1990): 901–37.

Bergman, David. *Gaiety Transfigured: Gay Self-Representation in American Literature*. Madison: University of Wisconsin Press, 1991.

Best, Sue. "Sexualized Space." *Sexy Bodies: The Strange Carnalities of Feminism*. Ed. Elizabeth Grosz and Elspeth Probyn. New York: Routledge, 1995. 181–94.

Bhabha, Homi K. *The Location of Culture*. New York: Routledge, 1994.

Black, Jeremy. *The British Abroad: The Grand Tour in the Eighteenth Century*. New York: St Martin's Press, 1992.

Bochner, Jay, and Justin D. Edwards, eds. *American Modernism across the Arts*. New York: Peter Lang, 1999.

Boone, Joseph Allen. *Libidinal Currents: Sexuality and the Shaping of Modernism*. Chicago: University of Chicago Press, 1997.

———. *Tradition Counter Tradition: Love and the Form of Fiction*. Chicago: University of Chicago Press, 1987.

———. "Vacation Cruises; or, The Homoerotics of Orientalism." *PMLA* 110 (January 1995): 89–118.

Bradbury, Malcolm. Introduction. *The Marble Faun*. By Nathaniel Hawthorne. London: Everyman, 1995.

Bremer, Sidney H. "Home in Harlem, New York: Lessons from the Harlem Renaissance Writers." *PMLA* 105 (1990): 47–56.

———. *Urban Intersections: Meetings of Life and Literature in United States Cities*. Chicago: University of Illinois Press, 1992.

Broe, Mary Lynn. *Silence and Power: A Reevaluation of Djuna Barnes*. Carbondale: Southern Illinois University Press, 1991.

Brown, William Wells. *The American Fugitive in Europe: Sketches of Places and People Abroad*. 1854. *The Travels of William Wells Brown*. Ed. Paul Jefferson. New York: Markus Wiener, 1991. 72–235.

———. *Clotel; Or, The President's Daughter*. 1853. *Three Classic African-American Novels*. Ed. William L. Andrews. New York: Mentor, 1990. 115–283.

Browne, Junius. *The Great Metropolis: A Mirror of New York*. Hartford, Conn.: n.p., 1867.

Burroughs, William. *Queer*. New York: Penguin, 1985.

Butler, Judith. *Bodies That Matter: On the Discursive Limits of "Sex."* New York: Routledge, 1993.

Butor, Michel. "Travel and Writing." *Mosaic* 8.1 (1974): 1–16.

Buzard, James. *The Beaten Track: European Tourism, Literature, and the Ways to "Culture," 1800–1918*. Oxford: Oxford University Press, 1993.

Caesar, Terry. "'Counting the Cats in Zanzibar': American Travel Abroad in American Travel Writing to 1914." *Prospects* 13 (1988): 95–134.

Chapman, Mary. Introduction. *Ormond*. By Charles Brockden Brown. Toronto: Broadview Press, 1999. 1–31.

Chauncey, George. *Gay New York: Gender, Urban Culture, and the Making of the Gay Male World, 1890–1940*. New York: HarperCollins, 1994.

Child, Lydia Maria. *Letters from New York*. 1844. New York: C. S. Francis, 1850.

"Claude McKay." *The Norton Anthology of African American Literature*. Ed. Henry Louis Gates Jr. and Nellie Y. McKay. New York: Norton, 1997. 981–83.

Cooley, John. "White Writers and the Harlem Renaissance." *The Harlem Renaissance: Revaluations*. Ed. Amritjit Singh et al. New York: Garland, 1989. 13–22.

Cooper, Wayne F. Foreword. *Home to Harlem*. Boston: Northeastern University Press, 1987.

Craft, William. *Running a Thousand Miles for Freedom; or, The Escape of William and Ellen Craft from Slavery*. 1860. Miami: Mnemosyne, 1969.

Crain, Caleb. "Lovers of Human Flesh: Homosexuality and Cannibalism in Melville's Novels." *American Literature* 66 (March 1994): 25–53.

Crane, Stephen. "Opium's Varied Dreams." 1896. *Stephen Crane: Prose and Poetry*. New York: Library of America, 1984. 853–58.

Crowley, John W. Editor's Introduction. *Genteel Pagan: The Double Life of Charles Warren Stoddard*. By Roger Austen. Amherst: University of Massachusetts Press, 1991. xxv–xli.

———. "Howells, Stoddard, and Male Homosocial Attachment." *The Mask of Fiction: Essays on W. D. Howells*. Amherst: University of Massachusetts Press, 1989. 56–82.

Dana, Richard Henry. *Two Years before the Mast*. 1840. New York: Signet, 1964.

Davis, Angela Y. *Blues Legacies and Black Feminism: Gertrude "Ma" Rainey, Bessie Smith, and Billie Holiday*. New York: Pantheon, 1998.

Derrick, Scott. "Making a Heterosexual Man: Gender, Sexuality, and Narrative in the Fiction of Jack London." *Rereading Jack London*. Ed. Leonard Cassuto and Jeanne Campbell Reesman. Stanford: Stanford University Press, 1996. 110–29.

Dorr, David F. *A Colored Man round the World: By a Quadroon*. Cleveland, 1858.

Dougherty, Michael. *To Steal a Kingdom: Probing Hawaiian History*. Waimanalo, Hawaii: Island Style Press, 1992.

Douglas, Ann. *Terrible Honesty: Mongrel Manhattan in the 1920s*. New York: Farrar, Straus, and Giroux, 1995.

Dulles, Foster Rhea. *Americans Abroad: Two Centuries of European Travel*. Ann Arbor: University of Michigan Press, 1964.

Duncan, James. Introduction. *Housing and Identity*. Ed. James Duncan. London: Croom Helm, 1981. 1–21.

Edwards, Justin D. "Henry James's 'Alien' New York: Race and Gender in *The American Scene*. *American Studies International* 36 (February 1998): 66–80.

Ellis, William. *Polynesian Researches*. London: John Murray, 1833.

Ernest, John. "The Reconstruction of Whiteness: William Wells Brown's *The Escape; or, A Leap for Freedom*." *PMLA* 113 (October 1998): 1108–21.

Erskine, John Elphinstone. *Journal of a Cruise among the Islands of the Western Pacific*. London: John Murray, 1853.

Faderman, Lillian. *Odd Girls and Twilight Lovers: A History of Lesbian Life in Twentieth-Century America*. New York: Columbia University Press, 1991.

Farrison, William Edward. *William Wells Brown: Author and Reformer*. Chicago: University of Chicago Press, 1969.

Fauset, Jessie. *Plum Bun*. 1929. Boston: Northeastern University Press, 1989.

Fern, Fanny [Sara Willis Parton]. "A Law More Nice Than Just." 1858. *The Norton Anthology of American Literature*. Ed. Nina Baym et al. 6th ed. New York: Norton, 1999. 825–26.

———. "The Working-Girls of New York." 1868. *The Heath Anthology of American Literature*. 2nd ed. Vol. 1. Toronto: Heath, 1994. 1955–56.

Fiedler, Leslie. "Home as Heaven, Home as Hell." *What Was Literature? Class, Culture and Mass Society*. New York: Simon and Schuster, 1982. 145–65.

Field, Andrew. *Djuna: The Life and Times of Djuna Barnes*. New York: Putnam, 1983.

Fisher, Rudolph. *The City of Refuge: The Collected Stories of Rudolph Fisher*. Columbia: University of Missouri Press, 1987.

Fitzgerald, F. Scott. "My Lost City." *The City: American Experience*. Ed. Alan Trachtenberg et al. New York: Oxford University Press, 1971. 140–50.

Foster, George G. *Fifteen Minutes around New York*. New York: De Witt and Davenport, 1854.

———. *New York in Slices*. New York: William H. Graham, 1849.

———. *New York Naked*. New York: De Witt and Davenport, 1850.

Foster, Shirley. "Making It Her Own: Edith Wharton's Europe." *Wretched Exotic: Essays on Edith Wharton in Europe*. Ed. Katherine Joslin and Alan Price. New York: Peter Lang, 1993. 129–45.

Foucault, Michel. *The Archaeology of Knowledge*. Trans. A. M. Sheridan Smith. New York: Pantheon, 1972.

———. *The History of Sexuality: Vol. 1: An Introduction*. Trans. Robert Hurley. New York: Vintage, 1978.

———. "Of Other Spaces." *Diacritics* 16.1 (1986): 22–27.

Franchot, Jenny. *Roads to Road: The Antebellum Protestant Encounter with Catholicism*. Berkeley: University of California Press, 1994.

Freud, Sigmund. *Civilization and its Discontents*. 1930. Trans. Joan Riviere. New York: Dover, 1994.

———. "Fetishism." *The Standard Edition of the Complete Psychological Works of Sigmund Freud*. Vol. 21. London: Hogarth Press, 1961. 152–57.

———. *Totem and Taboo*. 1913. Standard Edition. Vol. 13. 1–162.

Frow, John. "Tourism and the Semiotics of Nostalgia." *October* 57 (1991): 123–51.

Fuller, Margaret. *At Home and Abroad; or, Things and Thoughts in America and Europe*. Ed. Arthur B. Fuller. Boston: Roberts Bros., 1895.

———. *Memoirs of Margaret Fuller Ossoli.* 2 vols. Ed. R. W. Emerson, W. H. Channing, and J. F. Clarke. 1859. Boston: Roberts Bros., 1884.

———. *"These Sad but Glorious Days": Dispatches from Europe, 1846–1850.* Ed. Larry J. Reynolds and Susan B. Smith. New Haven: Yale University Press, 1991.

———. *Women in the Nineteenth Century.* New York: Norton, 1971.

Fussell, Paul. *Abroad: British Literary Travelling between the Wars.* New York: Oxford University Press, 1980.

Garber, Eric. "A Spectacle in Color: The Lesbian and Gay Subculture of Jazz Age Harlem." *Hidden from History: Reclaiming the Gay and Lesbian Past.* Ed. Martin Duberman et al. New York: Meridian, 1989. 318–31.

Gates, Henry Louis. *The Signifying Monkey: A Theory of Afro-American Literary Criticism.* New York: Oxford University Press, 1988.

General Evening Post (London), September 12, 1734 (os).

Gifford, James. *Dayneford's Library: American Homosexual Writing, 1900–1913.* Amherst: University of Massachusetts Press, 1995.

Giles, James R. *Claude McKay.* Boston: Twayne, 1989.

Ginsberg, Elaine K., ed. *Passing and the Fictions of Identity.* Durham: Duke University Press, 1996.

Green, Martin. *Dreams of Adventure, Deeds of Empire.* 1979. London: Routledge, 1980.

Grosz, Elizabeth. *Volatile Bodies: Toward a Corporeal Feminism.* Bloomington: Indiana University Press, 1994.

Gruesser, John C. "Afro-American Travel Literature and Africanist Discourse." *Black American Literature Forum* 24.1 (spring 1990): 5–20.

Hawthorne, Nathaniel. "Chiefly about War Matters." *The Writings of Nathaniel Hawthorne.* Vol. 17 of 22. Boston: Houghton, 1876. 361–86.

———. *The French and Italian Notebooks.* Ed. Thomas Woodson. Vol. 14. Columbus: Ohio State University Press, 1980.

———. *The Marble Faun.* 1860. London: Everyman, 1995.

Heath, William. "Melville and Marquesan Eroticism." *Massachusetts Review* 29.1 (spring 1988): 43–65.

Hedrick, Joan D. *Solitary Comrade: Jack London and His Work.* Chapel Hill: University of North Carolina Press, 1982.

Herbert, T. Walter, Jr. *Dearest Beloved: The Hawthornes and the Making of the Middle-Class Family.* Berkeley: University California Press, 1993.

———. "The Erotics of Purity: *The Marble Faun* and the Victorian Construction of Sexuality." *Representations* 36 (fall 1991): 114–32.

————. *Marquesan Encounters: Melville and the Meaning of Civilization.* Cambridge: Harvard University Press, 1980.

Herzig, Carl. "Roots of Night: Emerging Style and Vision in the Early Journalism of Djuna Barnes." *Centennial Review* 31 (summer 1987): 255–69.

Howells, William Dean. *A Hazard of New Fortunes.* 1890. New York: Bantam, 1960.

Huggins, Nathan Irvin. *Harlem Renaissance.* New York: Oxford University Press, 1971.

Hughes, Charles H. *The Neurological Practice of Medicine.* St. Louis: Hughes and Company. 1903.

————. "The Gentleman Degenerate: A Homosexualist's Self-Description and Self-Applied Title." *Alienist and Neurologist* 25 (February 1904): 62–70.

Hughes, Langston. *The Ways of White Folks.* 1934. New York: Vintage, 1987.

Ikonné, Chidi. *From DuBois to Van Vechten: The Early New Negro Literature, 1903–1926.* Westport: Greenwood Press, 1981.

Ivison, Douglas. "Travel Writing at the End of Empire: A Pom Named Bruce and the Mad White Giant." Unpublished manuscript.

Jakle, John A. *The Tourist: Travel in the Twentieth-Century North America.* Lincoln: University of Nebraska Press, 1985.

James, Henry. *The American Scene.* 1907. New York: Penguin, 1996.

Jefferson, Paul. Introduction. *The Travels of William Wells Brown.* New York: Markus Wiener, 1991. 1–20.

Jefferson, Thomas. *The Papers of Thomas Jefferson.* Ed. J. P. Boyd et al. Princeton: Princeton University Press, 1950.

Johnson, David E. "'Writing in the Dark': The Political Fictions of American Travel Writing." *American Literary History* 7 (March 1995): 1–27.

Johnson, James Weldon. *Black Manhattan.* New York: Knopf, 1930.

Jones, LeRoi. *Home: Social Essays.* New York: William Morrow, 1966.

Jongh, James de. *Vicious Modernism: Black Harlem and the Literary Imagination.* Cambridge: Cambridge University Press, 1990.

Kabbani, Rana. *Europe's Myths of Orient.* Bloomington: Indiana University Press, 1986.

Kannenstine, Louis. *The Art of Djuna Barnes.* New York: New York University Press, 1977.

Kaplan, Amy. "Imperial Triangles: Mark Twain's Foreign Affairs." *Modern Fiction Studies* 43 (spring 1997): 237–48.

————. *The Social Construction of American Realism.* Chicago: University of Chicago Press, 1988.

Kaplan, Caren. *Questions of Travel: Postmodern Discourses of Displacement.* Durham: Duke University Press, 1996.

Katz, Jonathan Ned. *Gay American History: Lesbians and Gay Men in the U.S.A.* New York: Avon, 1976.

Kellner, Bruce. *Carl Van Vechten and the Irreverent Decades.* Norman: Oklahoma University Press, 1968.

———. "Carl Van Vechten's Black Renaissance." *Harlem Renaissance: Revaluations.* Ed. Amritjit Singh et al. New York: Garland, 1989. 23–33.

Kerouac, Jack. *On the Road.* 1955. New York: Viking Press, 1985.

———. *The Subterraneans.* New York: Grove Press, 1958.

Kidd, Benjamin. *The Control of the Tropics.* New York: Macmillan, 1893.

Knopp, Lawrence. "Sexuality and Urban Space: A Framework for Analysis." *Mapping Desire: Geographies of Sexualities.* Ed. David Bell and Gill Valentine. New York: Routledge, 1995. 149–61.

Krauss, Rosalind. *The Originality of the Avant-Garde and Other Modernist Myths.* Cambridge: MIT Press, 1985.

Kröller, Eva-Marie. "First Impressions: Rhetorical Strategies in Travel Writing by Victorian Women." *Ariel: A Review of International English Literature* 21 (October 1990): 87–99.

Labor, Earle. "Jack London's Pacific World." *Critical Essays on Jack London.* Ed. Jacquleine Tavernier-Courbin. Boston: G. K. Hall, 1983. 205–22.

Labor, Earle, and Jeanne Campbell Reesman. *Jack London.* New York: Twayne, 1994.

Lane, Christopher. *The Ruling Passion: British Colonial Allegory and the Paradox of Homosexual Desire.* Durham: Duke University Press, 1995.

Lang, Jonathan C. "Some Perversions of Pastoral: Or Tourism in Gide's *L'Immoraliste.*" *Genders* 21 (1995): 83–113.

Larsen, Nella. *Quicksand.* 1928. New Brunswick: Rutgers University Press, 1986.

Latimer, Dean, and Jeff Goldberg. *Flowers in the Blood: The Story of Opium.* New York: Franklin Watts, 1981.

Lawrence, D. H. *Studies in Classic American Literature.* 1923. New York: Penguin, 1961.

Lears, T. J. Jackson. *No Place of Grace: Antimodernism and the Transformation of American Culture, 1880–1920.* New York: Pantheon, 1981.

Lee, A. Robert. "Harlem on My Mind: Fictions of a Black Metropolis." *The American City: Literary and Cultural Perspectives.* Ed. Graham Clarke. New York: St. Martin's, 1988. 62–85.

Leed, Eric. *The Mind of the Traveler: From Gilgamesh to Global Tourism.* New York: Basic Books, 1991.

Leverenz, David. *Manhood and the American Renaissance.* Ithaca: Cornell University Press, 1989.

Levine, Nancy J. "'Bringing Milkshakes to Bulldogs': The Early Journalism of Djuna Barnes." *Silence and Power: A Reevaluation of Djuna Barnes.* Ed. Mary Lynn Broe. Carbondale: Southern Illinois University Press, 1991. 27–34.

Levine, Robert S. "'Antebellum Rome' in *The Marble Faun.*" *American Literary History* 2 (spring 1990): 19–31.

Lewis, David Levering. *When Harlem Was in Vogue.* New York: Oxford University Press, 1979.

Lewis, Reina. *Gendering Orientalism: Race, Femininity and Representation.* New York: Routledge, 1996.

Lewis, R. W. B. *Edith Wharton: A Biography.* New York: Harper & Row, 1975.

Lippard, George. *New York: Its Upper Ten and Lower Million.* 1842. Upper Saddle River, N.J.: Literature House, 1970.

———. *George Lippard, Prophet of Protest: Writings of an American Radical, 1822–1854.* New York: Peter Lang, 1986.

Locke, Alain. *The New Negro.* New York: Knopf, 1925.

Lofland, Lyn H. *A World of Strangers; Order and Action in Urban Public Space.* New York: Basic Books, 1970.

Logan, Joshua, dir. *South Pacific.* USA, 1958.

London, Charmian. *The Book of Jack London.* London: Mills and Brown, 1921. 2 vols.

London Evening Post. January 27, 1737 (os).

London, Jack. *The Cruise of the Snark: A Pacific Voyage.* 1911. New York: KPI, 1986.

———. "Good-By, Jack." 1912. *Tales of the Pacific.* New York: Penguin, 1989. 111–20.

———. "The Heathen." 1909. *South Sea Tales.* New York: Macmillan, 1946. 151–96.

———. *The Letters of Jack London.* Ed. Earle Labor et. al. Stanford: Stanford University Press, 1988. 3 vols.

———. "The Sheriff of Kona." 1912. *Tales of the Pacific.* New York: Penguin, 1989. 121–34.

London, Joan. *Jack London and His Times.* New York: Doubleday, 1939.

Lucey, Michael. *Gide's Bent: Sexuality, Politics, Writing.* New York: Oxford University Press, 1995.

Lueders, Edward. *Carl Van Vechten.* New York: Twayne, 1965.

MacCannell, Dean. *The Tourist: A New Theory of the Leisure Class.* New York: Schocken, 1976.

Mailer, Norman. *The White Negro.* San Francisco: City Lights, 1959.

Martin, Robert K. "'Enviable Isles': Melville's South Seas." *Modern Language Studies* 12 (winter 1982): 68–76.

——. *Hero, Captain, and Stranger: Male Friendship, Social Critique, and Literary Form in the Sea Novels of Herman Melville.* Chapel Hill: University of North Carolina Press, 1986.

——. *The Homosexual Tradition in American Poetry.* Austin: University of Texas Press, 1979.

Mayne, Xavier [Edward Irenaeus Prime Stevenson]. *The Intersexes.* 1908. New York: Arno Press, 1975.

McClintock, Anne. *Imperial Leather: Race, Gender and Sexuality in the Colonial Contest.* New York: Routledge, 1995.

McKay, Claude. *Home to Harlem.* 1928. Boston: Northeastern University Press, 1987.

——. *A Long Way from Home.* 1937. New York: Harcourt Brace, 1970.

Melville, Herman. *Benito Cereno.* 1855. *Billy Budd and Other Stories.* New York: Penguin, 1983.

——. *Typee: A Peep at Polynesian Life.* 1846. New York: Penguin, 1972.

Metwalli, A. M. "Americans Abroad: The Popular Art of Travel Writing in the Nineteenth Century." *Exploration* 4.1 (1976): 15–24.

Michener, James A. *Tales of the South Pacific.* New York: Macmillan, 1949.

Mill, John Stuart. *Three Essays on Religion.* London: Longmans, 1874.

Mills, Sara. *Discourse.* New York: Routledge, 1997.

——. *Discourses of Difference: An Analysis of Women's Travel Writing and Colonialism.* New York: Routledge, 1991.

Morand, Paul. *New York.* New York: Holt, 1930.

Moreland, David A. "Violence in the South Sea Fiction of Jack London." *The Jack London Newsletter* 16 (January–April 1983): 1–35.

Mott, Frank Luther. *American Journalism: A History, 1860–1960.* New York: Macmillan, 1962.

Mulvey, Christopher. *Anglo-American Landscapes: A Study of Nineteenth-Century Anglo-American Travel Literature.* Cambridge: Cambridge University Press, 1983.

——. *Transatlantic Manners: Social Patterns in Nineteenth- Century Anglo-American Travel Literature.* Cambridge: Cambridge University Press, 1990.

Mulvey, Laura. *Fetishism and Curiosity.* Bloomington: Indiana University Press, 1996.

Mumford, Kevin J. "Homosex Changes: Race, Cultural Geography, and the Emergence of the Gay." *American Quarterly* 48 (September 1996): 395–414.

Nelson, Dana D. *The Word in Black and White: Reading "Race" in American Literature, 1638–1867.* New York: Oxford University Press, 1992.

Niles, Blair. *Strange Brother.* 1931. London: GMP, 1991.

Noel, J. *Footloose in Arcadia.* New York: Carrick & Evans, 1940.

Nord, Deborah Epstein. "The Urban Peripatetic: Spectator, Streetwalker, Woman Writer." *Nineteenth-Century Literature* 46 (December 1991): 351–75.

Obeyesekere, Gananath. "'British Cannibals': Contemplation of an Event in the Death and Resurrection of James Cook, Explorer." *Critical Inquiry* 18 (summer 1992): 630–54.

Oliver, Douglas L. *The Pacific Islands.* New York: Doubleday, 1968.

Olney, James. "'I Was Born': Slave Narratives, Their Status as Autobiography and as Literature." *The Slave's Narrative.* Ed. Charles T. Davis and Henry Louis Gates. Oxford: Oxford University Press, 1985. 148–75.

Osborne, Thomas J. *Annexation Hawaii: Fighting American Imperialism.* Waimanalo, Hawaii: Island Style Press, 1998.

Osofsky, Gilbert. *Harlem: The Making of a Ghetto.* New York: Harper & Row, 1963.

Park, Robert E. "The City: Suggestions for the Investigation of Human Behavior in the City Environment." *American Journal of Sociology* 20 (March 1915): 600–10.

Penley, Constance. *NASA/TREK: Popular Science and Sex in America.* London: Verso, 1997.

Porter, David. *Journal of a Cruise Made to the Pacific Ocean, in the U.S. Frigate Essex, in the Years 1812, 1813, and 1814.* Philadelphia, 1815.

Porter, Dennis. *Haunted Journeys: Desire and Transgression in European Travel Writing.* Princeton: Princeton University Press, 1991.

Pratt, Mary Louise. *Imperial Eyes: Travel Writing and Transculturation.* New York: Routledge, 1992.

Priebe, Richard. "The Search for Community in the Novels of Claude McKay." *Studies in Black Literature* 3 (summer 1972): 22–30.

Prince, Nancy. *A Narrative of the Life and Travels of Mrs. Nancy Prince.* 1850. *Telling Travels: Selected Writings by Nineteenth-Century American Women Abroad.* Ed. Mary Suzanne Schriber. DeKalb: Northern Illinois University Press, 1995. 114–29.

Probyn, Elspeth. *Outside Belongings.* New York: Routledge, 1996.

Raby, Peter. *Bright Paradise: Victorian Scientific Travellers.* London: Pimlico Book, 1996.

Rennie, Neil. *Far-Fetched Facts: The Literature of Travel and the Idea of the South Seas.* Oxford: Clarendon Press, 1995.

Reynolds, David S. *Beneath the American Renaissance: The Subversive Imagination in the Age of Emerson and Melville.* New York: Knopf, 1988.

Riis, Jacob A. *How the Other Half Lives.* 1890. New York: St. Martin's Press, 1996.

Roberts, Neil. "The Novelist as Travel Writer: *The Plumed Serpent.*" *D. H. Lawrence Review* 25.1–3 (1994): 130–39.

Robertson, Michael. *Stephen Crane, Journalism, and the Making of Modern American Literature.* New York: Columbia University Press, 1997.

Russell, John. *Paris.* New York: Dover, 1983.

Ryan, Mary P. *Women in Public: Between Banners and Ballots, 1825–1880.* Baltimore: Johns Hopkins University Press, 1990.

Ryan, Thomas Joseph. "'Scenes Well Worth Gazing At': The Effects of Hawthorne's Touristic Vision in *The Marble Faun.*" Diss. York University, 1976.

Said, Edward. *Orientalism.* New York: Vintage, 1978.

Santayana, George. *Works.* Vol. 6. New York: Triton, 1936.

Sarotte, Georges-Michel. *Like a Brother, Like a Lover: Male Homosexuality in the American Novel and Theatre from Herman Melville to James Baldwin.* Trans. Richard Miller. New York: Doubleday, 1978.

Sarup, Madan. "Home and Identity." *Travellers' Tales: Narratives of Home and Displacement.* Ed. George Robertson et al. New York: Routledge, 1994. 93–104.

Saunders, Peter. "The Meaning of 'Home' in Contemporary English Culture." *Housing Studies* 4.3 (1989): 177–92.

Saunders, Peter, and Peter Williams. "The Constitution of Home: Towards a Research Agenda." *Housing Studies* 3.2 (1984): 81–93.

Savoy, Eric. "The Subverted Gaze: Hawthorne, Howells, James and the Discourse of Travel." *Canadian Review of American Studies* 21 (winter 1990): 287–300.

Schick, Irvin Cemil. "Representing Middle Eastern Women: Feminism and Colonial Discourse." *Feminist Studies* 16 (summer 1990): 345–80.

Schriber, Mary Suzanne. "Edith Wharton and the Dog-Eared Travel Book." *Wretched Exotic: Essays on Edith Wharton in Europe.* Ed. Katherine Joslin and Alan Price. New York: Peter Lang, 1993. 147–64.

———. *Writing Home: American Women Abroad, 1830–1920.* Charlottesville: University Press of Virginia, 1997.

Scott, Bonnie Kime. "Djuna Barnes's Migratory Modernism." *American Modernism across the Arts.* Ed. Jay Bochner and Justin D. Edwards. New York: Peter Lang, 1999. 218–33.

Scruggs, Charles. "Crab Antics and Jacob's Ladder: Aaron Douglas's Two Views of *Nigger Heaven.*" *The Harlem Renaissance Re-examined.* Ed. Victor A. Kramer. New York: AMS Press, 1987. 149–84.

———. *Sweet Home: Invisible Cities in the Afro- American Novel.* Baltimore: Johns Hopkins University Press, 1994.

Seabrook, Jeremy. *Travels in the Skin Trade: Tourism and the Sex Industry.* London: Pluto Press, 1996.

Sears, John. *Sacred Places: American Tourist Attractions in the Nineteenth Century.* New York: Oxford University Press, 1989.

Sedgwick, Catherine Maria. "An Incident in Rome." *Graham's Magazine,* 1845, 13–27.

Sedgwick, Eve Kosofsky. *Between Men: English Literature and Male Homosocial Desire.* New York: Columbia University Press, 1985.

———. *Epistemology of the Closet.* Berkeley: University of California Press, 1990.

Silverman, Kaja. *Male Subjectivity at the Margins.* New York: Routledge, 1992.

Simmel, Georg. "The Metropolis and Mental Life." 1950. *Classic Essays in the Culture of Cities.* Ed. Richard Sennett. New York: Appleton, 1969.

Sinclair, Andrew. Introduction. *Tales of the Pacific.* Jack London. New York: Penguin, 1989. 7–15.

Smith, Harold F. *American Travellers Abroad: A Bibliography of Accounts Published before 1900.* Carbondale: Library of Southern Illinois University, 1969.

Smith-Rosenberg, Carroll. *Disorderly Conduct: Visions of Gender in Victorian America.* New York: Knopf, 1985.

Spivak, Gayatri. "Three Women's Texts and a Critique of Imperialism." *The Feminist Reader.* Ed. C. Belsey and J. Moore. Basingstoke: Macmillan, 1989. 175–96.

Spurr, David. *The Rhetoric of Empire: Colonial Discourse in Journalism, Travel Writing and Imperial Administration.* Durham: Duke University Press, 1993.

Stafford, Barbara Maria. *Voyage into Substance: Art, Science, Nature, and the Illustrated Travel Account, 1760–1840.* Cambridge: Cambridge University Press, 1984.

Stasz, Clarice. "Social Darwinism, Gender, and Humour in 'Adventure.'" *Rereading Jack London.* Ed. Leonard Cassuto and Jeanne Campbell Reesman. Stanford: Stanford University Press, 1996. 130–40.

Stein, Gertrude. *Three Lives.* 1909. New York: Vintage, 1936.

Stern, Madeleine. *The Life of Margaret Fuller.* New York: E. P. Dutton, 1942.

Sterne, Laurence. *A Sentimental Journey through France and Italy.* 1768. New York: Oxford University Press, 1991.

Stewart, Charles. *A Visit to the South Seas, in the U.S. Ship Vincennes, during the Years 1829 and 1830*. New York: John Haven, 1831.

Stocking, George W. *Victorian Anthropology*. New York: The Free Press, 1987.

Stoddard, Charles Warren. *Cruising the South Seas*. San Francisco: Gay Sunshine Press, 1987.

————. *For the Pleasure of His Company: An Affair of the Misty City: Thrice Told*. 1903. San Francisco: Gay Sunshine Press, 1989.

Stowe, Harriet Beecher. *Sunny Memories of Foreign Lands*. 2 vols. Boston: Phillips, Sampson, 1854.

Stowe, William W. *Going Abroad: European Travel in Nineteenth-Century American Culture*. Princeton: Princeton University Press, 1994.

Sundquist, Eric J. *To Wake the Nations: Race in the Making of American Literature*. Cambridge: Harvard University Press, 1993.

Taylor, Bayard. *Views A-foot*. New York: G. P. Putnam and Son, 1846.

Thompson, George. *New-York Life: The Mysteries of Upper-Tendom Revealed*. New York: Charles S. Atwood, 1849.

Thurman, Wallace. *Infants of the Spring*. 1932. New York: AMS Press, 1975.

Tietze, Thomas R., and Gary Riedl. "'Saints in Slime': The Ironic Use of Racism in Jack London's *South Sea Tales*." *Thalia: Studies in Literary Humour* 12 (summer 1992): 59–66.

Torgovnick, Marianna. *Gone Primitive: Savage Intellects, Modern Lives*. Chicago: University of Chicago Press, 1990.

————. *Primitive Passions: Men, Women, and the Quest for Ecstasy*. New York: Knopf, 1997.

Trachtenberg, Alan. "Experiments in Another Country: Stephen Crane's City Sketches." *Southern Review* 10 (1974): 269–78.

————. *The Incorporation of America: Culture and Society in the Guilded Age*. New York: Hill and Wang, 1982.

Twain, Mark. *Mark Twain's Letters from Hawaii*. Ed. A. Grove Day. New York: Appleton-Century, 1966.

Tylor, Edward B. *Primitive Cultures*. 2 Vols. 1871. New York: G. P. Putman's Sons, 1920.

Van Den Abbeele, Georges. *Travel as Metaphor from Montaigne to Rousseau*. Minneapolis: University of Minnesota Press, 1992.

Van Vechten, Carl. *Letters of Carl Van Vechten*. Ed. Bruce Kellner. New Haven: Yale University Press, 1987.

————. *Nigger Heaven*. 1926. New York: Farrar, Straus & Giroux, 1973.

Vance, William. *America's Rome*. 2 vols. New Haven: Yale University Press, 1989.

Weinauer, Ellen M. "'A Most Respectable Looking Gentleman': Passing, Posses-sion and Transgression in *Running a Thousand Miles to Freedom*." *Passing and the Fictions of Identity*. Ed. Elaine K. Ginsberg. Durham: Duke University Press, 1996. 37–56.

Welter, Barbara. "The Cult of True Womanhood: 1820–1860." *American Quar-terly* 18 (1966): 151–74.

Wharton, Edith. *A Backward Glance*. New York: Scribners, 1934.

———. *In Morocco*. 1919. Hopewell, N.J.: Ecco Press, 1996.

Whetter, Darryl. "Michael Ondaatje's 'International Bastards' and Their 'Best Selves': An Analysis of *The English Patient* as Travel Literature." *English Studies in Canada* 23 (December 1997): 443–58.

Williams, Raymond. "Metropolitan Perceptions and the Emergence of Modern-ism." *The Politics of Modernism*. London: Verso, 1989.

Williams, Tennessee. *Suddenly Last Summer*. 1958. New York: Signet, 1976.

Willis, Nathaniel Parker. *Pencillings by the Way*. Auburn: Rochester, 1853.

Withey, Lynne. *Grand Tours and Cook's Tours: A History of Leisure Travel, 1750 to 1915*. New York: William Morrow, 1997.

Woodcock, George. Introduction. *Typee: A Peep at Polynesian Life*. New York: Penguin, 1972. 7–27.

Woods, Gregory. "Fantasy Islands: Popular Topographies of Marooned Mascu-linity." *Mapping Desire: Geographies of Sexualities*. Ed. David Bell and Gill Valentine. New York: Routledge, 1995. 126–48.

Wright, Esmond. *The American Dream: From Reconstruction to Reagan*. Cam-bridge: Blackwell, 1996.

Wright, Nathalia. *American Novelists in Italy: The Discoverers, Allston to James*. Philadelphia: University of Pennsylvania Press, 1965.

Wright, Sarah Bird. *Edith Wharton's Travel Writing: The Making of a Connois-seur*. New York: St. Martin's Press, 1997.

———. Introduction. *Edith Wharton Abroad: Selected Travel Writings, 1888–1920*. Ed. Sarah Bird Wright. New York: St. Martin's Press, 1995. 1–37.

Yingling, Thomas. Rev. of *For the Pleasure of His Company* and *Cruising the South Seas*," by Charles Warren Stoddard. *American Literary Realism* 21 (spring 1989): 91–93.

Young, Robert J. C. *Colonial Desire: Hybridity in Theory, Culture and Race*. New York: Routledge, 1995.

INDEX